Power and policy
in liberal democracies

Edited by

Martin Harrop
University of Newcastle upon Tyne

Published by the Press Syndicate of the University of Cambridge
The Pitt Building, Trumpington Street, Cambridge CB2 1RP
40 West 20th Street, New York, NY 10011–4211, USA
10 Stamford Road, Oakleigh, Melbourne 3166, Australia

First published 1992
Reprinted 1993, 1994

Printed in Great Britain by Athenæum Press Ltd, Gateshead, Tyne & Wear

A catalogue record for this book is available from the British Library

Library of Congress cataloguing in publication data

Power and policy in liberal democracies / edited by Martin Harrop.
    p.   cm.
Includes bibliographical references and index.
ISBN 0 521 34579 0 (hardback)
1. Comparative government. 2. Policy sciences. 3. France – Politics and government. 4. Great Britain – Politics and government. 5. Japan – Politics and government. 6. United States – Politics and government. I. Harrop, Martin.
JF51 P664 1992
320.3 – dc20   91-2462   CIP

ISBN 0 521 34579 0 hardback
ISBN 0 521 34798 X paperback

UP

Contents

Figure

Tables

Contributors

All the contributors are, or have been, lecturers in politics at the University of Newcastle upon Tyne.

MICHAEL CLARKE is executive director of the Centre for Defence Studies, University of London. He lectured at the University of Manchester from 1975 to 1979 and at the University of Newcastle upon Tyne from 1979 to 1990. He has been a Guest Fellow at the Brookings Institution, Washington D.C., and an Associate Fellow at the Royal Institute of International Affairs, London.

PHILIP DANIELS is lecturer in politics at the University of Newcastle upon Tyne. Educated at Johns Hopkins University and the European University Institute (Florence), his main research interests are the European Community and West European politics. He has published widely on Italian politics.

ROD HAGUE is lecturer in politics at the University of Newcastle upon Tyne. Educated at Oxford and Manchester Universities, he is co-author of *Comparative government and politics* and co-editor with Michael Clarke of *European defence cooperation: America, Britain and NATO*.

MARTIN HARROP is senior lecturer in politics at the University of Newcastle upon Tyne. Educated at Oxford, Strathclyde and Yale Universities, he is co-author of two other wide-ranging texts, *Comparative government and politics* and *Elections and voters*. He also co-edited books on political communications in the British general elections of 1979, 1983 and 1987.

PETER JONES is senior lecturer in politics at the University of Newcastle upon Tyne. He has written on various subjects in political philosophy, including rights, democracy, freedom and social welfare, and is interested in the application of political philosophy to issues of public policy.

IAN NEARY is director of the Contemporary Japan Centre, University of Essex. Previously he taught for five years each at Huddersfield Polytechnic and the University of Newcastle upon Tyne. He is author of *Political protest and social control in prewar Japan* and is currently studying the relationships between the pharmaceutical industry and government in the UK and Japan.

ELLA RITCHIE is lecturer in politics at the University of Newcastle upon Tyne. Educated at Lancaster and London Universities, she has written on French politics and European Community politics.

Preface

This textbook seeks to integrate policy analysis with mainstream comparative politics. We try to give the reader an insight into policy analysis but to do so in a way which is grounded in a solid understanding of the political process in specific liberal democracies.

The project arose from our experience teaching an undergraduate course in comparative public policy at Newcastle University. We felt a need for a text lying between a pure introduction to policy analysis, on the one hand, and a traditional treatment of comparative government and politics, on the other.

Our starting-point is that we cannot understand public policy without discussing political institutions. But we want to understand political institutions largely in order to explain patterns of policy. So it is not a question of either an institutional or a policy approach. Rather the task is to try and combine the two.

We have arranged our material with that in mind. After an introductory chapter on the policy approach, the chapters are divided into three parts which form a sequence in which each part builds on what has gone before. Part 1 provides an introduction to the politics of four leading liberal democracies: France, Japan, the United Kingdom and the United States. These chapters set out the actors, arenas and agendas of policy in each country. They require little, if any, prior knowledge of the countries concerned beyond the factual information given in the appendix.

Part 2 turns from countries to sectors. Here we examine the policy process in our countries in four areas: industrial policy, health policy, ethnic minorities and law and order. These sectors vary widely in terms of the role played by the modern state within them. Each chapter therefore begins by assessing the place of the state in the sector and then discusses the policy agenda, the policy community and policy outcomes. We hope that the use of standard subheadings in parts 1 and 2 will ease comparisons among the countries and the sectors.

The chapters in part 3 use the earlier material to illustrate general features of comparative public policy. The perspectives adopted here are implementation, evaluation and comparison. The chapters on implementation and evaluation, in particular, reflect the distinctive emphasis within the policy perspective on what happens after a decision has been reached. We hope that by basing these chapters on the preceding discussion of countries and sectors, we will aid students' understanding of the policy approach and their appreciation of the intimate links between power and policy.

A book of this range inevitably has several authors. We like to think that sharing offices in the same building, teaching on the same course, commenting on each other's drafts, and receiving equally helpful comments from our students, has given the book more coherence than multi-authored texts sometimes achieve. If not, many a meeting will have been in vain! But our readers, as ever, will be the judge.

We are grateful to Alison Wright for compiling the index.

MARTIN HARROP

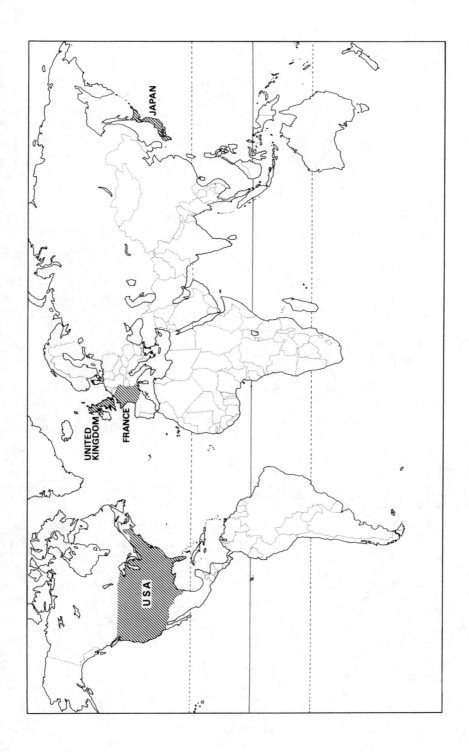

1   Introduction

Martin Harrop

Why has Japan found it easier than the United States to pursue a consistent industrial policy? Why does Britain provide health care collectively whereas France relies on private provision? Why is the United States government unable to ensure the safety of its citizens as they walk the city streets whereas personal safety is not even an issue in Japan?

These are the kinds of questions asked in the study of comparative public policy. They are questions which this book asks and seeks to answer. The comparative study of public policy is a relatively new approach in politics and we therefore begin this chapter by asking what is distinctive about it. What is the policy approach? Why study public policy comparatively? And what work has already been done in this area? We then go on to explain the selection of countries and policy areas discussed in this book.

The policy approach

Perhaps the best way to explain the policy approach is by contrasting it with the decision approach, an influential focus in political science. Political scientists working with a decision approach have studied who was involved in making important decisions and why those decisions went the way they did.[1] A policy, however, is a more general notion. Whereas a decision is a more or less explicit selection from a range of options, a policy involves a bundle of decisions and how they are put into practice. Typically, a policy will evolve and have consequences which go well beyond those envisaged by its original architects. Thus the key advantage of a policy focus over a decision approach is that it encourages us to trace a policy beyond the point of initiation to the point of delivery – to what happens out there in the world (hence the chapter on implementation in part 3). It is out there that politics can make a difference to the quality of people's lives: in providing a sense of security to the old, in providing prompt medical treatment for the sick and in ensuring equal opportunities for ethnic minorities. Whether or not this is what politics is, it is certainly

1

what politics is *for*. Politics is not just about who decides; it is also about the impact of decisions. We want to know not just what the policies are but also what they achieve (hence the chapter on evaluation in part 3). Thus the policy approach is a useful extension to a decision approach – though it is not a replacement for it.

Whereas students of decisions are often hard-nosed analysts who just want to know who won and why, many students of policy seek to evaluate and improve public policy. Policy evaluation, in other words, is a distinct branch of policy studies. Comparative public policy is particularly useful in expanding policy options and giving clues (sometimes misleading) about what might work elsewhere. A concern with evaluation and improvement is therefore an additional contrast between a decision approach and a policy focus.

Exactly how broad we want to make the concept of a policy is a matter of definition. There is much to be said for simple definitions and the simplest definition is Heclo's: a policy is a course of action designed to accomplish some end.[2] As Peter Jones points out in chapter 11, policies are concerned to make things happen or not happen. They are courses of action designed to promote, maintain or prevent states of affairs. This conveys two ideas: (1) that a policy is by definition linked, however remotely, to a purpose and (2) that this purpose serves to link together a set of actions. In the case of public policy, we can also stipulate that these actions are taken by the state or, in the case of contracted-out services, on behalf of it. Public policy therefore consists of purposive action by or for governments.

Beyond this simple definition, however, it is only necessary to be aware of the variety of uses to which the word 'policy' can be put. For example Hogwood and Gunn collect ten uses.[3] These include the general but perfectly legitimate use of the word policy to describe a sector or field of activity – industrial policy, health policy, for example. At the other extreme, the term 'policy' can be used to describe highly specific means of achieving broader objectives: for example, 'our policy is to increase the tax on company cars in order to reduce road congestion'.

A policy focus can be contrasted not just with a decision approach but also with an older, institutional tradition in politics. Institutional scholars described the formal institutions of government – legislature, executive and judiciary – and the constitutions which governed the relationships between these institutions. The result was a description of government rather than an analysis of politics.[4] But even the description of the formal governmental machinery was incomplete because it omitted to mention what the machinery was *for*; policy did not get a look in. By adopting a policy focus, we do not dispense with institutions, for they structure the policy process. For example, the key fact about policy formation in the United States is institutional, indeed constitutional: the President cannot command Congress. But a policy approach means we are now examining institutions more purposively, seeking to understand their impact on policy. Thus we must pay more attention to the bureaucracy than institutionalists did because we know that public 'servants' are the source of most policies. We must also pay attention to non-governmental institutions such as pressure groups for these too impinge on the policy process.

For 'new institutionalists' such as Hall, institutional factors play two fundamental roles in policy.[5] On the one hand, the organisation of policy-making affects the degree of power that any one set of actors has over policy outcomes. On the other hand, organisational position also influences an actor's definition of his or her own interests, by establishing his or her institutional responsibilities and relationships to other actors.

Why compare?

This book is about comparative public policy, rather than policy analysis in general. So why *comparative* public policy? The case is similar to the case for studying any form of politics comparatively: comparison is essential to understanding. 'What know they of England', asked Kipling, 'who only England know?' By examining policies comparatively, we can discover how countries vary in the policies they adopt, gain insight into why these differences exist, and identify some of the conditions under which policies succeed or fail. Comparative public policy is therefore a source of generalisations about public policy. In turn these are essential for understanding policy in any particular country.

The study of comparative public policy provides particular opportunities for cross-national learning. If neighbourhood watch schemes reduce crime in the United States, why not give them a try in France? If the United States could reduce deaths from coronary heart disease by a quarter in the 1970s, why not try to repeat the success among the Scots in the 1990s (whose hearts are the most unhealthy in the world)? What can the French and Japanese experience with national health insurance contribute to the American debate about whether public insurance should be introduced there? The practical benefits from studying policy comparatively are one of the distinctive strengths of the approach.

This does not mean that the national context is irrelevant to the policy process. Far from it. For the four large and powerful liberal democracies examined in this book, their histories, institutions and cultures constrain the policies they can adopt and the success new policies can achieve. For example, several chapters in this book stress the distinctiveness of Japan. Japanese policies cannot be exported as successfully as their products have been. It is naive for Americans and Britons to look at Japanese industrial policy and say, 'Let's copy that.' Learning from another country involves more than copying. In fact a practical test of one's understanding of comparative public policy is the ability to judge which policies can be transplanted to which countries. And a theoretical understanding can be measured by the ability to explain these judgements.

A comparative approach to public policy is particularly helpful when examining scarce events. By definition, no country has regular experience of responding to such rare occurrences as disasters or disorder. But world-wide there have been enough oil spills, for instance, to give some clues as to how public authorities do, and should, respond.[6]

Policies must be studied comparatively because that is the context in which an increasing number are formed. Policy-making in liberal democracies can no longer (if it ever could) be examined in isolation from other states. The EC impinges directly on policy processes in Paris and London. Economic competition from Japan forces the United States to consider how it can improve its own productivity. The mass media, themselves a world-wide business, quickly transmit and interpret new developments taking place anywhere in the global village. International yardsticks provide a club with which opposition parties can attack any governing party which is perceived to be 'falling behind'. The extent of globalisation varies by country (America is by virtue of its size more insular than Britain) and sector (industrial policy is more internationalised than is policy towards ethnic minorities). Nonetheless the context of policy-making, for many countries and some sectors, has become global.

We began this introduction with questions about differences between nations and that is indeed the most straightforward way into the study of comparative public policy. But comparison is not always cross-national. In fact the current interest in comparative public policy was stimulated by studies of the fifty American states which sought to discover why some spent more than others on particular areas of policy such as education.[7] Here the focus was on comparison within a country rather than between countries. But we can equally well take the policy sector rather than a geographical unit as our focus. We can ask such sectoral questions as: why are governments more heavily involved in maintaining law and order than in promoting the rights of ethnic minorities? Are physicians more or less successful than the police in claiming autonomy over the implementation of policy in their sector? Why are some sectors of policy more politicised than others? Sectoral comparisons are useful because they often point out similarities between nations. They are an antidote to easy generalisations about a particular country's policy style.

Studying comparative public policy

Public policy is a field but comparative public policy is a method. It is a way of studying public policy.[8] In reviewing comparative studies of public policy, therefore, it is natural to classify them by the method they used. Most fall into one of three categories: case studies (based on a sample of one), statistical studies (based on many cases), or focused comparisons (based on a few cases).

Case studies A case study of a particular sector in a specific country is not comparative in itself. Nonetheless case studies still provide most of the raw material for comparative analysis. For example, case studies of medical associations in all four countries examined in this book suggest some decline in the political clout of organised medicine over the last twenty years or so. Our confidence in this conclusion is strengthened precisely because it has been reached independently in several countries. Armed with a general observation like this, we can seek a general explanation. Have medical associations lost ground because of some public loss of faith in orthodox medicine, for example, or because the medical profession has become polarised between hospital doctors and private practitioners?

The problem with case studies is that they accumulate rather than cumulate. Case studies only survive in the memory of the discipline if they have some general significance (and then they live for ever). As a student of comparative public policy, you should not feel you must remember all the details of every study you look at. Read as much as you can but only remember the points which have value beyond the case. Comparative public policy is one subject where the ability to forget is a definite virtue!

Comparison is one way to force out the overall relevance of case studies. Indeed comparison can sometimes lead to reinterpretation of the original conclusions of a case study. For example, Eckstein examined the success of the British Medical Association (BMA) in its negotiations with the government in the 1950s over such issues as payment methods for physicians.[9] He attributed the BMA's success to factors specific to Britain – notably the free hand which the Ministry of Health had in regulating medical care as a result of a general consensus in Britain behind the principle of the National Health Service. However, Marmor and Thomas showed that medical associations were equally successful in comparable negotiations in Sweden and the United States, despite a different policy-making environment there.[10] What really matters, say Marmor and Thomas, is the general point – physicians are an extremely powerful lobby, particularly where their pay is concerned – not the details of a particular country. This exercise could probably be repeated with many other case studies. Case students describe 'how' but should not think they have explained 'why'.

Case studies should be selected because of their general significance. If not, they are not strictly case studies; a 'case', by definition, falls under a wider principle. Paradoxically, unusual cases are particularly significant. When sleep researchers discovered The Man Who Never Went To Sleep, they descended on him in droves. To find out why the rest of us sleep, they had only to discover what else was distinctive about this poor soul. (They never did.) The same applies to public policy. To find out why most liberal democracies fund medical care collectively means discovering how they differ from the United States, which is one of the few democracies to rely on private health insurance. These 'deviant cases', as they are called, are essential to the testing of theories.

In reality case studies are chosen for more practical reasons. This 'case book' is an example. We examine several countries and several sectors but from a 'multiple case studies' perspective. We chose countries we knew something about and sectors in which we were interested. Further, and again typical of the subject, we spend more time on the cases than on comparisons between them. This reflects the intellectual difficulty of genuinely comparative work, the wide range of expertise needed, and the under-development of theory as a guide to observation. The comparative method is forceful but its power is rarely unleashed.

Statistical studies   At the opposite extreme to the single case study stand statistical projects based on all liberal democracies, all industrial societies or even all countries. Such research typically seeks to explain why countries vary in the extent and patterns of their public expenditure. Why do some countries tax at higher rates than others do? Why do some countries spend a higher proportion of public expenditure on welfare than others do? These are statistical variables and the factors used to explain them are also numerical. They include social factors (such as urbanisation), economic factors (such as affluence) and political factors (such as how many years parties of the right have been in power since the war).

Despite the statistical basis of these studies, researchers still disagree on the interpretation of the results. The two rival schools are the 'socioeconomic determinism' approach, led by Wilensky, and the 'politics matters' school, led by Castles.[11] Wilensky argues that economic development is the root cause of the development of the welfare state. To predict what fraction of a country's total income will be devoted to social security schemes such as pensions and income maintenance, one must first of all ask how affluent the country is. The wealthier the country, the more it spends on public welfare provision – in proportionate as well as in absolute terms. Compared to these socio-economic factors, politics is of little importance. It mattered little whether a regime was communist or liberal democratic. It matters even less whether a liberal democracy is governed by the left or the right. As Wilensky puts it, 'economic growth makes countries with contrasting cultural and political traditions more alike in their strategy for constructing the floor below which no one sinks'.[12]

Not surprisingly, political scientists took umbrage at this dismissal of the importance of their subject. The counter-attack was led by Castles. He noted that Wilensky's study was based on sixty countries varying greatly in affluence. For very poor countries it does not matter whose hand controls the till because the till is empty. For affluent liberal democracies, on the other hand, the notion of political choice makes more sense. And indeed later research suggested that political factors do exert at least some influence on public expenditure patterns in liberal democracies. Centralised states (such as Britain) and those where parties of the left have predominated in office (such as Sweden) tend to spend more on welfare than do federal states (such as the USA) and those where the right has been more influential (such as Italy). Holding other factors constant, countries such as Austria in which Catholic parties have been a major ruling force also tend to be high spenders. On a world scale, these differences may be subtle but in the context of this study of liberal democracies they cannot be ignored.

In general this statistical research consists of complicated manipulation of simple data. Expenditure figures tell us how much is spent (at least on those programmes for which international bodies, such as the Organisation for Economic Co-operation and Development (OECD), collect data) but not why the money is spent, how it is spent, for whose benefit, and with what consequences. Furthermore, public programmes must be examined in conjunction with private traditions. Unemployment benefit may be limited in Japan but does this matter to a worker employed by a large company with a tradition of career-long employment? For these reasons, statistical analysis based on many countries provides essential background for qualitative comparisons but is not a replacement for them.[13]

Statistical relationships can be used to identify deviant cases – countries which diverge from the expected pattern. Why, for example, does Japan spend much less on welfare provision or Britain spend less on medical care than we would expect, given these countries' overall level of affluence? We can then seek qualitative explanations for these exceptional cases. Perhaps Japan spends less on welfare because looking after old people is still regarded as the responsibility of the family rather than the state. Perhaps Britain is economical with health care spending because the government can control expenditure through the National Health Service. These illustrations show that statistical studies and case studies are not contradictory but work together in combination. In particular statistical patterns provide a criterion for selecting deviant cases.

Francis Castles' *The Comparative History of Public Policy* is an example of this approach.[14] Castles asked eight specialists on particular countries to explain what was distinctive and/or puzzling about the public policy profile of the countries concerned – and why. The authors were therefore required to locate their country in a comparative context. For example the Japanese specialist wondered why Japanese growth rates had been far higher and its social welfare spending far lower than in the rest of the industrialised world. This strategy of 'taking exception' usefully combined the general with the particular, the normal with the exceptional.

Focused comparisons   These studies fall between case studies and statistical analysis. They compare a small number of countries or sectors. Typically a single sector is compared across two countries. For example, Heclo examined the origins of unemployment insurance, old age pensions and earnings-related supplementary pensions in Britain and Sweden.[15] He concluded that the bureaucracy was the main agency of policy formulation in these areas. More recently Kudrle and Marmor have compared the growth of social security programmes in the United States and Canada, concluding that the presence of elements of left-wing ideology and Tory paternalism in Canada explains its edge in spending and programme development.[16] As a third example, Grant, Paterson and Whitson examined policy-making towards the chemical industry in Britain and Germany, and were struck by the similarity within the sector rather than the difference between the nations.[17]

Studies such as these remain sensitive to the details of particular countries and policies while retaining some ability to test explanations. But their explanatory power is limited. If two countries have a similar policy, the explanation almost certainly lies in some other similarity between them – of which there will be a large number. However, in practice comparison of even a small number of countries and/or sectors does seem to enhance understanding, whatever the methodologists may say about the limitations of such a small sample. Focused comparison is therefore a useful technique, and one which is as suited to student projects as to professional monographs.

Selecting countries

This book examines France, Japan, the United Kingdom and the United States. As table 1.1 shows, these are large, affluent, powerful and long-established nation-states. They provide four of the 'G7' countries (a group of economically strong non-communist states), the others being Canada, Italy and West Germany.

Now that the United States has finally removed restrictions on the voting rights of blacks, all four countries are clearly liberal democracies. Indeed these countries contain a majority of all the people in the world today living in societies with a long, unbroken democratic tradition.[18] However the very size and importance of these countries means they cannot be regarded as representative liberal democracies. Our selection contains none of the younger democracies of Southern or Eastern Europe, nor is the Third World represented.

Our selection is also skewed away from the smaller democracies which are in fact more numerous: Austria, Belgium, or the Netherlands, for example. Some smaller democracies offer a style of government which is unrepresented in this book – a 'consensual' style of democracy in which coalition governments, proportional representation (PR), and a tradition of sharing political decisions with powerful interest groups combine to restrain majority rule.[19] Significantly, most democracies use PR but none of our countries has a tradition of doing so (though France has tried out a vast range of electoral systems).

Even though our four countries do not cover the range of liberal democracies, they are nonetheless a diverse group. They have enough in common to make comparison possible but sufficient diversity to make comparison interesting. The most important contrast is between the two countries with a strong state tradition – France and Japan – and the pair where the state tradition is weaker – Britain and, especially, the United States. This is not a matter of political institutions: of the two 'strong' states, one (France) is presidential while the other (Japan) is parliamentary. The same applies to the two 'weak' states: the USA is presidential while Britain is parliamentary. Rather, the strength of a state is a much broader characteristic, covering the capacity of the state to be more than a prisoner of social forces, to choose its partners and, with them, impose its vision on society. This capacity is sustained by tradition as much as by institutions. It reflects expectations, particularly among elites, about the legitimate areas and style of state intervention.

Dyson, for example, contrasts 'state' and 'state-less' societies. State societies such as France and Japan defer to state authority and regard state intervention in many sectors as legitimate. As chapter 2 notes, there

Table 1.1. *Basic statistics on the four countries*

	France	Japan	United Kingdom	United States	Year
Basic					
Area (km²)	547,030	372,310	244,820	9,372,610	1988
Population (million)	55.8	122.6	56.9	246.0	1988
Population density (people per km²)	102	329	233	26	1988
Population growth 1980–5 (% per year)	0.5	0.7	0.1	1.0	—
Religion	76% Roman Catholic	Most both Shinto and Buddhist	50% Church of England, 13% Roman Catholic	33% Protestant, 22% Catholic	1980s
Military					
Last foreign invasion	1940	1945	1066	1812	—
Deaths in military battle 1816–1980 (thousands)	1,965	1,371	1,295	664	—
Economic					
Gross Domestic Product (GDP) (billion $)	950	2,856	826	4,881	1988
GDP per head ($)	17,004	23,325	14,477	19,815	1988
GDP growth 1980–8 (% per year)	1.9	4.1	2.8	3.0	—
Investment (% of GDP)	24	33	17	18	1965–86 average
Public expenditure (% of GDP)	48	30	47	36	1980s
Top rate of personal income tax	57	50	40	28	1989
Government final consumption (% of GDP)	17	10	21	18	1985
Labour force					
Labour force (million)	24.0	60.2	27.9	122.0	1987
Agricultural employment (% of labour force)	7	9	2	3	1985
Manufacturing employment (% of labour force)	21	24	22	19	1985
Service employment (% of labour force)	53	55	56	67	1985
Trade union membership (% of labour force)	18	29	37	18	1980s

Budget					
Revenue (billion $)	197.4	341.0	312.7	854.1	1988
Expenditure (billion $)	217.5	423.0	314.5	1,004.6	1988
Trade					
Trade (% of GDP)	21.5	17.7	30.2	11.7	1988
Main trading partner	Germany	USA	Germany	Canada	1985
Main import (% of total)	Oil (13)	Oil (27)	Electrical machinery (13)	Motor vehicles (16)	1985
Main export (% of total)	Chemicals (14)	Electrical machinery (27)	Oil (16)	Electrical machinery (15)	1985

Sources: The Economist, *The World in Figures* (London: Hodder and Stoughton, 1987) and *Book of Vital World Statistics* (London: Hutchinson, 1990); Charles Taylor and Michael Hudson, *World Handbook of Political and Social Indicators* (New Haven: Yale University Press, 1983); CIA, *The World Factbook 1988* (Washington: CIA, 1988); R. Rose and R. Shiratori, *The Welfare State East and West* (New York: Oxford University Press, 1986); R. Rose, *Politics in England*, 5th ed. (London: Macmillan, 1989).

is a tradition of 'public order' in France which has no real equivalent in the (relatively) 'state-less' societies of Britain and the United States. These 'state-less' societies are more sceptical of the right, and the ability, of the state to lead society.[20]

A strong state is not necessarily an effective state. Indeed a strong state tradition may be a disadvantage in creating an economy which is internationally competitive. Gaullist grandeur helped to build up French industry in the 1950s but left an ideal of national independence which could not be sustained in the interdependent world of the 1990s. For states, as for any other organisation, effectiveness equals capacity *plus* flexibility.[21] The strength of a state is a characteristic, not in itself a virtue or a vice. Even as a characteristic it is very broad, giving an overall picture but not portraying the variation between policy sectors within a country.

Why do our countries vary in the strength of their states? This is an outcome of at least three historical processes: state-building, industrialisation and war.

State building is a particularly crucial influence on the contemporary capacity of the state. This is clearest in the case of the United States, which was built on a deliberate and successful attempt to pre-empt centralised and authoritarian rule.[22] By contrast, in Japan military and bureaucratic leaders imposed a form of top-down modernisation which meant the country went from feudalism to modernity while preserving an authoritarian and hierarchical political culture. Thus, although Japan's constitution was imposed by the Americans after 1945, the state traditions of the two countries could hardly be further apart.

The strength of a state is also influenced by its role in *industrialisation*. The greater the involvement of the state in this process, the stronger its contemporary position tends to be. Britain and the United States industrialised early so the process was relatively unplanned. In Britain, in particular, the development of commercial capitalism and later economic modernisation was largely spontaneous, establishing a hands-off relationship between government and the private sector which exists to this day. But in Japan industrialisation was largely state-sponsored, as the country sought to develop in the period before the first war and to reconstruct its economy, with American help, after the second. In France, post-war development was not just state-sponsored but also state-undertaken, with the state playing a more direct role in production than it did in Japan.

These varying histories produce contrasting difficulties in adapting to the contemporary international economy. In the market-oriented societies of Britain and the United States, the task is to develop means through which governments can steer the economy towards success in international markets. In the state-oriented societies of France and Japan, the task is to lighten the touch of the state so that markets and companies are more open to the stimulus of international competition.

The more *military threats* a country experiences, the more the state develops its capacity to extract resources from society. Again the contrast is between the United States and Britain, on the one hand, and France and Japan, on the other. As table 1.1 shows, the United States and, to a lesser extent, Britain have suffered fewer military casualties than France and Japan over the last 150 years. Unlike France and Japan, neither the United States nor Britain has been invaded in modern times. The wars fought not just by France but also on its territory have given the state a more military orientation than in either Britain or the United States. In Japan a military-dominated regime fought successive wars from the late nineteenth century in order to acquire a sphere of influence, fearing that if it did not, it would itself become the prey of stronger powers. More recently the 'fifteen-year war' to 1945 solidified the ethos of co-operation between Japanese society and state.

The chapters on each country introduce the policy-making process and are arranged as shown below. These chapters describe the who, where and what of policy. The 'who' are the political actors (such as parties), the 'where' are the arenas of battle (such as the assembly) and the 'what' is the agenda (such as a national concern to reverse economic decline). To see policy-making as *actors competing in arenas over agendas* is inevitably partial; for example, only by implication do we consider who is not involved in the process, and what is kept off the agenda and by whom.[23] But the conclusion to each chapter raises broader questions about how the overall process of policy-making in each country can be interpreted.

Organisation of the country chapters

The national situation
The constitution
Actors
   Executive
   Bureaucracy
   Parties
   Pressure groups
Arenas
Instruments
Interpretation

The introductory section on the *national situation* describes the broad agenda of the country, particularly in terms of its relationship to the international economy. The national situation provides a broad context for policy. These sections also summarise changes in the agenda since 1945.

Constitutions also provide a framework for political activity and are an indication of elite attitudes to the wielding of power. Although the study of constitutions was long unfashionable in political science, constitutions cannot be ignored in liberal democracies which do, on the whole, abide by them. Small details, such as the electoral system, have large consequences for the distribution of power.

We turn next to the main *actors* in the policy process – the political executive, the bureaucracy, parties and pressure groups. These institutions, and especially the relationships between them, shape the content, direction and style of a country's policies. Each country offers a distinct configuration here: strong bureaucracies in France and Japan, a single dominant party in Japan and a tradition of untrammelled party government in Britain.

In the United States, all the 'actors' (except for pressure groups) are themselves fragmented. The political executive, the civil service and the parties are not so much actors as *arenas* in which policy is made. For this reason the American chapter does not attempt to distinguish between actors and arenas. In the other countries, the distinction is slightly more robust and the section on arenas allows us to discuss the cabinet, the assembly and the courts as arenas where policy is at least ratified. We also examine the territorial arena of policy-making here.

The *instruments* of policy are a neglected topic. Anything which gives effect to policy influences policy. In all four countries, administrative regulation, rather than law, is the main instrument of policy but the procedures for issuing regulations vary between countries, offering particular scope to the executive in France. This section also examines planning and budget-making as policy instruments.

Selecting sectors

Any classification of sectors runs the risk of ignoring overlap between them. As Anderson points out, political scientists discuss sectors but politicians confront problems which have no respect for sectoral boundaries.[24] For example a decision about whether to import or manufacture a weapons system can have implications for foreign, defence, regional, industrial and employment policy. Just as governments set up interdepartmental committees, so political scientists need 'inter-sectoral' awareness.

This book examines the policy process in four sectors: industry, health, ethnic minorities and law and order. Just as we asked how representative our four countries are of all liberal democracies, so we can ask how typical these sectors are of the range of activities performed by the modern democratic state. This question raises the curiously under-developed issue of how policy areas should be classified.[25] We make four distinctions here.

1. One distinction among policy areas is between domestic and foreign policy. Our selection is restricted to domestic sectors. Neither foreign nor defence policy is included explicitly. Yet although our selection is restricted to domestic policy, the growing international dimension to policy cannot be ignored. Industrial policy, for example, is largely motivated by the desire to secure or maintain a place for the country's economy within a world economic order. Just as foreign policy is tending to involve more actors (such as firms) so domestic policy is now increasingly internationalised. Thus the distinction between domestic and foreign policy is declining in significance.

2. Another distinction among policy areas is between the basic functions of government and those acquired as part of the twentieth-century expansion in the state's activities. Here our selection covers a wide range. Basic functions of the state, which are performed by or for the state if they are performed at all, are represented in the book by law and order and immigration control. By contrast policy towards ethnic minorities is an example of a sector where the involvement of the state is more recent, marginal and controversial. Here the state uses weaker instruments: symbolic statements of minority rights, some regulation of behaviour (such as anti-discrimination legislation, and a more or less committed effort to promote good practice.

3. Sectors can also be classified by whether they acquire resources from, or apply them to, the population.[26] States must acquire money through taxes; they must also persuade people to administer the state and fight (and die) in its wars. If necessary states will use physical power to achieve these ends. This function of acquiring resources is under-represented in this book. The most relevant sector is industrial policy but here governments seek not so much to acquire resources directly but rather to create prosperity which will, among other things, ease the task of acquisition by increasing tax revenues.

The application of resources is represented in this book by health policy. Ensuring the provision of prompt medical treatment, whether through public or private means, is an important and expensive task of the contemporary democratic state. Together with education, health care in most democracies takes the highest proportion of public employees of any policy sector.[27] Indeed employment in health and education is continuing to increase in all liberal democracies. The state's successes here have contributed to its legitimacy and eased the process of acquiring resources. Health and education are also important because they are examples of sectors where policy is implemented by professionals who claim autonomy in their work. The relationship between policy-makers and professionals is an important theme in the study of policy-making in liberal democracies.[28]

4. A final way of classifying policies is to use Lowi's distinction between regulative, redistributive and distributive policies.[29] Regulative policies embody rules of conduct with sanctions: in industrial safety laws, for example. Redistributive policies seek to reallocate resources between groups: through progressive taxation, for example. Distributive policies convey tangible benefits to individuals or groups but without explicit competition within the sector: agricultural subsidies from which all farmers can benefit, for example.

Lowi's classification concerns policies rather than sectors and examples of each type of policy can doubtless be found in every sector. However none of our areas exemplify distributive policies as clearly as the agricultural sector does. For long periods after 1945 cosy communities of farmers' associations and agriculture ministries worked together to get as much money out of the public purse (the pork barrel) as they could. Pork barrel politics is an important form of policy-making which is not fully represented in our book.

The arrangement of the sectoral chapters is shown below. The opening section discusses the extent and, where relevant, the development of state involvement in the sector. The contrasts here are generally by sector rather than nation. The second section examines the policy agenda – the concerns of the policy community within each sector. Again we find considerable similarity between countries in the agenda within each sector.

Organisation of the sectoral chapters

State involvement
Policy agenda
Policy community
Policy outcomes

The third section describes the policy community. This comprises actors with a common interest and focus on a particular area. As a result, they have some common concerns and often a shared outlook – including a willingness to abide by the informal rules of the policy-making game within that particular sector. The policy community normally extends beyond government to include interest groups and, on occasion, commentators. For example, in the case of the health sector, the main members of the community are politicians and bureaucrats in the health and finance ministries, medical associations, the representatives of insurance organisations and health care administrators, and, on occasion, other health-care pressure groups. Routine policy is often made in specialised communities like these though, as we will see, wider social and political forces impinge on decisions reached. Indeed when a sector becomes politically 'hot', new actors (such as top politicians) enter the arena and policy-making styles change, at least temporarily. Even on routine policy, our use of the word 'community' is not intended to imply any identity of interests or values among its members.[30]

The final section of the sectoral chapters appraises policy outcomes – what policies have achieved, and failed to achieve, in the sector. This reflects the concern of the policy approach with what is achieved out in the field.

NOTES

1. For a classic study, see R. Dahl, *Who Governs?* (New Haven: Yale University Press, 1961). Later critics suggested the decision approach ignored 'non-decisions' which are kept off the agenda. See S. Lukes, *Power: A Radical View* (London: Macmillan, 1974).

2. H. Heclo, 'Policy Analysis', *British Journal of Political Science*, 2 (1972), pp. 83–108.

3. B. Hogwood and L. Gunn, *Policy Analysis for the Real World* (Oxford University Press, 1984), pp. 13–19.

4. A classic example was S. Webb and B. Webb, *Soviet Government: A New Civilisation?* (London: published by the authors, 1935). This described the formal organisation of the Soviet state in minute detail in the apparent conviction that everything worked as Stalin's propagandists alleged.

5. P. Hall, *Governing the Economy* (Oxford: Polity, 1986), p. 16. See also the section on policy-making institutions in Philip Daniels's chapter on industrial policy in this book.

6. In reality, however, governments seem to learn more from their own disasters than from other countries'. See Robert J. Jackson, 'Crisis Management and Policy Making', in R. Rose, ed., *The Dynamics of Public Policy* (London: Sage, 1976), pp. 209–37.

7. For a review of this literature, see H. Jacob and M. Lipsky, 'Outputs, Structures and Power: An Assessment of Changes in the Study of State and Local Politics', *Journal of Politics*, 30 (1968), pp. 510–38. This research showed that political factors were not a major influence on expenditure on particular sectors but that treating outputs in non-financial terms generally produced a bigger role for political variables.

8. This point is made in a useful literature review by E. Feldman, 'Comparative Public Policy: Field or Method?', *Comparative Politics*, 10 (1978), pp. 278–305.

9. H. Eckstein, *Pressure Group Politics* (London: Allen and Unwin, 1960).

10. T. Marmor and D. Thomas, 'Doctors, Politics and Pay Disputes: "Pressure Group Politics' Revisited" ', *British Journal of Political Science*, 2 (1971), pp. 412–42.

11. H. Wilensky, *The Welfare State and Equality* (Berkeley: University of California Press, 1975) and F. Castles, ed., *The Impact of Parties* (London: Sage, 1982). For more recent and qualified statements by each school, see H. Wilensky et al., 'Comparative Social Policy', in M. Dierkes, H. Weiler and A. Antal, eds., *Comparative Policy Research* (Aldershot: Gower, 1987), pp. 381–457 and F. Castles, 'Introduction' to *The Comparative History of Public Policy*, pp. 1–15. These are also the sources of the findings summarised in the next paragraph.

12. H. Wilensky, *The Welfare State and Equality*, p. 27.

13. This point is make by Castles in his introduction to *The Comparative History of Public Policy*.

14. (Oxford: Polity, 1989). The chapter mentioned in this paragraph is T. Pempel, 'Japan's Creative Conservatism: Continuity under Challenge', pp. 149–91.

15. H. Heclo, *Modern Social Politics in Britain and Sweden* (New Haven: Yale University Press, 1974).

16. This summary is from Wilensky, 'Comparative Social Policy', p. 406. See also R. Kudrle and T. Marmor, 'The Development of Welfare States in North America', in P. Flora and A. Heidenheimer, eds., *The Development of Welfare States in Europe and America* (New Brunswick, N.J.: Transaction Books, 1981), pp. 187–236.

17. W. Grant, W. Paterson and C. Whitson, *Government and the Chemical Industry* (Oxford: Clarendon Press, 1988).

18. A. Lijphart, *Democracies* (New Haven: Yale University Press, 1984), p. 38.

19. This model of consensus democracies is developed in Lijphart, *Democracies*, ch. 2.

20. This summary is from S. Wilks and M. Wright, *Comparative Government–Industry Relations* (Oxford: Clarendon Press, 1987), p. 279. See also K. Dyson, *The State Tradition in West Europe* (Oxford: Martin Robertson, 1980).

21. This point is discussed further in ch. 12. Scandinavian social scientists have shown particular interest in the notion of flexibility, generally suggesting that an extensive welfare state, far from producing stagnation, in fact encourages the workforce to accept the need for change in the work-place. See for example K. Nielsen and O. Pedersen, 'Is Small Still Flexible?', *Scandinavian Political Studies*, 12 (1989), pp. 343–72.

22. L. Hartz, *The Liberal Tradition in America* (New York: Harcourt, Brace and World, 1955).

23. See Lukes, *Power: A Radical View*.

24. C. Anderson, 'The Logic of Public Problems', in D. Ashford, ed., *Comparing Public Policies* (London: Sage, 1978), pp. 19–41.

25. For a classification of state agencies, which distinguishes delivery, regulatory, transfer, contracts and control agencies, see P. Dunleavy, 'The Architecture of the British Central State, Part I', *Public Administration*, 67 (1989), pp. 249–75.

26. The distinctions between acquiring, dividing and applying resources are made

in a useful text by M. Burch and B. Wood, *Public Policy in Britain*, 2nd ed. (Oxford: Blackwell, 1989).

27. R. Rose, ed., *Public Employment in Western Nations* (Cambridge University Press, 1985).
28. P. Dunleavy, 'The Professions and Policy Change', *Public Administration Bulletin*, 36 (1981), pp. 3–16.
29. T. Lowi, 'Public Policy and Bureaucracy in Britain and France', in D. Ashford, ed., *Comparing Public Policies*, pp. 177–96.
30. The literature abounds with conflicting definitions of 'communities' and 'networks'. In general a community implies at least some shared values among its members, whereas a 'network' is a more neutral and narrower term, implying only regular interaction among participants. For a review of these terms, see R. Rhodes, 'Policy Networks: A British Perspective', *Journal of Theoretical Politics*, 2 (1990), pp. 293–317.

FURTHER READING

A good general introduction to policy analysis (which we have not sought to repeat here) is B. Hogwood and L. Gunn, *Policy Analysis for the Real World* (Oxford: Oxford University Press, 1984). On comparative policy analysis, a bulky sector-based collection is *Comparative Policy Analysis*, ed. M. Dierkes, H. Weiler and A. Antal (Aldershot: Gower, 1987). For an impressive country-based selection, see *The Comparative History of Public Policy*, ed. F. Castles (Oxford: Polity, 1989). This covers all our countries except France. The *Impact of Parties* (London: Sage, 1982), also edited by Castles, can be read as an extended reply to H. Wilensky's influential *The Welfare State and Equality* (Berkeley: University of California Press, 1975).

Part 1

Countries

2 France

Ella Ritchie

The national situation

After the Second World War France entered a sustained period of rapid state-led economic growth. Between 1945 and 1974 France was transformed from a predominantly agricultural economy with a small, uncompetitive and highly protected industrial sector, to a competitive industrial economy. By 1974 only 12 per cent of the workforce was employed on the land compared to 30 per cent in 1940.[1]

The active role played by the state in post-war reconstruction continued a tradition of direct government involvement in the economy dating back to the seventeenth century. The main priority of the post-war bureaucracy, dominant in the Fourth Republic, was to modernise France and to transform it into a leading power within Europe. This drive to modernisation was given a political impetus with the Presidency of General de Gaulle (1958–69), whose policies were built on the twin pillars of economic modernisation and national grandeur.

Post-war governments set about strengthening the French economy by increasing the public sector and by introducing measures to strengthen the private sector. The nationalisation of the Bank of France was completed and several other private banks and insurance companies were taken into state control. The government also nationalised the gas, electricity and coal industries. In addition it introduced a large number of measures to protect and stimulate private industry.

In addition to these economic measures France instituted a system of indicative planning. A Planning Commissariat was set up which produced five yearly Plans to guide the direction of the economy. The First Plan, issued in 1948, was particularly useful in outlining the direction that post-war reconstruction should take. In the 1950s and early 1960s the Plan continued to be a useful instrument for setting targets for economic growth. However as the French economy has become more open to international forces and the state has controlled less investment the Plan has become less important as a method of strategic resource allocation.[2]

Membership of the European Coal and Steel Community in 1951 and of the European Economic Community in 1957 was a significant factor in the development of the post-war French economy. The wider European market opened up trade opportunities for French industry, which was generally well placed to compete with its European counterparts. France reaped substantial benefits from the Common Agricultural Policy which provided support for French farmers and a large market for France's surplus production.

One of the problems facing France in its drive to modernisation was stagnation in the labour force. In order to counteract this the government followed fairly liberal immigration policies until the mid-1970s. Between 1946 and 1980 some 3 million people migrated to France. In 1961 France absorbed a massive resettlement of French Algerians (*pieds noirs*) following the decolonisation of Algeria. France rapidly became a multi-racial and multi-ethnic society and by the 1970s the government was faced with the social problems caused by an increasingly diverse nation.

During the post-war period the state took on an increasing role in the provision of welfare services, such as health, education and housing. To a certain extent these welfare policies mitigated the uneven distribution of the economic benefits which emerged as a result of economic growth. However, there remained a tension in society arising out of a continued divergence in economic rewards. Groups such as small farmers, unskilled workers and regional minorities have continually pressured the state to improve their conditions.

After 1974 France was hit by the world economic recession and increasing energy costs caused by the oil crisis. Economic performance deteriorated as the country experienced increasing unemployment, rising inflation, decreasing investment and a decline in exports. Membership of the European Monetary System in 1979 meant that it became increasingly difficult for French governments to pursue an independent monetary policy. Within the European Community companies in West Germany and Italy began to be fierce competitors to the French. The increasingly assertive role of the European Community in competition policy meant that it became more difficult for French governments to use the traditional range of policy instruments, such as public procurement policy and industrial subsidies, to protect French industry. The growing internationalisation of products and markets which took place in the late 1970s and 1980s further inhibited the government's use of traditional protectionist policies. The post-war goal of seeking national independence in all fields – military, technology, energy and agriculture – was called into question as policy-makers began to realise the international and financial constraints on traditional French priorities.

The effects of the international economic environment on national policy-making were brought into sharp focus at the beginning of the Socialist Presidency of François Mitterrand in 1981. Mitterrand's expansionist economic policies of reflating the economy were sharply at odds with the policies of economic restraint which were being followed by other countries in the West.[3] During 1982 external opposition to Mitterrand's policies helped to weaken the franc and to aggravate the economic crisis in the country. The European Community put considerable pressure on the Socialist government to deflate the economy and reduce the budget deficit.

Mitterrand was faced with a choice of 'going it alone' by pulling out of the European Monetary System and introducing further protectionist policies for French industry, or taking the 'European solution', which meant sacrificing the socialist economic programme in favour of more deflationary policies. Despite considerable opposition from the Socialist Party Mitterrand chose the latter solution and effected a U-turn in economic policy: from a dash for growth to austerity and restraint. From 1983 onwards the Socialist government abandoned its reflationary policies and, in concert with other OECD countries, began to pursue policies based on the market economy. In 1984 the new Prime Minister Laurent Fabius instituted measures designed to cut back the public sector and deregulate the economy.

The election of a government of the right in 1986, committed to economic liberalism, further challenged the consensus of state-led growth. The new government's policies of deregulation, liberalisation and privatisation, whilst limited in practice, led to a further erosion of the traditional methods of state intervention in France. Nevertheless, whilst the notion of the strong interventionist state lost some of its appeal, traditional techniques such as state procurement policy and subsidies continued to be used in the 1980s to support French industry. The state still played a more interventionist role in directing the economy than in either the UK or the USA.

In parallel to these domestic changes France was managing a new set of international relations in the post-war period.[4] After the painful experience of decolonisation France continued to play a very active role in Third World politics. France also maintained an independent defence strategy, marked by the decision of General de Gaulle to leave the integrated military command structure of NATO in 1966. France was also one of the key actors in the European Community. France realised at an early stage that its strategic and economic interests lay within the Community and during the 1950s French politicians, such as Jean Monnet and Robert Schuman, played an influential role in establishing the European Coal and Steel Community and the European Economic Community. Whilst General de Gaulle, who assumed power in 1958, did not share the supranational aspirations of Monnet he accepted French membership of the European Community because he realised that the Community would help France to achieve two important and related policy objectives – strengthening France's role in the world and modernising the French nation.

During the 1960s and 1970s France dominated Community politics, the shape of its institutions and the outcome of its policies. In 1974 the French President Giscard d'Estaing initiated the European Council, which brought together Heads of Government on a regular basis to discuss community policy. The Franco-German alliance, dominant for most of the 1960s and 1970s, was responsible for the launching of the European Monetary System in 1979. However, during the 1980s France's leadership role in the Community began to be increasingly challenged by the changing balance of power within the enlarged Community, although support from France remained a necessary precondition of any major reform.

The constitution

The Fifth Republic, set up by General de Gaulle in December 1958, has brought political stability to France in the form of a strengthened executive, relatively enduring governments and stable parliamentary majorities. The 1958 constitution gave France a system which is a hybrid between a presidential and a parliamentary regime. The President was to be the 'guardian of the nation', and the 'arbiter in policy making'. He was given the right to choose the Prime Minister who in turn had the right to nominate the government; in practice Presidents have intervened extensively in choosing both senior and junior ministers. Parliament had limited power to force the resignation of the government (though not of the president), and the government was held nominally responsible to Parliament for its policies.

The direct election of the President, introduced by de Gaulle in 1962, together with the practices of all three conservative Presidents, de Gaulle (1958–69), Pompidou (1969–74) and Giscard d'Estaing (1974–81), led to a concentration of power, authority and decision-making around the presidency. Most significantly, compared to previous republics, until 1986 each President was backed by a political party or coalition which held the majority of seats in the National Assembly and consequently was able to steer policies through Parliament and to create a reasonably united governmental machine. Within this framework Presidents remained pre-eminent. Over time Presidents accumulated areas which they considered to be their own domain: foreign and European affairs, defence and colonial policy, key financial and industrial matters and many social and environmental issues. In addition Presidents soon made it clear that they would intervene in any matter which interested them.

If Presidents shared power with their Prime Ministers, often leaving the day-to-day running of the government to them, they always had the upper hand. Both governments and Prime Ministers were often circumvented by the infrastructure of committees and advisers with which Presidents surrounded themselves. Consequently, the Cabinet itself was relatively weak both as a decision-making forum and as an arena for resolving political disputes.

When the left came to power in the presidential and parliamentary elections of 1981, it inherited a regime constructed for and around the Gaullist and Giscardien administrations. François Mitterrand, the new President, had heavily criticised the right-wing Presidents for their abuse of power and their 'colonisation' and penetration of the state machinery. The Socialists were committed to reducing the power of the President and to revitalising Parliament. In practice, however, until the power-sharing experience of March 1986 to May 1988, Mitterrand continued to take decisions in much the same way as his predecessors had done, relying heavily on personal advisers and politically sympathetic civil servants. Although he did initially try to revitalise Parliament, for example, by increasing the opposition's role on committees, he soon came to dominate it, using the same constitutional devices, such as turning contentious legislation into votes of confidence, as had Giscard d'Estaing.

In the parliamentary elections of March 1986, the French electorate failed to give President Mitterrand a working majority within the Assembly. Instead the right-wing coalition was returned with a narrow and precarious majority. Short of provoking a constitutional crisis, Mitterrand had little option but to choose as his Prime Minister the Gaullist leader, Jacques Chirac,[5] and for the main to endorse a conservative government chosen by Chirac. France entered a period of *cohabitation* where a left-wing President was forced to share power with a right-wing Prime Minister and government. The novel experience of *cohabitation* in some ways proved a test for the constitution and led to the reworking of many of the ground rules which had built up over the previous twenty-eight years. Temporarily the balance of power between the President and the Prime Minister was changed. During this period the Prime Minister became more significant in policy-making and there was a revitalisation of Parliament as both leaders worked hard to appeal to their party support in the National Assembly.

Political conflict between Mitterrand and Chirac was minimised for two reasons. First, both men had set their sights on winning the 1988 presidential election and hence neither wanted to cause a political crisis by overstepping his constitutional position. Secondly, there was some convergence of policy between the two leaders in areas such as foreign policy and economic affairs. In practice during this period the President remained dominant in foreign policy – especially in the fields of defence, Franco-German relations and disarmament. In domestic matters, such as industrial policy, health and law and order, the Prime Minister and the government took more responsibility.

In the May 1988 parliamentary elections no single party emerged with a majority in the National Assembly. In this instance Mitterrand appointed a largely Socialist government under a moderate Socialist Prime Minister, Michel Rocard. Since May 1988 the role of the Prime Minister has once again been downgraded with the President resuming control over most matters of policy.

Actors

Executive

The Executive in the Fifth Republic, and more specifically the President and, between 1986 and 1988, the Prime Minister, are the key actors in the French system. The President or Prime Minister will intervene directly in the drawing up of legislation in particular circumstances, such as when the policy involves several conflicting ministries. In practice this means that Presidents do not confine themselves to matters falling into their reserved domain but range widely across the policy agenda.

All members of the executive are assisted by personal teams of advisers called ministerial *cabinets*.[6] These are entirely separate from the Cabinet of government ministers. Between 1959 and 1981 approximately 90 per cent of *cabinet* members were civil servants seconded from their posts to work with ministers as policy advisers. The remainder were party activists, industrialists or academics. The typical *cabinet* consists of about ten members who assist the minister both politically (relations with Parliament, constituency matters, speech writing) and administratively (co-ordination of the civil service, liaising with key bureaucrats in Brussels, following through policy initiatives). In a sense the *cabinets* combine the functions carried out in the United Kingdom by ministers' private offices and the top echelons of the civil service. They are an invaluable support for a minister in a system which tends to be dominated by a powerful administration.

Unlike the work of the civil service, which is neatly laid down in lists of functions and fields of jurisdiction, the *cabinet*'s work has no defined boundaries. Instead each *cabinet* accumulates its own administrative territory and political power by bargaining, precedent and unwritten rules. Consequently the power and style of *cabinets* vary enormously depending on the calibre of the minister and the strength of the ministry.

The personal staff of the Prime Minister and the President have become particularly important during the Fifth Republic. The Prime Minister's *cabinet* supervises the day-to-day workings of the ministries and deals with inter-ministerial disputes. The President's personal staff, consisting of the General Secretariat and the *cabinet*, occupy a more strategic position in the policy-making process. Presidential aides not only provide the President with advice and ideas on policy and strategy but also help him to co-ordinate policy and to follow through policy initiatives. This is evident in European community policy. Since the 1950s European Community policies have been co-ordinated in France by an inter-ministerial committee, the SGCI.[7] The SGCI acts as a two-way link between Brussels and the French administration. Although the SGCI is nominally under the control of the Prime Minister, since 1969 it has always been headed by a member of the President's personal *cabinet*. Consequently, Presidents have been well informed about community policy and have been able to exert considerable control over the position which French ministers and bureaucrats take in Brussels.

Bureaucracy

The Fifth Republic has been described as a 'technocrat's paradise'. Higher civil servants are seen as the key decision-makers within the political system because they form a prestigious elite, representing and serving a highly interventionist state, which has been able to penetrate the world of politics and industry. In France training as a top civil servant is the key to a successful career in many fields. Many ministers, Members of Parliament and leading industrialists are former civil servants or civil servants on secondment.

French civil servants are organised into *corps* or professional groups. Each *corps* has its own rules, norms, privileges and, most importantly, identity. The *corps*, which were largely set up under Napoleon, wield an enormous influence over the administration. The administrative structure of many ministries has been shaped around the function of the *corps*. Certain ministries have become the stronghold of one particular corps, for example the Finance Ministry and the *Inspection des finances*. Other ministries find themselves caught between different corps. For example, in the Ministry of the Environment policy is often the outcome of battles between the *corps des mines* (mining engineers) and the *corps des ponts et chausées* (bridges and roads engineers).

Top civil servants are recruited by competitive entry to post-graduate colleges, the *grandes écoles* (technical schools) and the *Ecole Nationale d'Administration* (ENA). The ENA is the training school for the five *grands corps*: the *Inspection des Finances*, the *Conseil d'Etat* (Council of

State), the *Cours des Comptes* (Court of Accounts) the Prefectoral and Diplomatic *corps*, and for the generalist class of civil servants – the *administrateurs civils*. Students at the ENA are taught by serving civil servants and are quickly socialised into the norms of the top administration. Anne Stevens found that people trained at the ENA had a good grasp of strategic thinking[8] and Peter Hall, in a comparative study of economic policy-making in France and Britain, notes that 'French civil servants felt responsibility for the direction of industry, generally capable of undertaking it and entitled to do so, when their British counterparts were far more hesitant.'[9]

The *grands corps* are the most prestigious administrators; large numbers are detached from the *corps* at any one time and are seconded to high posts in other parts of the administration, to work as personal aides to ministers, or to industry or politics. Many leave the administration at mid-career to take up posts in public corporations or in private industry. Members of the *grands corps* are strategic actors in the policy-making process. They set the climate for policy debate, help to shape the political agenda and regulate the output of policy. As top administrators and as ministerial aides they may also be vital initiators of policy. Within industry they also influence business strategy. There is considerable evidence to suggest that during the 1960s and 1970s the widespread presence of former civil servants within the public and private sectors of industries contributed to a shared ethos of state-led economic expansion.[10] It may be that in the more international context of business in the 1980s and 1990s this particular influence is declining. Faced with the competitive pressures associated with the completion of the internal market by 1993, the private sector is beginning to turn to managers who have a training in international management skills in preference to publicly trained administrative and technological elites.[11]

While the top echelons of the administration are relatively innovative and forward thinking in France, the lower echelons are often bureaucratic and inflexible. The centralised and regulated state produces a complex and hierarchical administration. Frustrated citizens have to deal with a huge and often bewildering bureaucracy. The problems associated with inflexible administrators has long been a source of alienation, for example among ethnic minority groups.

Parties

Historically, political parties have been weak in France, both as a focus for particular political ideologies and as influences on the output of government. The tradition of localism and the fragmented nature of the party system in the late Third and Fourth Republics meant that deputies were important not through parties but independently of them.

In the Fifth Republic this has changed. Most significantly, the structure of the party system has polarised into two camps, left and right, grouped around four main parties. Urbanisation and the decline of issues such as church versus state has meant that parties representing specific interests have declined. The introduction of a simple majority two-ballot electoral system encouraged coalition building within the right and the left and led to a simplification of the party system.

The most significant factor influencing the shape of the party system has been the institutional structure of the Fifth Republic.[12] The power and authority of the presidency has effected a restructuring of the party system. This has taken place through a number of mechanisms. First, parties have realised the importance of the presidency. To be politically significant parties must not only attain a sound electoral and parliamentary base but must also be able to offer a credible presidential candidate. Party leaders have also become aware of the need to form coalitions and to back one candidate on the second ballot in order to stand a chance of winning the great political prize of the presidency. Secondly, once elected, deputies realise that toeing the party line may be the key to a successful political career. They are therefore prepared to tolerate party discipline in the National Assembly. Finally, Presidents need organised party support in the National Assembly to get their legislation passed; they also need the support of parties to get elected. These factors have led to stronger, more coherent and better disciplined parties.

On the left, the two main parties are the Socialists (*Parti Socialiste*, PS), and the Communists (*Parti Communiste Français*, PCF). During the Fifth Republic the Socialists have emerged as the dominant party on the left. The PCF has, since 1958, suffered an inexorable decline in electoral support, party membership and political credibility. The right is more fragmented; the main forces are the Gaullists (*Rassemblement pour la République*, RPR) and the non-Gaullist right (since 1978 federated under the banner of the *Union pour la Démocratie Française*, UDF). The introduction of proportional representation for the 1986 legislative elections helped the extreme right *Front National* Party to win thirty-five seats in the National Assembly and to gain a national platform for its policies. However, proportional representation was not used in 1988 and *Front National* representation was virtually eliminated (see appendix, p. 284).

On the right, party structures remain weak. The RPR is a party dominated by its leadership. Factions within the party tended in the 1980s to be grouped around personalities rather than issues. The constituent parties of the UDF, the *Parti Républicain*, and more especially the *Parti*

Radical and the *Centre des Démocrates Sociaux*, are more decentralised and organised around local *notables*. Internal infighting was rife both within the UDF and between the UDF and the RPR during the 1980s. On the left, party discipline remains strong in the PCF, whereas the Socialist Party is constructed around a number of factions, and it is these factions which are important in shaping policy.

While parties are largely dominated by the executive they are on some occasions a constraint on policy-making and, to a limited extent, policy initiators. Between 1958 and 1981 the primary role of political parties was to provide political and electoral support for the President. This period saw the emergence of a well-organised and disciplined Gaullist majority, supported by a minority of non-Gaullist Conservatives. This Conservative majority backed the President's policies in Parliament. Under the Mitterrand administration of 1981–6 the Socialists largely supported the President's policy in Parliament, although Mitterrand, and more especially his second Prime Minister Laurent Fabius, experienced some difficulties in selling moderate socialist policies and the post-1982 austerity programme to the Socialist Party. Party influence over the administration tended to be more assertive in the early phases of the Socialist government. Ministers, conscious of the potentially hostile administrative environment, surrounded themselves with party activists as advisers.[13] By the time of the second Socialist administration in 1988 they had reverted to the more traditional pattern of using civil servants as their personal advisers and consequently the party lost an important channel of influencing the government.

Generally speaking opposition to the government has been weak during the Fifth Republic because the government dominates procedural arrangements in Parliament and all parliamentary committees. The growth of majority government in the Fifth Republic means that governments do not now fear being overturned on crucial issues. Nevertheless the parties have effectively checked the government on occasions, either through amendments, questions or delaying tactics. For example, Mitterrand's controversial decentralisation legislation of 1982, which sought to dismantle many aspects of the Napoleonic centralised state and hence threatened to disturb the well-feathered nests of local politicians, provoked hundreds of parliamentary amendments.

Between March 1986 and May 1988 political parties became more significant in the policy-making process both within Parliament and in outside arenas. The difficulties of *cohabitation* and the narrowness and complexity of the Conservative majority in the Assembly meant that Chirac was unable to take a parliamentary majority for granted. The attempt to appeal to the right wing of the Conservative parties and to gain the support of the *Front National* meant that the government sometimes lost the support of the centrists within the majority. The tightening of immigration legislation, changes in working and employment practices and social security policy were amended in the Assembly by both the left opposition and some centrist sections of the majority. Since 1988 when the Socialists again became the largest party in Parliament, the Conservative parties have been riddled with infighting and have consequently been relatively weak as an opposition force.

The role of the party in policy formation is multifaceted. The broad thrust of a government's policy will be formulated outside office and it is at this stage that a party may have an important input. Often the philosophical underpinnings of a party's policy perspectives will be generated and articulated by groups and interests which surround it. For example, during the 1981–6 opposition period the two major Conservative parties (the RPR and the UDF) became, for the large part, committed to neo-liberalism, a move that was resonant with the policy stances of the right in most major Western countries. It was institutions such as the political clubs, the Gaullist *Club de l'Horloge* and the *Club 89*, and the Giscardien *Club Perspectives et Réalités*, and certain key conservative intellectuals,[14] who propounded these ideas vociferously before the parties drew up their manifesto in 1984. The party leaders themselves organised the ideas into an electoral programme, *Plateforme pour gouverner ensemble*. In this platform a series of policy intentions such as deregulation, liberalisation and privatisation were laid down. However the detail of the policies, and hence their real content, was left to the government to define.

Pressure groups

It is often argued that under the Fourth Republic pressure groups exerted enormous influence on policy, whereas since 1959 their role and influence has considerably diminished. Whilst it is true that de Gaulle and other leaders publically had a great disdain for pressure groups, in practice French governments, like their counterparts elsewhere in Western Europe, depend upon the support, or at least the acquiescence, of key socio-economic groups to govern effectively. France was traditionally depicted as a state whose citizens had a low level of participation in interest groups compared to other countries in Western Europe but it appears that this pattern changed in the 1970s and 1980s as groups representing both interests and causes proliferated.[15]

The fragmentary nature of pressure groups in France, their ideological and philosophical divisions and the weakness of peak organisations has often enabled governments to circumscribe the political power of individual groups by a process of divide and rule. Thus although, for example, certain business interests have a close and cosy relationship with the Ministry of Industry, others such as the CNPME, the organisation representing medium-sized business, has not managed to gain a foothold. In practice individual businesses often try to influence national government or the European Community directly.

There are numerous bodies such as the Planning Commission, the Economic and Social Council and Regional Planning bodies which formally incorporate interests into the decision-making process. Hence there is to some extent an institutionalisation of pressure groups. In practice, however, this process of incorporation may not amount to much because the major decisions about resource allocation tend to be made outside these bodies. Nevertheless there are some elements of neo-corporatism in France. Some professional groups, such as lawyers, have a very close relationship with their tutelage ministry.[16] One of the farming unions, the FNSEA, has sought to colonise the agricultural ministry and it is often unclear where the interest of the groups ends and the interest of the administration begins.[17]

Trade unions have historically carried little weight in the policy-making process.[18] By the end of the 1980s only about 13 per cent of the French workforce belonged to a trade union.[19] The unions are ideologically fragmented and competitive. Although there are no formal links between trade unions and parties of the left as found in the UK, there is often an overlap in personnel at the activist level and close informal contact. The *Confédération Générale du Travail* (CGT) is the oldest and largest trade union confederation in France and is closely linked with the Communist Party. The second biggest union, the *Confédération Française Démocratique du Travail* (CFDT) is Christian Socialist in origin but has renounced its confessional links and has largely aligned itself with the Socialist Party. Although these and smaller confederations each tend to be concentrated in a particular industrial sector there is still considerable competition between unions, both at a national and a local level. Consequently, evolving a joint national industrial strategy has been a laborious task. The natural hostility of the CGT and some sections of the CFDT to government and managers has meant that accommodation has been practically non-existent.

The election of a Socialist government in 1981 which was publicly committed to an *ouverture* (opening out) to the unions led to the possibility of a more effective say for them in policy-making. Initially CFDT leaders were consulted by the government and were influential in drawing up the 1983 Auroux law which gave a greater influence to workers in decision-making within firms. However once the austerity measures imposed by the Socialists began to bite the unions became estranged from the government and were consulted less about policy.

Arenas

The policy-making process takes place in a number of different arenas depending on the actors involved, the stage of the process and the nature of the policy. For example, under the constitution of the Fifth Republic the President is largely responsible for defence – hence the arena for defence policy-making is to be found in the advisers and committees for defence which surround the presidency and which work with the Defence Ministry and defence staff. The stage of the process will also be important in determining the arena; political leaders may initiate a policy but they will leave detailed formulation and implementation to the administration. Finally, the nature of the policy itself will also be of significance in determining the arena. The majority of policy-making is routine rather than political; however, a seemingly technical issue, routinely handled by the administration, may suddenly erupt into a politically sensitive issue if it touches the interests of an important group in a minister's constituency, and hence may move from one arena to another. Because of their administrative expertise ministerial *cabinets* are usually well equipped to deal with technical issues on behalf of their ministers. This tends to increase the degree of control which the executive has over the minutiae of policy. Actors in the policy process will know that the arena for a policy may well influence its outcome – hence bureaucrats often try to hide policies in technical committees, and politicians may defuse a politically contentious issue by placing it under judicial review.

The broad arena for the initiation of policy lies with the executive rather than with Parliament. Although legislation formally proceeds through the National Assembly and Senate, over 90 per cent of bills are initiated by the government. From a very early stage in the Fifth Republic the government used its constitutional right of decree to force through policies without Parliament's approval. As in most liberal democracies the French Parliament does little more than scrutinise and approve legislation. In the Fifth Republic there have only been six parliamentary committees. Their large membership makes them unwieldy and relatively ineffective. In contrast to the Fourth Republic, where specialised committees worked closely with interest groups, committees in the Fifth Republic have not generally been important arenas for policy-making. However the fragile nature of the government's majority since 1988 has to some extent reinvigorated the parliamentary committee system.

The President, Prime Minister and individual ministers, working closely with their *cabinets*, are all in a position to identify and initiate a policy, although they will rarely follow a decision through to its conclusion. These initiatives may be as a response to a manifesto, or to an important pressure group, or, in some cases, to an unforeseen event. Once the initiative has evolved the President and his staff (until March 1986 in tandem with the Prime Minister) will initiate discussion of the proposal through small groups of Ministers, *conseils restreints* and inter-ministerial committees. The Cabinet will only act as a ratifier of policy.

The main arena for policy-making will be within the administration which will either work out the details of policy initiatives from above or will make policy itself. The administration is divided into about twenty ministries organised hierarchically. As in most other Western democracies there are hundreds of committees and commissions which mushroom around the traditional ministry structures. One characteristic of the French administrative system is the creation of *administrations de mission*, or special policy units to deal with particular questions. These missions have a special status within the administration.

Many policies involve inter-ministerial committees. The journey of a dossier between ministries is usually a slow and hazardous one. This is for two main reasons. First, ministries tend to see problems from different standpoints, either because of the *corps* working within the ministries, or because of the interests which they represent. Secondly, ministries tend to assess their power in terms of the areas which they control and hence are reluctant to 'lose' policy areas to another ministry. It is often up to the ministerial *cabinets* to sort out these disputes.

The growing Europeanisation of French policy-making has inevitably widened the national policy-making arena. In areas such as agriculture, trade, industry and increasingly the environment, policy-making takes place through bilateral exchanges between Brussels and Paris. The increasing importance of the Community has undoubtedly undermined the power of the nation-state as an arena in which forces compete to shape policies. As the policy competences of the Community have grown, groups increasingly use links with the EC as a way of circumventing national government. Community policy-making is well co-ordinated in France through the SGCI, the committee which acts as a filter between the national ministries and French civil servants in the Permanent Representation in Brussels. The close control effected by the SGCI over the French position in Brussels means that French Ministers are well briefed over the policy positions which they should take. This sometimes leads to inflexibility by the French in the Council of Ministers.

Normally the arena for policy-making is shielded from the public eye, taking place in committee rooms deep inside ministries. Occasionally, however, the public may have a ringside seat for the policy debate; this may be because the issue is leaked to the media, or because it is by nature a public affair – in France, where taking to the streets has been described as a 'public sport' this is not uncommon. In 1986 it was estimated that there were over 500 major demonstrations in Paris alone. Often direct action reaps rewards. For example the battle over university reform in 1986, in which university students demonstrated against plans to tighten selection procedures and to increase tuition fees, was largely fought in the streets and on television. Student and public opposition eventually led to the withdrawal of the proposed reforms and the resignation of the minister responsible for universities.

The judicial arena has become increasingly important in policy-making.[20] Judicial review of new legislation by the Council of State has been a long tradition in France. In addition the 1958 Constitution set up a nine-person Constitutional Council to police the boundaries between the law-making domain of Parliament and the decree-making domain of the government. Both the Council of State and the Constitutional Council have become more important arenas. During the 1970s and 1980s Parliament frequently had recourse to the judicial arena in its search for ways of obstructing and amending government legislation. For example, Mitterrand's controversial nationalisation was subject to close scrutiny and amendment by both the Council of State and the Constitutional Council. During the period of *cohabitation* Mitterrand used the judicial arena to slow down or amend contentious legislation proposed by the Chirac government.

France has traditionally had a highly centralised system of government. The system of Prefects (renamed Commissioners for the Republic in 1982), who represent the state in each of the ninety-three departments, has ensured that central government has considerable control over other levels of government. Government departments have field agencies in the provinces but these agencies are subject to control from Paris and to a certain extent by the Prefects. This means that key areas of the state's activities, such as education and policing, are subject to rigorous control by the central authorities. Nevertheless local interests have always been well protected in France. Most deputies and ministers, as well as many top civil servants, hold multiple local offices and they usually take their local responsibilities very seriously by lobbying on their constituents' behalf.

During the 1980s considerable efforts were made by the Mitterrand administration to decentralise the state's functions.[21] The powers of local government were considerably strengthened, the regional tier of government became elected and between 1982 and 1988 the financial resources of local authorities were doubled.[22] One of the effects of these changes has been to increase the policy-making capacity of regional and local authorities. For example during the 1980s local authorities were increasingly using their own finances to pay for municipal police forces. The growing influence of the European Community in shaping French policy has been used by the regions to strengthen their own power vis-a-vis the centre. By 1988 six regions and four departments had their own offices in Brussels to lobby the community in areas such as industrial policy.

Instruments

Policies are enacted by *lois*, *décrets* and *arrêtés*. Laws (*lois*) are voted by Parliament but are generally initiated by the government through the Prime Minister. In many cases laws give only a very general framework and have to be complemented by decrees (*décrets*) and administrative rules (*arrêtés*) before they can be implemented by the administration. Membership of the EC has meant that EC law overrides national law.

The constitution gives the right of initiative to ministers for legislation concerning their own departments. The majority of bills (*projets de lois*) are drawn up by the department concerned although about one in ten bills is drawn up directly by the President or the Prime minister, or alternatively, may be modified by the President or Prime Minister on discussion in the Council of Ministers before being presented to Parliament. After laws have been passed they are promulgated by being signed by the President, the Prime Minister and all interested ministers. During the *cohabitation* experience Mitterrand frequently used the tactic of delaying his signature on certain contentious legislation – for example, the repeal of the proportional representation system of election and the reintroduction of the single member two ballot system – while the constitutionality of the legislation was tested.

The importance of decrees has increased under the Fifth Republic. First, only certain specified fields of policy are covered by laws: civil rights, criminal procedure, taxation, the electoral system, nationalisation and privatisation, local authorities, education and property. All other areas are covered by governmental decrees. Secondly, even within the law-making sphere, the government has the right to seek the authorisation of Parliament, for a limited period, to rule by decrees in special areas which eventually have to be ratified by a bill through Parliament. The effect of these two clauses has been to transfer power to the executive and away from Parliament. Thirdly, laws now give much less detail of policy and often even the substance of a law is to be found in the accompanying decrees. Constitutionally, the Prime Minister has the authority to draw up decrees but for technical and practical reasons this power has normally been delegated to individual ministers. The minister will delegate the details of drawing up the decree to a member of his *cabinet* (usually an administrative lawyer from the Council of State) or to his civil servants. If a decree is very complex and involves several ministries it will be discussed in an inter-ministerial committee. The more important decrees are discussed in the Council of Ministers; others are signed by the author of the decree and by the Prime Minister or President and inserted into the *Journal Officiel*.

The most detailed stipulations about how policies are to be enacted are drawn up in *arrêtés* and *circulaires*. Because of their technical nature these tend to be drawn up by the administration; in some cases they are signed by a minister, in others by civil servants who have received the appropriate *délégation de signature*. In practice these *arrêtés* may be very important – once legislation has been passed, the administration can delay drawing up the appropriate enabling legislation, so in a sense they can veto or adopt the decision at this stage. A classic example is the contraception legislation (Neuwirth law) passed by Parliament in 1967 which took years to be fully implemented because of the reluctance of the administration, under pressure from the anti-contraception lobby, to clarify the technical details of the legislation.

France is unusual among West European nations in that it has an indicative planning machinery. Initially the Plan was conceived as a method of setting targets and goals for the economy. This involved four linked processes: study and forecasting, concertation and co-ordination, decision-making and implementation.[23] Most commentators are agreed that the planning mechanism was more effective in the 1950s than later. During the recession of the 1970s the planning mechanism as it was originally devised had little place in giving direction to the economy. Further, the Planning Commissariat has no real sanctions which it can impose and no resources to allocate. It has, over time, become dominated by the Ministry of Finance. The Socialist decentralisation of some planning functions to regional level has further complicated its task, and despite the development of more complex models the Plan has been downgraded. The 1986 Conservative government's emphasis on market forces meant that the Plan became less important as an economic instrument. Mitterrand stressed the importance of returning to Monnet-style planning when he was re-elected in 1988 but it seems unlikely that this will be possible in an era when the French economy is more exposed to international pressures. Whilst the economic objectives of the Plan have not generally been met, the commitment of the state to the process of planning has had an important impact on the culture of French economic policy-making. Both the tradition of directing state resources to particular areas and the close links between public and private sectors of industry can be partially attributed to the culture of planning.

The annual budget is a further instrument for the government to use to influence economic policy.[24] However the French budget has neither the symbolic importance of the British budget nor the political significance of the American budget. The impact of the annual budget, which sets out the expenditure and revenue patterns for the following year, is to some extent subsumed under the more strategic five year National Plan. Moreover, in France most public expenditure is not included in the budget. The extra-budgetory sector, which includes education, local authorities, nationalised industry and social security, amounts to about two-thirds of total government expenditure.[25]

The budget is voted every year in January under the Finance Bill. About 90 per cent of the total revenue is raised from taxes; the remaining 10 per cent comes from non-taxation income (such as social insurance and pension contributions), grants and capital revenue. Projections of expenditure are largely calculated in terms of ministries, despite numerous attempts to reshape the budget to the sectors used in the National Plan. The bulk of the budget is made up of continuing expenditure with little money for new items. As in most countries the budgetary process is incremental, consisting largely of bargaining between the spending ministries and the Ministry of Finance. Every year each ministry presents a statement of expenditure for the forthcoming year to the Ministry of Finance. The Ministry of Finance will attempt to cut back the estimated expenditure. The Prime Minister and his staff arbitrate in cases where the two ministries cannot resolve their differences. In very rare cases (approximately six a year) the President and his staff will become involved in budgetary disputes. In contrast to Japan there is little influence from the governing party in the preparation of the annual budget and Parliament's role in scrutinising and challenging the budget is usually limited to detail.

Interpretation

Policy-making in the Fifth Republic has been subjected to a variety of interpretations.[26] Most approaches to French policy-making take the state as a starting point. In the 1960s and 1970s writers on French politics emphasised the state's potential for autonomous action. In this view the state was seen as able to act independently from both interest groups and even politicians. It was argued that the French state had the capacity to successfully impose its policies through control of financial resources, a prestigious civil service and jurisdictional authority. Marxist theorists, while stressing that the French state is powerful, added the condition that it is not autonomous but acts as an instrument of dominant class interests.[27] More recently neo-Marxists have applied the model of state capitalism to contemporary France.[28]

Within the 'statists' some writers emphasise the institutional capacity of the state. Peter Hall in a comparative study of economic policy in France and the UK argues that an 'institutional' approach has some value in explaining why France, while facing similar economic challenges to Britain in the post-war period, has followed a different path.[29] France has had a policy of state-led growth whereas Britain has lacked a coherent economic policy. Hall argues that the way in which policy-making is organised affects policy outcome. Hence for Hall one of the contributory factors in France's relatively successful economic policy was its capacity to manage industry. He stresses 'the formal rules, compliance procedures and standard operating practices that structure the relationship between industries in the various units of the polity and the economy'.[30]

In accounting for the strong state some interpretations emphasise the power of its civil servants. Numerous studies have characterised the Fifth Republic as a 'technocracy',[31] stressing the powerful position of the bureaucracy at the centre of the policy-making elite. It is argued that under the Fifth Republic senior civil servants have assumed leadership positions not only within the administration but also within business and politics. Their strategic position has enabled them to dominate the policy process.

There is considerable evidence for this theory. The Gaullists' long period of office gave them the opportunity to place supporters in key administrative posts and hence there was a politicisation of the bureaucracy. At the same time there was a bureaucratisation of political institutions since many civil servants entered the world of politics, particularly through ministerial *cabinets*. These two processes strengthened the position of a powerful elite with access to all the sources of power within the state. However the weakness of this theory is that it fails to give enough weight to the difference between technical background and current functional responsibility.[32] Many in-depth case studies of the role of administrative *corps* stress the differing priorities and policy goals of each *corps* and the competition between them. A classic example is the study by Jean Pierre Thoenig[33] of clashes of interest over planning policy in the Department of the Environment between the bridges and road engineers, on the one hand, and the mining engineers on the other. This type of analysis illustrates how the state machinery is made up of a myriad of different parts which do not always interact smoothly to pull in the same direction; in extreme cases this rivalry and competition between the *corps* leads to policy inertia. Policy-making from this perspective tends to be more incremental and reactive than 'statist' models suggest. However the state is undoubtedly powerful even if it is not monolithic.

While competition does exist between members of the administration, a shared background facilitates good informal contact between elites. This easy interchange between elite groups is one of the strengths of the French system, particularly in areas such as industrial policy. Some critics maintain however that this cohesion amongst elite groups has some disadvantages. In particular close contacts and overlap in personnel may lead to closed policy-making communities which are not sufficiently adaptive to change or to the incorporation of new groups. The system also reduces democratic control.

Recent theories of state power have emphasised that states may not be uniformly weak or strong; they may easily impose policies in one sector but be caught in a stranglehold by interested parties in another. Theda Skocpol[34] develops a theory of the conditions under which states have the capacity to achieve their goals: control of financial resources (such as a national central bank and strategic ownership of parts of the economy), a prestigious and status-conscious career civil service with predictable access to key executive posts and authoritative planning agencies. Most of these conditions apply to contemporary France, as does Skocpol's point about the dynamics and complexity of the state's position:

Whether originally autonomous or not, state intervention in socio-economic life can, over time, lead to a diminution of state autonomy and a reduction of any capacities which the state may have for coherent action.[35]

Ezra Suleiman writing within this perspective[36] argues that a centralised state is not necessarily all powerful. In many areas the French state is hemmed in and constrained by the relationship it has with particular sections of society. Far from concentrating power, centralisation 'offers a remarkable advantage to private groups; they need not disperse their efforts in accordance with jurisdictional dispersal as is the case with decentralisation'.[37] He argues that in order to understand the power of the state one must look at the relationship, historically derived, between the state and groups.[38]

Many commentators deal with the complexity, incoherence and fragmentation of the policy process by using the concept of 'network analysis' or 'policy communities'. This approach has long been an established methodology in France for understanding the complex web of interrelationships between central and local government.[39] It is argued that for most of the Fifth Republic policy communities have been stable and cohesive. Yves Meny emphasises two critical factors which underpin this stability.[40] First, the power and influence of the *grands corps* which have an unchallenged control of the policy-making process. Secondly, the ability of the state to legitimise key interest groups into policy communities by granting them special favours and, equally importantly, the capacity of the state to exclude groups which it does not favour. Because of the closed system of policy-making in France, outsider groups find it extremely difficult to enter policy arenas and consequently in frustration resort to direct action. The exclusion of many groups leads to problems in implementing policy. Meny argues that the growing importance of the European Community in domestic policy-making and the increasing decentralisation of power has begun to change the policy-making framework. Within this scenario it is possible that policy communities will themselves be subject to change.

Another approach which seeks to explain the paradox of a strong state which is often hindered by its incapacity to implement policies is Hayward's theory of a dual policy style.[41] Hayward argues that on the one hand the state is highly coercive and on the other that it proceeds by 'negotiated mutual accommodation and compromise':

although French policy making may be characterised as having a predominantly reactive, short term and piecemeal approach to problem solving, at the summit of the French state there is an informal nucleus of executive power capable of challenging the routine norms and attempting to impose an active, longer-term and comprehensive style of policy-making and implementation.[42]

This model can be used for characterising the state as a whole or for understanding particular sectors.

It is very difficult to arrive at a coherent synthesis of different interpretations of French politics. Clearly policy-making is a complex matter and a government's capacity to act and the nature of its responses to problems may differ not only across sectors but over time. The changing context of policy-making in the 1980s with the increasing blurring of domestic and European policies makes some of the earlier interpretations of French policy-making seem redundant. The strategy of economic independence so vigorously pursued by de Gaulle has become unaffordable for a country the size of France. During the 1980s there was increasing recognition that the need to develop European strategies was in conflict with the French protectionist tradition. Nevertheless it is important not to overlook the continuities in French policy-making. Whilst the context and output of policy-making may be changing, the key actors and dominant style are likely to remain constant.

NOTES

1. For a good background discussion of post-war economic and social changes see H. Ehrmann, *Politics in France* (Boston: Little, Brown, 1983), pp. 18–51.
2. See D. Green 'The French Plan: The Demise of French Planning', *West European Politics*, (1978), pp. 60–76.
3. For a discussion of the international constraints on Mitterrand's economic policy see the introduction to V. Wright and H. Machin, eds., *Economic Policy and Policy-Making Under the Mitterrand Presidency 1981–84* (London: Francis Pinter, 1985), pp. 1–44, and P. Hall, 'Socialism in One Country: Mitterrand and the Struggle to Define a New Economic Policy', in P. G. Cerny and M. A. Schain, eds., *Socialism, the State and Public Policy in France* (London: Francis Pinter, 1985), pp. 81–107.
4. For a short background to France's changing international role in the post-war period, see P. Godt, ed., *Policy-Making in France* (London: Francis Pinter, 1989), part 4, chapters by D. Moisi, P. Moreau Defarges and M. C. Smouts.
5. Mitterrand did veto some of Chirac's suggestions, most notably Jean Lecanuet, leader of the UDF, with whom he had previously had very public disputes.
6. For a short discussion of the role of *cabinets* in the Fifth Republic see E. Searls, 'The Fragmented French Executive', *West European Politics* (May 1978), pp. 161–76.
7. The committee responsible for co-ordinating EC policy is the *Comité interministériel pour la coopération économique européene* and its *Secrétariat général*.
8. A. Stevens, 'The Higher Civil Service and Economic Policy-Making', in P. G. Cerny and M. A. Schain, eds., *French Politics and Public Policy* (London: Methuen, 1980), p. 83.
9. P. Hall, *Governing the Economy: The Politics of State Intervention in Britain and France* (Oxford University Press, 1968) p. 279.
10. See, for example, ibid., pp. 164–91 and J. E. S. Hayward, *The State and the Market Economy* (Brighton: Wheatsheaf, 1986), pp. 17–38.
11. For a discussion of this point see J. Hayward, 'Conclusion: The State and Modernisation', in P. Hall, J. Hayward and H. Machin, eds., *Developments in French Politics* (London: Macmillan, 1990).
12. See P. Cerny, 'The New Rules of the Game in France', in P. G. Cerny and M. A. Schain, eds., *French Politics and Public Policy* (London: Methuen, 1981), pp. 26–47.
13. A. Stevens, 'L'Alternance and the Higher Civil Service', in P. G. Cerny and M. A. Schain, eds., *Socialism and the State: Public Policy in France* (London: Francis Pinter, 1985), pp. 143–66.
14. Most notably Guy Sorman whose works *La Solution libérale* and *La Révolution américaine* were extensively referred to by the radical right in the UDF and RPR in the early 1980s (source: personal interviews).
15. See P. Hall, 'Pluralism and Pressure Politics', in P. Hall, J. Hayward and H. Machin, eds., *Developments in French Politics*, pp. 77–92.
16. E. N. Suleiman, 'State Structures and Clientelism: The French State Versus Notaires', *British Journal of Political Science*, 17 (1987), pp. 257–79.

17. For a discussion of the FNSEA see John T. S. Kessler, 'Agricultural Reform in Mitterrand's France', in J. Ambler, ed., *The French Socialist Experience* (Philadelphia: Institute for the Study of Human Issues, 1985), pp. 60–91.
18. See J. Hayward, 'Conclusion', in P. Hall, J. Hayward and H. Machin, eds., *Developments in French Politics*, pp. 54–67.
19. P. Hall in ibid., p. 79.
20. See A. Stone, 'Legal Constraints to Policy-Making: The Constitutional Council and the Council of State', in P. Godt, ed., *Policy-Making in France*, pp. 28–42.
21. See S. Mazey, 'Centre–Periphery Relations in the Fifth Republic: The Legitimization of Local Politics', in Godt, *Policy-Making in France*, pp. 42–57 and Y. Meny, 'The Socialist Decentralization', in G. Ross, S. Hoffman and S. Malzacher, eds., *The Mitterrand Experiment* (Oxford: Polity, 1987), pp. 248–63.
22. The total revenue of communal budgets grew to 135 million francs in 1987. *Bulletin d'information statistique, D.G.C.L. supplement No. 56, Démocratie Locale*.
23. See H. Machin, 'Economic Planning: Policy-Making or Policy-Preparation', in Godt, ed., *Policy-Making in France*, pp. 127–42.
24. For a general survey of the French budget see G. Lord, *The French Budgetary Process* (London: University of California Press, 1973).
25. Ibid., p. 24.
26. For a useful survey of some of these interpretations see S. Mazey, 'Policy-Making in France, the Art of the Possible', *West European Politics*, (1986), pp. 412–27 and Y. Meny, 'The National and International Context of French Policy Communities', *Political Studies*, 37 (1989), pp. 387–99.
27. See for example, H. Claude, *Gaullisme et grande capitale* (Paris: Editions Sociales, 1960).
28. See for example, P. Birnbaum, *The Heights of Power* (University of Chicago Press, 1982) and P. Bourdieu *La Noblesse d'état* (Paris: Editions du Minuit, 1989).
29. P. Hall, *Governing the Economy*.
30. Ibid., p. 19.
31. A classic example is J. Meynaud, *Technocracy* (London: Faber and Faber, 1965).
32. See E. N. Suleiman, *Power Politics and Bureaucracy in France* (Princetown University Press, 1974) especially ch. 14, pp. 372–83.
33. J. P. Thoenig, *L'Ere des technocrates: le cas des ponts et chausées*, 2nd ed. (Paris, L'Harmattan, 1987).
34. P. B. Evans, D. Rueschemeyer and T. Skocpol, *Bringing the State Back In* (Cambridge University Press, 1985). See introductory chapter by Skocpol pp. 3–37 and ch. 11 by Evans, Ruescherneyer and Skocpol, pp. 347–69.
35. Skocpol in *Bringing the State Back In*, p. 29.
36. For a summary of Suleiman's thesis see *BJPS* (1987), pp. 257–79.
37. Ibid., p. 261.
38. Ibid., p. 279.
39. For example P. Gremion, *Le Pouvoir périphérique* (Paris: Editions du Seuil, 1976).

40. Y. Meny, 'The National and International Context of French Policy Communities', *Political Studies*, 37 (1989), p. 39.
41. J. E. S. Hayward, 'Mobilising Private Interests in the Service of Public Ambitions: The Salient Element in the Dual French Policy Style?', in J. J. Richardson, ed., *Policy Styles in Western Europe* (London: Allen and Unwin, 1982), pp. 111–46.
42. Ibid., p. 116.

FURTHER READING

For an informative background on the French political system see V. Wright, *The Government and Politics of France*, 3rd ed. (London: Unwin Hyman, 1989); on the Mitterrand Presidency see S. Mazey and M. Newman, eds., *Mitterrand's France* (London: Croom Helm, 1987). On the administrative elite see E. N. Suleiman, *Elites in French Society* (Princeton University Press, 1978). F. Wilson, *Interest Group Politics in France* (Cambridge University Press, 1987) provides a useful survey of interest groups. On policy-making see the excellent collection in P. Godt, ed., *Policy Making in France* (London: Pinter, 1989). On policy style see J. E. S. Hayward, 'Mobilising Private Interests in the Service of Public Ambitions: The Salient Element in the Dual French Policy Style?', in J. Richardson, ed., *Policy Styles in Western Europe* (London: Allen and Unwin, 1982). Y. Meny, 'The National and International Context of French Policy Communities', *Political Studies*, 37 (1989), pp. 387–400 gives a clear overview of the changing context of policy-making. P. Hall, J. Hayward and H. Machin, eds., *Developments in French Politics* (London: Macmillan, 1990) also emphasises the changing European and international context of the policy-making process.

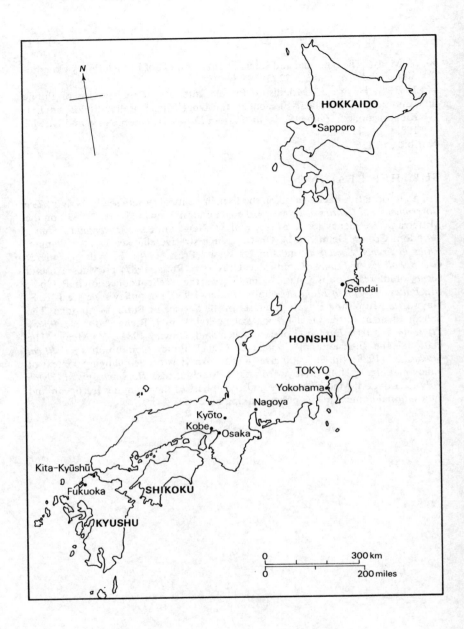

3   Japan

Ian Neary

The national situation

Japan's post-war growth rate resulted in its becoming one of the most powerful economies in the world by the late 1980s. Though the double-digit growth rate of the 1960s is not likely to be repeated, the economy is expected to continue to grow at around 4 per cent per year.

With the exception of small coalfields which are in the process of being run down even further, Japan has negligible natural resources; most raw materials consumed by the economy have to be imported. The only resource that Japan has is its highly skilled population of 123 million people.[1] It is often concluded therefore that the explanation for Japan's economic power resides in the way in which central government has allocated scarce resources among the population. The policy process has, it is argued, effectively served the Japanese people to bring them an enviable degree of economic prosperity and political stability.

So successful have the policies been that many suspect an 'unfair' degree of co-operation between government and industry; a degree which, it is suggested, would not be tolerated in Western liberal democratic societies.[2] The central headquarters of Japan Inc. are said to exercise a degree of control over the 'economic animals' who populate the four islands which has enabled them to compete unfairly with the other advanced capitalist countries. Racist implications of this model aside, it betrays a considerable ignorance of policy-making in Japan over the last forty years. In terms of the resources directly distributed by the central government Japan is the least active of all the four states in this study. From the early 1950s the Japanese have endeavoured to maintain a policy of 'cheap government' and this has been the major single theme of most policy formulation in the 1980s. If the state exerts a considerable degree of central control it does so without committing itself to high levels of expenditure or the imposition of high rates of taxation.[3] Moreover, the Japan Inc. model posits a static simple relationship between the administration and the actors within the political arena when history suggests a complex and changing mosaic of inter-relationships at the level of policy-making. Japan is a capitalist country whose processes of development have bequeathed its current political system with numerous unusual characteristics. But it is a capitalist society which has adopted many of the features of the liberal democratic political process.

The constitution

Japan adopted a modern written constitution in 1889 and held its first general election in 1890. The imperial constitution was erected around the institution of the Emperor but, despite the fact that there was a legislature, one of whose houses was elected, most of the executive power was reserved to the imperial advisers. In any case in the early years the electorate was composed of only 1 per cent of the total population. Nevertheless, over the next fifty years the notion of representative government became an accepted part of the policy-making process and by the late 1920s universal manhood suffrage had been granted and party politics appeared the norm.

Many of the advances made in the application of democratic practice were reversed in the 1930s as the civil and military bureaucracy regained control of the political structure. But, despite its many failings, the experience of operating within a modern, written constitutional structure prepared both populace and power holders for the changes insisted on by the Americans in the post-war period.

The occupation of Japan ended in 1952, by which time a political structure at least as democratic as that in the USA had been created. Formally, the new constitution was an amendment to that of 1889, but in practice the old one was abolished and replaced by one which was devised using the British Cabinet system as a model. The Emperor, once central to the system, was not included in it, and was not given even the residual powers wielded by some West European monarchs. In theory, the Diet is central to the political system. In the words of the constitution, it is 'the highest organ of state power and . . . the sole law making authority of the state'. It is composed of two houses, of which the Lower House is the more important as the majority party here has formed the government on every occasion since 1955, before which there were coalition Cabinets. Moreover, the Lower House is granted the final word over the budget and foreign affairs and most of the Cabinet, and the Prime Minister, are members of this body.

A complex Diet committee system was created in the late 1940s. This is charged with the duty of overseeing the policy-making process but in Japan, as in the UK, most political power is wielded by members of the Cabinet and in particular the Prime Minister. The Cabinet is composed of 'not more than twenty members' of whom twelve will be the ministers representing the twelve departments[4] plus the directors general of the more important sections of the Prime Minister's office such as the Defence Agency and the Economic Planning Agency. Despite wide powers granted to it by the constitution, the Cabinet is responsible to the Diet and nearly all its members have been Diet members, 80 per cent from the Lower House.

In keeping with the American concept of separation of powers, the court system was separated from the Ministry of Justice and established as an independent structure supervised by the Supreme Court. The Chief Justice is appointed in theory by the Emperor, though in fact by the Prime Minister with Cabinet approval, as are the other fourteen justices. These judges are appointed in practice for life but the constitution provides that the appointment of a new judge to the Supreme Court will be reviewed by the people at the first Lower House election after his appointment and in each Lower House election that falls ten years thereafter. If a majority of voters were to vote against him he would be removed from office but all appointments have been approved by overwhelming majorities.

Actors

Executive

Although designed by the American framers of the post-war constitution as a Cabinet system of government, in practice the Cabinet exerts very little influence on the execution of policy. Its twice-weekly, fifteen-minute sessions merely give formal approval to decisions made elsewhere. Most decisions are made within the appropriate ministry and boundaries between ministries are well defined and protected. However, sub-governmental conflict is growing in importance as complex issues arise which cross departmental boundaries.

Ministers themselves will often be ill equipped to deal with complex problems as they lack experience within the ministry. The rapid circulation of Cabinet posts between senior members of the ruling party has resulted over the last twenty years in very few ministers occupying their posts for more than twelve months. Between November 1964 and June 1987 the average time in office of ministers was less than twelve months for all members of the Cabinet except for the Prime Minister (36.7 months), the Minister of Finance (16.4), the Foreign Minister (15.9) and the Minister of International Trade and Industry (13.2).[5] Ministerial careers in Japan are shorter than in most liberal democracies and certainly briefer than in France, the US and the UK (see table 3.1). Co-ordination of the

Table 3.1. *Ministerial careers, 1945–80*

	Average duration (years)	One-post ministers (%)
France	3.4	50
Japan	1.9	77
UK	4.6	54
USA	3.0	93

Note: The first column shows the duration of a career in government. The second column shows the proportion of ministers who occupy just one post during their career.

Source: J. Blondel, *Government Ministers in the Contemporary World* (London: Sage, 1985), appendix 2.

sub-governmental processes has been the major function of the permanent vice ministers (the most senior civil servant in each ministry) who meet regularly to decide on issues requiring the co-ordination of more than one ministry. These vice ministers will also be the chief source of advice for the political leaders and will exert a more important influence over the direction of a ministry than the minister. And yet these too will rarely occupy their posts for very long. Most high-flying bureaucrats will only spend two years in any particular post and the climax of any bureaucratic career will be two years or less spent as permanent vice minister prior to retirement at the age of fifty-five. As very few of the senior decision-makers will spend any time working outside the ministry this creates a very high degree of loyalty to the ministry and an ability to resist outside pressure for policy innovation.

Where conflict cannot be resolved by career bureaucrats, the minister or Prime Minister may act as broker in negotiations. Recently the increased need to resolve such sub-governmental conflict, the increased need to take into account the interests of foreign actors and the growing importance of issues that have a strong ideological component has meant that more problems are being resolved within the Liberal Democratic Party. More decisions are passed on to the highest level – the Prime Minister.

Nakasone (Prime Minister 1982–7) relished this high-profile role and even went so far as to suggest that the constitution be revised to allow for the direct election of a presidential-style Prime Minister. While not going so far, other commentators have suggested that the Prime Minister needs to play a more active role in policy co-ordination and needs an extended secretariat to carry out this role. Nakasone's successors have not sought to develop their office in this direction and have not tried to encourage the development of an overall policy direction. In contrast to constitutional theory, the central executive elite is fairly passive and at the highest levels no chief executive has devised a policy style equivalent to 'Thatcherism' or 'Reagonomics'.

Bureaucracy

Occupation reforms barely touched the bureaucratic hierarchy despite the overall American aim of democratising the political structure. Indeed the American administrators deliberately chose to retain the existing official networks as a legitimating buffer between them and the people of Japan. There remains a strong feeling among senior civil servants that they are less public servants than public mentors.

At the core of the bureaucracy lie the twelve ministries plus the Prime Minister's office – this core is fixed, there is no equivalent to the regular changing number and nature of ministries of the kind seen in the UK. Outside this there are public corporations whose number and authority have changed over time and have in fact grown. The number of major government agencies grew from 40 to 45 between 1955 and 1982 and the number of public authorities increased from 33 to 94 in this same period. Since the 1960s continued efforts have been made to hold down the size of the publicly employed sector such that the total establishment is just over 5 million, including educational and military personnel. This is a level of 45 per thousand population compared to 109 in the UK, 83 in France and 82 in the USA.[6]

Parties

The most important special characteristic of the Japanese political system is the uninterrupted control of the political structure by the Liberal Democratic Party (LDP) since its formation in 1955. Over three decades very close and complex relationships have developed between the national bureaucracy and the committees and sub-committees that exist within the LDP headquarters, to the extent that it is difficult to consider the bureaucracy as politically independent in any but the most technical of decisions. However, electoral support for the LDP has not been constant. From a peak of nearly 60 per cent in the first House of Representatives election after the LDP was formed its support has hovered around 45 per cent since the mid 1970s. There have been times when the LDP seemed to be on the brink of losing its majority in the Lower House and thus control over government.

In the 1989 House of Councillors elections the LDP lost its overall majority and it seemed possible that it could suffer a similar setback in the next Lower House election. After a very expensive campaign that may have cost over 100 million dollars, the LDP was returned with a comfortable majority in February 1990. It faced problems working with an unco-operative second chamber but its overall control of the policy process remained intact.

However, the LDP has internal divisions which have suggested fragility. Almost every LDP Diet member belongs to a faction of which at any one time there will be between five and eight. The rivalry between these groups has at times been so intense that it has come close to splitting the party. In 1980 the failure of one leading faction to vote against an opposition motion of no confidence forced the Cabinet to resign and a general election to be held less than twelve months after the previous election. It has even been suggested that a faction might leave the party and enter into a grand coalition of the centre parties with the Democratic Socialists, the Komeito and perhaps even the Japan Socialist Party.

Though periodically condemned by the party's leadership, factions play a significant role in the life of the LDP and they are likely to continue to do so. Factions benefit both leader and followers. The aim of each faction leader is to become president of the party and thus Prime Minister. He therefore expects his faction members to obey his wishes in the elections to this post. In return for their support he is able to provide access to money which members can use, especially at election time, to increase their chances of re-election. Faction leaders can also ensure selection for their members in government positions from Cabinet level downwards. No faction is large enough to guarantee the success of its leader and so coalitions have to be formed. Then, when the Prime Minister selects his Cabinet he has to reward his supporters as well as giving some positions of influence to rivals so as to maintain party unity.

Though important determinants of the outcome of the leadership selection process, factions contribute little to the policy process. It is personal ties rather than ideological commitment that bind the faction and support for any single controversial cause will cut across the faction lines. Recently, political commentators have placed far more stress on the influence of *zoku* – the 'policy tribes' that exist within the LDP.[7] The word *zoku* is used rather loosely to indicate those members of the LDP who have a special interest in a specific policy field and who occupy influential positions within the party. Having no formal existence the membership of these 'tribes' is difficult to pin down, but it would include all those who have served for more than ten years on an LDP standing committee or Diet Committee, plus all ex-ministers of that particular department.[8] Each ministry will be keenly aware of those powerful LDP politicians who have a specific interest in its affairs and these individuals will be circulated with details of all significant policy proposals before they are formally introduced. Any suggestion of strong opposition to these proposals will usually lead to amendment or withdrawal.

Opposition parties have little access to the policy process. In the mid-1950s there was only one opposition party with representation in the Diet, the Japan Socialist Party (JSP). Then, in the 1960s, the Japan Communist Party (JCP) improved its popular image to the extent that it was able to command up to 9–10 per cent of popular support in general elections. Meanwhile, the Buddhist lay organisation Soka Gakkai, the fastest-growing 'new religion' of the 1960s, grew a political arm – the Komeito or Clean Government Party. By 1976 it had become the second largest of the opposition parties, a position it has since maintained. All this time support for the JSP was declining from almost one-third of the popular vote in 1956 to less than one-fifth by the 1980s. Although the JSP improved its share of the vote in the 1990 election, its chances of achieving power by itself seem small and attempts to negotiate electoral pacts with the other opposition parties have so far ended in failure.

Pressure groups

There can be little doubt that the most persuasive pressure-group activity is by big business through its three organisations: the Keidanren (Federation of Economic Organisations), Nikkeiren (Federation of Employers Associations) and the Keizai Dōyukai (Committee on Economic Development). Each of these seeks to persuade policy-makers to create an environment conducive to stable economic growth and, though their perspectives on a specific issue may vary, they tend to act in a complementary rather than a competitive manner. Of the three it is the Keidanren which is the most important. It represents the 700 largest corporations plus nearly 100 of the biggest financial/commercial institutions and over 100 trade associations such as the Japan Iron and Steel Federation, and the Japanese Automobile Manufacturers Association. Virtually all the major corporations of Japan are represented in this body. It has over thirty committees engaged in opinion gathering and research. The Keidanren attempts to influence opinion in myriad ways, but most important are the daily contacts between its bureaus, on the one hand, and individuals in various ministries, especially the Ministry of International Trade and Industry, on the other. It will keep in close contact with the LDP at executive level, through factions and their leaders, and with the policy specialists who are interested in the appropriate policy area. Moreover, so close is the contact between the Keidanren and the administration that, for example, MITI and the Keidanren even exchange junior officials for short periods to ensure that links between them during their careers will continue smoothly. Similar links also exist between key trade associations such as the Electrical Manufacturers Federation and the Automobile Manufacturers Association and the relevant sections of MITI.[9] The Keidanren and/or trade associations have negotiated directly with their counterparts in Britain on such matters as export limitation agreements. Indeed, there is usually a representative of the Keidanren with quasi-diplomatic accreditation at the Japanese Embassy in London and in other major capitals. So, the government/business relationship goes beyond the simple sharing of information as the Keidanren often acts as an adjunct of government.

The influence of the agricultural community over policy-making within the Ministry of Agriculture (MAFF) has been a major feature of post-war politics as the LDP has depended on the voters from rural communities almost as much as on the cash contributions from urban-based big business. Furthermore, agricultural employment is still more common in Japan than in any of the other countries in this book (see p. 10). The influence of Nōkyō (the Federation of Agricultural Co-operatives) within MAFF is great. Nōkyō is composed of several major co-operative federations in the areas of agricultural production and sales, purchases and credit. Collectively these organisations claim to include every farm family in Japan. In rural areas the Nōkyō office (which now includes banking facilities) may be as important as local government. At regional and national levels the federations push for legislative and bureaucratic decisions favourable to agricultural interests and particularly to rice farming. A local Nōkyō may receive and formally channel funds to a candidate for the Diet (usually though not always the LDP). Elsewhere local Nōkyō leaders will give informal support to one particular candidate. The official circle of Nōkyō supporters is around 90 but a much larger group of at least 150 LDP Diet members will represent predominantly farming constituencies.[10]

Medium- and small-scale business has not been able to exert much influence on the policy process despite the fact that collectively it employs more Japanese workers than the big corporations. It was only from the early 1970s that the LDP began to pay more attention to the Japan Chamber of Commerce and Industry (which now represents approximately 11 million small businesses) and to the smaller but more active Medium and Small Business Political League (membership about 300,000). There are two reasons for this increased emphasis on smaller businesses. First, the Communist Party was very successful from 1973 in organising small businesses into its own group, the Federation of Commercial and Industrial Organisations.[11] Secondly, though rural communities remain a solid source of support for the LDP, and disproportionately influential because of the small population of rural constituencies, it became clear to the LDP that an increase in its urban base would be one way of stopping the decline in electoral popularity that began in the 1950s.

Other organisations exist which support more specific sectional interests. The Japan Medical Association represents doctors and thus has developed close links with the Ministry of Health and Welfare (MHW). The Japan Teachers Union tries unsuccessfully to influence changes in education policy at lower levels while organisations founded by representatives of the private universities have had more success in changing the course of policy in the higher education sector. The Buraku Liberation League has campaigned since 1955 to win official recognition of the poverty and discrimination against the sector of society they represent (see chapter 8).

Organised labour is not insignificant in size, but rather like its equivalent in France, its effectiveness as a pressure group has been diluted by divisions between different national centres. About 29 per cent of the total workforce belong to a union, but 90 per cent of union members are organised within (and tend to identify with) their enterprise where most of the important decisions about wages and working conditions are made. Ambitious, talented workers may spend some time as full-time officials in the enterprise union but most will want to return to their positions in the workforce where they may expect promotion and higher wages. None of the national centres can afford to pay their permanent staff such rates and the national centres are relatively weak with few resources. Moreover nearly 40 per cent of the 12,500 unions in Japan lack any affiliation with a national federation.[12]

Of the main centres the largest was the Sōhyō (General Council of Japanese Trade Unions, membership 4.5 million). There were three other national centres: Dōmei (Japanese Confederation of Labour) with about 2.2 million members, Churitsu Roren (Federation of Industrial Unions) with less than 1.5 million and Shinsanbetsu (National Federation of Industrial Unions) with about 65,000.[13] Moreover, there is another group of unions, Kinzoku Rōkyō (International Metal Workers Federation: Japan Chapter), which is composed of the unions within the largest and most prestigious companies in the four sectors of steel, electrical goods, automobiles and ship building. This group represents over 2 million workers in such companies as Toyota, Nissan, Sumitomo and Hitachi and has no links with the other federations.

It may be, however, that at least some of this division will soon cease. In November 1987 a new national centre was formed from most of the unions in the private sector – Rengō (an anacronym for Zen Nihon Minkan Rōsō Rengōkai). Sōhyō decided to join this organisation in November 1989. With 8 million members and hopes to increase this to 10 million in the early 1990s, Rengō has the potential to become a key element in Japanese politics. In 1984–5 the precursor to Rengō entered into negotiations with the Prime Minister and various ministries over the content of the budget proposals. Some suggested that this could lead to increased incorporation of the representatives of organised labour into the LDP-dominated policy-making process.[14] On the other hand, its formation could just as easily lead to the creation of a United Socialist alternative to the conservative LDP.

Below the national level of policy-making, citizens' movements and consumer groups have been perhaps the most effective in stimulating policy formulation. It was mainly the activities of locally based citizens' movements that focused national attention on the problems caused by industrial pollution such as water-born inorganic mercury in Minamata Bay and atmospheric pollution in Yokkaichi. Moreover, in other areas local groups have been successful in resisting plans to site factories in their region or insisting on the use of pollution prevention equipment.

Two general remarks can be made about pressure group activity in Japanese politics. First, 'successful' organisations which manage to make a real input into the decision-making process tend to become auxiliary to the administrative structure and closely interlinked with the LDP. In particular, exchange of junior personnel early in their careers, and the practice of bureaucrats taking up positions in industry or politics after retirement in their early fifties, creates a group of actors within these institutions who have a set of shared attitudes towards the world. Secondly, those groups which lie outside the central arena of politics have very little ability to influence the creation of policy and are consulted, if at all, only after decisions are made by the administrators.

Similarly the role of groups in the process of implementation varies according to their relationship to the central institutions. Those groups which have the closest relations with the LDP and the bureaucracy play an important role not only in policy formulation but also in its implementation. This is most obvious in the activities of the Nōkyō agricultural co-operatives since it is through the local groups of this body that MAFF policy is actually carried out at the 'rice roots' level. However, the Keidanren and in particular the individual Federations of Manufacturers will also play an important part in implementing policy. Once a particular policy has been agreed between the appropriate ministry and the representatives of the industry it will usually be left to the industrialists to carry out the plan. This is one way in which the central authorities can exert considerable influence on the economic actors without becoming involved in direct economic intervention. Even groups such as the Baraku Liberation League, which have no ideological sympathy with the ruling party find themselves closely involved in the administration of schemes established to benefit their members.

Arenas

The most visible yet perhaps least important arena of the policy-making process in Japan is the passage of bills through the two houses of the Diet. Despite its central role in the formal political structure, neither in its plenary sessions nor during the hearings held by the many committees do Diet members make substantial contributions to the structure or content of the legislation under consideration. Normally over 80 per cent of bills proposed by the government become law and of these most, again more than 80 per cent, originate in the government. However, as one might expect, Cabinet proposals generally have less success when the Cabinet's position is unstable because it is unable to dominate both houses of the Diet. This happened in the periods 1947–55, 1975–80 and 1983–6. But even when it has a comfortable majority in both houses the Cabinet may not be able to ensure success for all legislative proposals. Relations between the government and opposition parties are not as combative as in, say, the United Kingdom. Opposition does not oppose for its own sake; even the JSP supports over half of the government's measures. Conversely, the government may be persuaded by the united criticism of the opposition parties not to proceed with the introduction of a measure. Although its importance can be overrated, there is a cultural predisposition in Japan to prefer compromise to confrontation. At times the LDP has been persuaded that it would suffer more loss of support from trying to steamroller a measure through the Diet than it would gain from passing the measure into law. But there are other ways in which opposition parties exercise influence. Committees rarely affect the substance of bills but they may be able to influence them in ways which are marginal to the proposal as a whole but of great importance to specific groups within Japanese society. The opposition may also be able to prevent the passage of a proposal by creating institutional delays so that a bill remains unapproved at the end of a Diet session. Such bills must begin anew at the start of the next session but will usually only be re-introduced if the government is particularly determined to see them enacted.

It is often suggested that politics in Japan is dominated by the bureaucracy. Ministers are never in a post long enough to command their departments and even the Prime Minister exerts less control over the policy-making process than does his equivalent in other Western democracies. The core arena of policy-making, it is argued, lies within the ministries, particularly within their lower echelons. Policy proposals which emanate from this hub of the bureaucracy, sometimes following consultation with pressure groups but more often without, are submitted to senior officials and ministers for the approval which they invariably receive.

If this simplified model was an accurate representation of the decision-making system in the 1950s, it no longer portrays the complex reality of policy formulation. Two major changes have occurred. First, the influence of those bureaucrats at the pinnacles of the ministerial hierarchies has increased as the greater scope and complexity of policy-making has necessitated the co-ordination of the activities of different agencies to eliminate duplication of effort. Secondly, the LDP has been able to assert more control over the bureaucracy. More than forty years of dealing with each other have brought about changes within the standard operating procedures of both organisations. Top-level bureaucrats are in constant touch with key figures in the LDP and all agencies cultivate links with the appropriate groups within the party. Conversely, there is evidence of 'partisanisation' of the bureaucracy which ensures that only those personnel who are in sympathy with the outlook of the LDP are promoted to positions of seniority.[15]

Parallel to the working of each agency there is a committee active within the LDP many of whose members are also on the appropriate Diet committee. In addition special committees may be established to examine issues of ephemeral importance. The recommendations of these committees are co-ordinated by PARC – the Policy Affairs Research Council. The influence of these committees extends even to the stage prior to any decision since there will be considerable exchange of views between lower ranking personnel and the members of the appropriate committee. At the earliest stage of the formulation of a policy, the 'rule of anticipated reaction' will ensure that if the party is considered not to be ready for the policy it will not be proposed.[16] In Japan, as elsewhere, most decisions are about matters which are dealt with by agency officials, who will of course be working within a framework, an ideology, which has developed over the last forty years, moulded by successive interactions with the political sector of the polity.

Proposals of greater importance will first be circulated in draft form to those who are influential within the particular policy field. The composition of the *zoku* ('policy tribe') is hard for outsiders to discern but each agency will have its own list which will include ex-ministers, chairmen and key members of the appropriate committee and members of PARC who are known to take an interest in the particular issue. Having amended the proposal after consideration of the views of these grandees, it will be submitted to the LDP committee which will in turn pass the proposal to PARC. At each stage of its progress through this labyrinth it may be altered in form or content. When it emerges from this process it is returned to the ministry for the endorsement of the minister who will then seek Cabinet approval for the introduction of the proposal to the Diet.

Not all proposals will require Diet approval and some may necessitate the approval of other ministries. Where two or more ministries are involved in a proposal or where a proposal has very broad implications for society (for example, the Equal Employment Opportunities Law), an advisory council will be set up. At any one time there will be a large number of these – over 200 – most of which have a life of about two years and a membership of 20 to 30. Membership of these councils is decided by the ministry but it includes representatives of academia, the client groups involved (for example, the JMA in MHW matters) and of course, representatives of the bureaucracy. How far these can give impartial advice, or are intended to do so, is a matter of some doubt. In most cases the chairman is in effect appointed by the sponsoring ministry. He will set the parameters of the enquiry and the information received will often be filtered through the bureaucracy. Thus many conclude that the advisory councils do not serve primarily to provide outside inputs into the policy process but rather to co-opt groups and other sectors of the bureaucracy into a particular policy decision.[17]

The heavily centralised Meiji state permitted minimal autonomy at the local government level and although one aim of the occupation reforms was to decentralise the political structure, the national government has retained or regained an extensive degree of control over local authorities. Local governments may not enact any ordinance that conflicts with national law. Much of the business they conduct is delegated to them by central government and directly supervised by its representatives. Central ministries will impose their will on branches of the local administration through 'administrative guidance'. Most crucially, only one-third of local government revenue comes from local taxes and there are strict controls on local borrowing. As a result, central government can exercise pervasive influence through its control over finance.

Despite this, there is some scope for innovative policy-making by local government which is particularly noticeable when opposition parties are in control. Local governments influenced by the Socialist Party have been consistently more receptive to requests from the Buraku Liberation League from the 1950s up to the present day. Provision of free health care for the elderly was pioneered by rural health authorities in the early 1970s.

Some of the less developed prefectures have launched their own technology parks in attempts to attract 'high-tech' industry into their region.

Central government and the LDP exert considerable control; the prefectural and municipal authorities have very limited autonomy compared to similar units in the USA. On the other hand they exert a degree of self-control which is very similar to that of French local government. Moreover, whereas in the UK the power of local authorities has been gradually restricted over the last decade, in Japan there appears to be increasing scope for local deviation, innovation and experimentation.

Instruments

While always remaining within the limits laid down by the constitution, laws establish the frameworks within which policy is devised. When new problems are identified, fresh legislation is introduced to provide the guidelines for coping with these new issues. Most government in Japan, though, does not proceed through formal laws but rather via less formal instruments of ordinances devised within the ministries in order to accomplish the wider goals of the laws. In this the Japanese system differs little from that of other liberal democracies. There are, however, three instruments which are used in Japan which are not found in a similar form in the other countries: planning, basic laws and administrative guidance.

Planning is regarded as a key function of government. This notion stems from a number of sources: the Confucian political culture which legitimates state intervention in the regulation of many aspects of life, the perceived necessity in the late nineteenth century and early post-war era for the state to act to ensure rapid economic development, and the related need to plan other sectors of social life to underpin this. The Japanese government has made economic plans, defence plans and construction plans though it has to be said that not all have had the success of the economic plans which have usually had priority. However, this goal-setting function has, for the most part, been achieved in a way consistent with cheap government.

Basic laws occupy a special place within Japanese legislation as they are intended to be general statements of principle from which to develop a set of policies often involving several ministries and requiring further legislation. For example, the Basic Law on Education passed in 1947 describes the basic principles for education which were implemented in a later act establishing the school system. Similarly the Basic Law on Pollution was passed in 1967, followed a few years later by laws which set specific standards for permitted levels of pollution in the atmosphere, sea, rivers, etc. Of course, the implementation of these laws then requires further detailed regulations to be worked out by the appropriate ministries. However, it is the purpose of basic laws to indicate that the state has taken a lead in establishing a set of standards which the citizenry are encouraged to maintain, preferably without the imposition of sanctions.

Administrative guidance is a phrase used particularly by foreign observers of Japan's political economy to describe how the government is able to win the compliance of specific corporations with its plans. Indicative economic plans for periods of five to ten years have been in operation since the early 1950s, although recent plans have been much looser than the earlier ones. Within the overall plan there were micro-economic programmes aimed at the development of specific industries. Recent examples of this are the planning activities of such agencies as MITI to facilitate the 'structural adjustment' of the aluminium, steel and ship building industries. But the plans are not just concerned with recession cartels – they also promote the formation of research associations for new technologies such as biotechnology or information technology. They also organise industry-wide responses to international pressure such as the 'restraint' on automobile exports to the USA.

Rarely is there any legal requirement for a company to pay the fee to join a research association, abide by production limitations agreed by the cartel or cut back on export efforts. The industry will allow itself to be guided by the administration for two reasons. First, it will have been closely involved in the process which led to the particular strategy – the agency will have made considerable efforts to win the agreement or acceptance of the proposals by all the key actors. Secondly, the ministry directly or indirectly will be responsible for the granting of licenses and permits for a whole range of activities. If a particular company proves reluctant to co-operate with the ministry's plan it may have difficulties obtaining the necessary permission the next time. During the 1950s MITI controlled access to foreign currency and foreign technology which enabled it to exert considerable influence over major corporations. Many of these powers no longer exist but the habit of listening closely to the appropriate section of government is maintained and there are still ways in which companies can be rewarded for doing so. With the careful use of such resources, ministries within the Japanese government have been able to channel economic change in their preferred directions.

Budget making is another important process through which the government is able to exert an influence on the economic system and an examination of it demonstrates the extent to which the activities of bureaucracy and LDP are inextricably interconnected. Nowadays the budget formation process is almost an all-year-round activity. It begins soon after the start of the fiscal year on 1 April when the ministries begin to formulate their budget requests for the following year. During the summer months the ministries will put together mini-budgets which are submitted to the Finance Ministry by 31 August. It is important that at this stage the proposals have the support of the appropriate section of the LDP's PARC. The leaders of the divisions and bureaus in the ministry will try to win the support of the key members of the *zoku* who will usually also be members of the appropriate PARC sub-committee.

In September the officials of the ministries will attend meetings at the Ministry of Finance (MoF) explaining their requests to the budget examiners. Then at the same time as the MoF examiners are scrutinising these requests, senior officials consider the overall proposals in terms of taxes and the total budget figure. By early December the draft budget will be put to the ministerial budget conference to ratify and modify. As the MoF budget nears completion, the PARC will put together a Budget Compilation Programme which will be discussed by the Cabinet before the release of the MoF draft. Once the two have been formally released there will be a period of 'revival negotiations' as appeals are made to top officials in the MoF and some supplementary funds are made available in response to appeals from individual ministries and LDP leaders. At this stage influential LDP members will try to win funding for pet projects – ones which will often be of direct benefit to their constituents. A final session will be held between top officials of the LDP and government to produce a budget which will then receive the formal approval of Cabinet.[18]

This process has remained largely unchanged since the 1950s but the margin for negotiation has decreased. In the 1970s each ministry would request an amount 25 per cent greater than the current year and in several years the annual growth of the General Account budget was close to 20 per cent. From the early 1980s tight control has been imposed on most ministries and overall growth restricted to single figures with the target of preventing any expansion. As the margin for manoeuvre has been restricted and discussion over policy has become a zero-sum game, so the role of the LDP politicians has increased. Ministries, almost as much as outside interest groups, may rely on the intervention of well-placed politicians to ensure the approval of their policy programmes.

While the general account budget is funded from tax revenues, the Fiscal Investment and Loan Programme (FILP) income derives from government trust funds, principally post office savings, postal life insurance and national pension programmes. It provides working capital to governmental financial institutions such as the Japan Development Bank as well as such politically sensitive bodies as the Housing Loan Corporation, the Agriculture, Forestry and Fisheries Finance Corporation and the Medical Care Facilities Finance Corporation. During the 1950s and

1960s FILP money was channelled through the Japan Development Bank to support the development of power plant and the shipbuilding industry. More recently loans have been made for the development of pollution control, housing programmes and energy saving. The total amount of money available through FILP is about 40 per cent of the General Account budget and represents a source of funds that can be applied for political purposes as it is not subject to the same strict constraints as the general budget. It can be used to encourage sectors of the electorate to support either an individual politician or the LDP as a whole. As the LDP has teetered on the edge of losing its overall majority in the past twenty years these funds have been a useful way of securing votes.

Interpretation

There can be little doubt that the political structure of Japan is highly centralised. This general characteristic can be explained by the deliberate attempt made by the revolutionary bureaucrats of the latter half of the nineteenth century who, having engineered the downfall of the Shogun, placed the Emperor at the centre of their new political edifice and constructed a centralised state around him. Fundamental to the new political network was the civil and military bureaucracy. Following defeat in 1945 the military was removed from a position of dominance but the authority of the civil bureaucracy emerged from the American occupation at worst unscathed and, some would argue, in an even stronger position than a decade earlier.[19]

Moreover, there was no other body willing or able to take the lead in the most important task which faced Japan, that of economic reconstruction. Using a variety of policy instruments, the economic ministries were able to cajole industry into accepting their plans. It is not clear precisely how far the economic growth of the 1950s and 1960s occurred as a result of this planning but nonetheless it was the government, particularly the economic agencies, which were able to take much of the credit. There developed, then, the 'bureaucratic primacy' model of politics in Japan in which *the state* is said to play the dominant role within the society and economy and all private groups are in a state of subjugation to the state bureaucracy.[20] Where consultation fails to convince, policy can be imposed.

Whether this model of Japanese decision-making fully explained the nature of policy-making in the 1950s is uncertain. But as an explanation of the policy-making process in Japan of the 1980s and 1990s it is clearly inadequate. Political groups, mainly of course within the LDP, and private interest groups play a key role in all major decisions. The relationships between the bureaucratic structure and the LDP are complex but it seems reasonable to conclude that in most areas it is increasingly the LDP which has the upper hand. If the trend within the policy-making process in the late 1940s and 1950s was one of the bureaucratisation of politics, then the reverse process of the politicisation of the bureaucracy has been well underway for at least the last ten years. Moreover, the longer the LDP remains in power, the tighter its control over the bureaucracy will become, both institutionally and ideologically. Outside groups are making a more significant contribution to policy discussion but only in controlled circumstances. Groups with access to the LDP, and Diet members through factions or *zoku*, may be able to exert some influence on policies as they pass through the LDP apparatus.

The Diet plays a more important role now than it did in the 1950s. Through their ability to question and perhaps embarrass ministers and the Prime Minister, Diet members may be able to mobilise public opinion to oppose a specific measure or to support significant change in a proposal. If the LDP is only prepared to use its majority as a last resort then it may be prepared to make concessions and even, when its popularity is at a low level, to withdraw a bill entirely.

So the hegemony of the bureaucracy in Japan is not what it was. The bureaucracy has been forced to share power with LDP politicians and on occasion both have had to make concessions to demands from within the Diet. There has been some pluralisation within the policy-making system but no one would suggest it is an open, plural structure with the state acting as mere umpire.

An examination of the balance of forces in each ministry or specific policy-making arena suggests wide variation. The Ministry of Agriculture has become politicised to the extent that some have been prompted to describe it as 'a support arm of the LDP'.[21] Here the bureaucracy is under heavy pressure to work in co-operation with the LDP and Nōkyō. Meanwhile the MHW relationship with the JMA and the pharmaceutical industry is antagonistic and thus the MHW has a greater degree of freedom to devise policy within the formal constraints set by the MoF and LDP. At least one ministry was for a time virtually captured by one of the factions. For much of the 1970s and 1980s the Ministry of Construction was dominated by the Tanaka faction and Diet members from this faction would impose 'unreasonably difficult' tasks on the bureaucracy to win preferential treatment for their constituents.[22]

Although political domination is not so obvious in the prestigious economic agencies such as MoF, MITI and the Economic Planning Agency, political intervention has come to play an important role in substance and presentation. As Japan opened her markets to international competition in the 1960s, it became less easy for these agencies to control domestic economic activity. When access to foreign currency, finance and technology became open the range of sanctions available was substantially reduced. Moreover, as Japan moves out of the era of high growth and the policy of financial restraint is maintained, all issues become politicised as issues become zero-sum games in which decisions are made, ultimately, by the politicians.

The overall theme, then, is one in which the policy-making process has become exceedingly complex as more actors are involved in policy arenas in advisory committees, *zoku*, and party factions. Underlying this is the increased importance of the LDP as its institutional structure becomes locked into that of the formal bureaucracy. In a sense, then, the process has become less state centred, but without becoming group dominated. Much popular writing about Japan seems to be premised on the assumption that Japan is some form of a corporate state and even those who are keen to stress the ability of interest groups to influence the policy-making process admit that access to the system is not as easy for some as others.

Completely excluded from top-level deliberations are the representatives of labour. Union leaders may be found on the councils which advise the Ministry of Labour and occasionally on similar bodies which suggest policy to other ministries. It might be argued that little would be served by including the leaders of the union federations since they represent at most only a fraction of organised labour in Japan. Even if these groups were to take part in negotiations within the bureaucracy they would be unable to secure the compliance of their membership let alone of the working population as a whole.

Overall, the policy-making process seems to be becoming increasingly politicised, not in the sense that representatives of political parties outside the LDP are becoming involved in the process but in that increasingly it is elected politicians who are taking decisions. Politicians are responsive to pressures within the party, the electorate and the international environment to which the bureaucrat will be insensitive if not immune. Moreover, election results seem to be having a great influence on trends in the policy process. When the LDP control over the Diet rests on a slender majority no Prime Minister is going to risk alienating the small business community by suggesting a value added tax or propose changes to the subsidy of rice production for fear of losing the rural vote. However, with LDP control of the Diet secure for a few years it was reform in these areas which was advocated by Prime Minister Nakasone and by Takeshita, his successor.

Is it possible then to talk of a Japanese policy style? Muramatsu and Krauss have suggested that it might be useful to speak of 'patterned pluralism' in Japan. Japanese policy-making is characterised by a strong state interacting with pluralist elements. These pluralist elements are composed of 'fairly consistent coalitions of actors with relatively predictable degrees of influence on policy making'.[23] To a greater extent than in most countries there is a strong tendency for public policy-making to become privatised. Close relations have been established between the bureaucrats, interested parties and the policy professionals in the ruling party and where possible there seems to be a preference for resolving conflicting interests in negotiation between representatives of these groups. Most ministries have a tradition of formulating plans for the sector of the economy or society over which they have charge or at least to contributing to the planning process of other agencies (most obviously the Economic Planning Agency). So the ministries are oriented towards an anticipatory approach to active problem solving. Further, since many of the key actors will be involved in the policy process prior to any decision being made, a consensus will usually be created which will allow the policy to be implemented smoothly. Not, of course, that even the Japanese bureaucracy can plan for all eventualities. The 'oil shocks' of the 1970s caught the planners by surprise and the various projects to find alternatives for oil-based products had only just been launched when oil prices plummeted making the alternatives no longer attractive. Moreover, there have been occasions when government has imposed its decisions on sections of the population, most recently in the restructuring and privatisation of the national railway system. Nevertheless there is no reason to suppose that Japan is moving in the direction of reactive problem solving whose decisions are imposed on substantial sectors of society, the direction that Richardson suggests most post-industrial societies are travelling.[24]

NOTES

1. Moreover, the population is concentrated in densely populated industrial regions. Seventy per cent of Japan's population lives in urban areas and 50 per cent lives in the urbanised strip along the Pacific coast between Tokyo and Kobe.
2. For example, M. Wolf, *The Japanese Conspiracy* (London: New English Library, 1984).
3. See figures in table 1.1, p. 10.
4. Ministry of Finance, Ministry of International Trade and Industry, Ministry of Agriculture, Forestry and Fisheries, Ministry of Health and Welfare, Ministry of Transport, Ministry of Justice, Ministry of Foreign Affairs, Ministry of Education, Ministry of Posts and Telecommunications, Ministry of Labour, Ministry of Home Affairs, Ministry of Construction.
5. J. A. A. Stockwin et al., *Dynamic and Immobilist Politics in Japan* (London: Macmillan, 1988), p. 43.
6. Quoted by Rix in ibid., p. 65.

7. For example, Yung H. Park, *Bureaucrats and Ministers in Contemporary Japanese Government* (University of California Press, 1986).
8. This definition is suggested in *Jiminto Seiken*, S. Sato and T. Matsuzaki, (Tokyo: Chuo Koron Sha, 1986), pp. 264–6.
9. G. K. Wilson, *Business and Politics* (London: Macmillan, 1985), p. 92.
10. A. D. George, 'The Japanese Farm Lobby and Agricultural Policy Making', *Pacific Affairs*, 54 (1981), pp. 409–30.
11. P. A. Berton, 'Japanese Eurocommunists: Running in Place', *Problems of Communism* (July/August 1986), p. 13.
12. T. J. Pempel, *Policy and Politics in Japan* (Philadelphia: Temple University Press, 1982), p. 96. This also provides a useful summary of the characteristics of enterprise unions.
13. Figures from *Gendai Yogo no Kiso Chishiki* (Tokyo: Jiyukokuminsha, 1984), pp. 407–8.
14. Nakano Minoru, *Nihon Seisaku Kettei no Henyo* (Tokyo: Toyo Keizai Shinposha, 1986), pp. 294–5.
15. See Park, *Bureaucrats and Ministers*, ch. 4.
16. Ibid., pp. 100–2.
17. Nakano, *Nihon Seisaku Kettei no Henyo*, pp. 80–6.
18. For a detailed analysis of the budget process see J. C. Campbell, *Contemporary Japanese Budget Politics* (University of California Press, 1977).
19. 'The purge left the bureaucracy almost unscathed in the composition of its personnel.' H. Baerwald, *The Purge of Japanese Leaders under the Occupation* (University of California Press, 1959), p. 83.
20. Chalmers Johnson develops this notion in *MITI and the Japanese Miracle* (Stanford University Press, 1982).
21. Nakano, *Nihon Seisaku Kettei no Henyo*, p. 103, Park, *Bureaucrats and Ministers*, p. 131.
22. Ibid., p. 95.
23. 'The Conservative Line and the Development of Patterned Pluralism', M. Muramatsu and D. Krauss in K. Yamamura and Y. Yasuba, eds., *The Political Economy of Japan*, vol. 1, (Stanford University Press), pp. 337, 538.
24. J. Richardson, *Policy Styles in Western Europe* (London: Allen and Unwin, 1982).

FURTHER READING

Neither of the two basic introductory textbooks to Japanese politics are perfect. J. A. A. Stockwin's *Japan: Divided Politics in a Growth Economy* (London: Weidenfeld and Nicolson, 1982) is highly readable but a little dated now. B. M. Richardson and S. C. Flanagan's *Politics in Japan* (Boston: Little, Brown and Company, 1984) is a fuller if duller treatment which describes the Japanese political system framed in the language of the structural functional approach. *Crisis and Compensation – Public Policy and Political Stability in Japan. 1949–1986* (Princeton University Press, 1988) by K. E. Calder provides not only a magisterial overview of the developments in postwar politics but also a review of six policy areas: agriculture, welfare, land use, defence, small business and regional policy. *The Political Economy of Japan*, vol. 1, *The Domestic Transformation*, ed.

K. Yamamura and Y. Yasuba (Stanford University Press, 1987) provides detailed analyses (many of them by Japanese political scientists) of numerous aspects of the Japanese political structure. A full statement of the 'revisionist' view – which argues that Japan's social, political and economic structures are fundamentally different to those of North America and Western Europe – is to be found in Karel von Wolferen, *The Enigma of Japanese Power* (London: Macmillan, 1989).

4   The United Kingdom

Martin Harrop

The national situation

Relative economic decline has been the major problem confronting British governments over the post-war period. Compared to France, Japan and the United States, Britain's growth rate has been low (see p. 142). As a result, Britain has slipped down the league table of industrial nations, a fall which has accelerated the inevitable decline in international influence caused by the retreat from empire.

The history of public policy in post-war Britain is primarily the story of how governments have fumbled to reverse this relative decline. Lacking a tradition of co-operation between the state and the private sector, government policy has oscillated between the ideological solutions of controlling the market, on the one hand, and freeing the market, on the other. Only in the late 1980s, as the Labour Party became more sympathetic to the market in response to the electoral success of Mrs Thatcher's right-wing administration, did this pattern show signs of change.

Relative decline has produced recurring electoral difficulties for governments. In eight out of twelve post-war elections, the governing party's share of the vote fell, indicating popular dissatisfaction with government performance. In office both major parties suffered spectacular by-election defeats and massive swings against them in mid-term opinion polls. This disillusionment gave the centre parties, untainted by office, the chance to secure a substantial protest vote in the 1970s and 1980s. However the bias of the electoral system prevented the centre parties from achieving the major breakthrough in Parliament to which they felt entitled. British politics remained dominated by the conventions of a two-party system.

Continuing hostility between the parties reflects, and helps to sustain, class divisions in Britain. Even though industrial change has weakened class solidarity, related divisions – between North and South, white and black, established classes and an expanding underclass – have grown in significance, producing symptoms of social disorder such as inner-city riots in the mid-1980s. British politics remains highly sensitive to distribu-

71

SCOTLAND

Glasgow

Edinburgh

NORTHERN
IRELAND

Belfast

Newcastle
upon Tyne

Leeds

Liverpool

Manchester

ENGLAND

Birmingham

WALES

Cardiff

Bristol

LONDON

0   150 km
0   100 miles

tive issues, as seen for example in the strident opposition to the flat-rate poll tax abandoned by the Conservatives at the start of the 1990s. Distributive squabbles detract attention from the problem of relative decline and the need to adapt to Britain's new position as a European state rather than a world power.

For much of the post-war period, governments seemed incapable of solving the problem of relative decline. It is not that the British state is inherently weak; in fact, Britain is a well-regulated society and the regulations are, on the whole, enforced. Rather, the difficulty lies in the state's capacity to form and implement an overall strategy to reverse decline. Anthony King puts the point well:

On the one hand, the British system is – certainly as compared with the American – highly centralised and effective; if central government takes a decision within its area of competence, such as deciding to raise a tax or to change the law relating to trade unions, then that decision sticks and is implemented. But, on the other hand, British governments often find it extraordinarily difficult to make their decisions stick when those decisions are not self-executing but instead depend for their successful execution on others in the society, whether industrialists, or bankers, or trade unionists, or ordinary citizens ... It may or may not be appropriate to describe modern Japan as 'Japan Inc.' but no one in their wildest dreams would think to describe modern Britain as 'Britain Inc.' The necessary elite cohesion is simply lacking.'[1]

One problem among many was the trade union movement. Labour organisations have usually been suspicious of major change and in the 1970s they succeeded in vetoing it. Both the Conservative government of Edward Heath and the Labour administration of James Callaghan ended up in unsuccessful conflict with the unions – and both paid the price of electoral defeat. It was left to Mrs Thatcher's governments to transform this situation in the 1980s. Through legal reforms, she tilted the balance of industrial power decisively away from the trade unions and towards management. Her victory over the miners in the bitter strike of 1984–5 was a visible statement of the declining power of organised labour – and of the difficulty which British governments have of achieving change through consensual means. Mrs Thatcher also strengthened the powers of the central state at the same time as privatising many nationalised corporations. In the second half of the 1980s these changes contributed to some improvement in Britain's economic performance and to a more positive national mood. In the opinion polls, optimism about Britain's prospects exceeded pessimism every year between 1982 and 1988, reversing the pattern of the previous Labour administration.[2] But it remains to be seen whether Mrs Thatcher's radical reforms produced more than a temporary halt to Britain's long-term decline.

Since 1945, the most dramatic single change to the policy environment came from Britain's belated entry to the European Economic Community (EEC) in 1973. The distinction between domestic and European policy has blurred and every major government department now has an EC dimension to its work. After initial problems of adjustment the British governmental machine adapted well to the policy style of the EC, which is based on log-rolling, consensus-building and package deals. Government, and indeed many local authorities and interest groups, have recognised the importance of the European arena. As the process of European integration continues, so another adjustment will be needed. Domestic policy-makers will have to recognise that the EC is ceasing to be just an arena within which national governments make deals. Increasingly the EC is becoming an actor in its own right, with a sharper, more direct policy style.

The constitution

Of the four countries, Britain is the only one without a written constitution. Nonetheless its political system is based on traditions which limit its flexibility at least as much as any written constitution would do.

British politics is based on an adversarial two-party system. British government is party government since control of both the executive and assembly rests with the victorious party. The first-past-the-post electoral system usually delivers a majority of seats in the Commons to the leading party even though no party has won a majority of votes since 1931. The governing party wields extensive executive powers until the next election. The factors which limit executive authority elsewhere – a strong second chamber, a written constitution, a federal system, an autonomous assembly, an assertive judiciary, open government – are largely absent in Britain.

The task of the opposition is to oppose. British politics thrives on conflict even more than Japanese politics seeks to suppress its open display. Because the electoral system discriminates against minor parties with evenly spread support, the opposition benches are dominated by a single party which seeks to act as a government in waiting. Government and opposition MPs face each other across the chamber of the Commons, separated only by a symbolic sword's length. Debates are robust but often superficial, giving an adversarial feel to British politics which is quite unlike any of the other countries examined in this book.

The foundations of adversarial democracy have decayed somewhat in Britain, especially since 1974, but the building remains largely intact. Four factors lie behind this decay. First, the capacity of the electoral system to manufacture a Commons majority for a single party has declined; the growing geographic axis in voting means a hung Parliament is likely before the century is out.[3] Secondly, in the 1970s (though not so much since 1983), MPs became slightly less reliable 'lobby fodder' for the governing party. This reflected the emergence of more professional, well-educated back-benchers as well as developments in the select committee system. More independently minded MPs were given greater opportunities to express their autonomy from their party. Thirdly, at the executive level, ministers and civil servants have become slightly more willing to express individual views which go beyond the official line of the governing party. Fourthly, and most important, there is growing scepticism about the quality of governance produced by adversary politics.[4] Support for electoral reform, which would force parties into a more co-operative posture, has widened. But the leaders of the two major parties remain resolute defenders of the current electoral system. Electoral reform is still unlikely until a hung Parliament arrives and even then its introduction is far from certain. It is ironic that an unwritten constitution should prove to be so inflexible.

Actors

Executive

The political executive in Britain can be looked at in several ways: as government by the Prime Minister, by the Cabinet, or by ministers.[5] The literature offers a tired debate about the balance of power between the Prime Minister and the Cabinet. It is more helpful to begin by thinking about the British executive in terms of government by ministers. We can then see how, if at all, the Prime Minister and the Cabinet fit into this picture.

The two dozen or so departments of central government are headed by ministers who are formally responsible to Parliament for all the actions of all their officials. Ministers are oriented first and foremost to their department, not to broader government strategy. They see their role as initiating or at least selecting policy, piloting measures through Parliament and party, and spotting political hot potatoes at an early stage. Ministers are judged by their departmental work and in consequence they are unlikely to give as much weight to their broader role as a Cabinet all-rounder. As one minister said, 'The main thing is the department. This absorbs all your energies. There is not enough time to read cabinet papers – although admittedly I am a slow reader – and personally I always tell my officials that my job is here at the centre.'[6]

Table 4.1. *Extent of ministerial specialisation,*
1945–80

	Specialists %	Not specialists %	Not known %	Total %
France	26	66	8	100
Japan	22	35	43	100
UK	13	77	10	100
USA	31	52	17	100

Source: J. Blondel, *Government Ministers in the Contem-*
porary World (London: Sage, 1985), appendix 2.

A distinctive feature of British ministers is their generalist ethos. This broad approach is encouraged by the relatively brief period which a minister spends in a particular job. As Blondel notes, 'the culture of prime ministerial governments is one of almost continuous changes in the composition of Cabinets. There is restlessness in almost all such governments almost all of the time'.[7] Compared to the other countries in this study, few ministers in Britain have a background in the subject matter of their department (see table 4.1). What British ministers do have is experience in the art of being a minister. Britain has far fewer 'one-post' ministers than the USA or Japan (see p. 52) and the notion of a ministerial career, progressing from junior minister to a minister, and then from a minor department to a major office of state, is better developed. When Headey interviewed a sample of fifty ministers, he found that almost half thought the qualities of an intelligent layperson were necessary and sufficient for a good minister. Less than a third mentioned executive, managerial or administrative skills.[8]

However the consequences of this generalist ethos are unclear. It might just encourage ministers to take a short-term, partisan view of policy. Short-term policy initiatives may help the minister to achieve promotion in the next reshuffle. If so, why worry about long-term problems? They can be safely left to the minister's successor. As King has suggested, the discipline of knowing one would have to live with the consequences of one's decisions would be a valuable constraint.[9]

All ministers who head departments are now members of the Cabinet but junior ministers, who are increasing in number, do not sit in Cabinet. The Cabinet comprises between twenty and twenty-five members and its weekly meetings now act more to ratify policies than to form them. The full Cabinet provides a court of appeal, capable of resolving politically sensitive issues which cannot be dealt with lower down the chain, but it is not a major decision-making arena. When Cabinet does become a policy-making site, as in 1976 when James Callaghan's Labour administration debated whether to accept the terms of a loan from the International Monetary Fund, this is often a sign of a government's political weakness rather than of its strength.

As with the United States Congress, the real significance of Cabinet lies in its committees. It is in these, or rather in the informal discussions which surround them, that the real work is done. Though still shrouded in secrecy, Cabinet committees are crucial to the operation of the modern political executive in Britain. A permanent system of Cabinet committees, serviced like the Cabinet by the Cabinet secretariat, was first established by the post-war Labour government. In addition to the standing committees, such as the Economic Strategy committee, most Prime Ministers set up several hundred Cabinet committees during their tenure though only a few meet regularly at any one time. Many committees sprout sub-committees: for instance the Falklands 'War Cabinet' technically reported to the Overseas and Defence Committee. Some committees are mixed, containing civil servants as well as ministers. Ministers are usually selected to serve on committees because their department has an obvious interest in the topic.[10] Decisions formally reached in committee carry the authority of Cabinet and Prime Ministers will want the minister chairing the committee to resolve the issue at committee level if possible. Indeed Prime Ministers themselves spend considerable time in committee. It is not so much that Cabinet committees are the effective point of decision; the policy will probably have been stitched up even before the committee ratifies it. Rather, Cabinet committees are the bodies which anchor the policy-making process, giving agendas, timetables and an overall structure to the flow of policy.

Where does the Prime Minister fit into all this? Prime Ministers lead the government through appointing ministers, chairing Cabinet, answering to Parliament and the people, and acting as a natural focus of authority, especially in a crisis. Beyond that the job is what the occupant chooses to make of it. In contrast to United States or French Presidents, Prime Ministers have no statutes setting out their authority. Yet neither do Prime Ministers have to work within formal constraints. Indeed in one sense the powers of the British Prime Minister are exceptionally strong. In contrast to many other countries, Prime Ministers can rearrange ministries just as easily as they can reshuffle ministers.

The role of the Prime Minister in policy-making also varies by sector. Traditionally Prime Ministers have been more closely involved in defence, foreign affairs and economic policy than in narrower, more domestic sectors such as transport or agriculture.

At the top, procedures are always flexible. The significance of a high-level meeting depends more on who is there than on its formal status. In truth we should look at the British executive not as government by particular positions, whether Prime Minister, Cabinet or minister, but rather as government by a few people at the top. Mrs Thatcher's penchant for informal meetings with relevant and/or trusted ministers was probably not as unusual as was often maintained during her tenure.[11] Nor was there anything unique in Mrs Thatcher's method of making strategy through a robust response to unanticipated events.

But formal institutional support is, of course, available to the Prime Minister. True, this is remarkably limited when compared with, say, a US or a French President. Harold Wilson described 10 Downing Street as 'a small village', a description which would hardly fit the White House metropolis.[12] Nonetheless Wilson was satisfied with the support available to him and saw no need for a Prime Minister's Department: 'everything a prime minister could expect to create is already there in the Cabinet Office'. (This office consists of civil servants who provide administrative support to the Cabinet, its committees and the Prime Minister.)

In addition to the Cabinet Office Mrs Thatcher had her own small Policy Unit of nine people. Mrs Thatcher also established an Efficiency Unit to identify savings through improved public sector management. In addition, from 1970 to 1983, a small Central Policy Review Staff (thirteen to twenty people), based in the Cabinet Office, attempted to provide a synoptic, non-departmental perspective on policy. But it did not establish a reputation sufficient to ensure its survival.

In general Prime Ministers, like the Supreme Court in the United States, must rely on others to execute their will. It is departments which supervise the implementation of policy and it is therefore through ministers – selecting, encouraging, co-ordinating and dismissing them – that Prime Ministers provide leadership.

Bureaucracy

Ministries, it has been said, are the largest communities in government which can command people's loyalties.[13] Of Britain's twenty-four departments, about half pre-date the Industrial Revolution though some, such as the Treasury, go back much further.[14] The varying age of departments means they vary in ethos. Differences in departmental style are a strong feature of central government in Britain.

The British civil service has traditionally accepted a limited political role. Senior civil servants offer confidential policy advice to ministers but they have much less contact with legislators than American bureaucrats do. In comparison with other democracies British civil servants are also particularly likely to see themselves in the modest role of brokers – mediating conflicts of interest rather than imposing grand solutions.[15] In this connection they spend a substantial proportion of their time in quiet discussions with pressure groups. Despite occasional complaints from ex-ministers about obstruction from the civil service, most civil servants are happy to accept political leadership from their ministers; there is no tradition of bureaucratic assertiveness as found in France and Japan. In fact what civil servants want more than anything else from ministers is decisiveness: 'the great bogey of the civil service is a minister who cannot make up his mind, who vacillates, who delays decisions'.[16] However at the top level in the civil service the distinction between politics and administration becomes less clear. One reason for this is that top civil servants are appointed by the Prime Minister. This is a significant weapon in the Prime Minister's armoury.[17] Mrs Thatcher's long tenure of office enabled her to initiate some penetration of the bureaucracy of the kind which the LDP has achieved in Japan.

Although the departments formulate much routine policy themselves, most of their higher-level business (and much of their routine stuff too) is inter-departmental. As a result, policy-making is no longer as narrow and confined as it was. For example, government policy towards North Sea oil involved several divisions of the Department of Energy; the Foreign Office, which wanted a policy which would be internationally acceptable; the Treasury, concerned about the economic implications; and the Inland Revenue, which had to collect tax from the oil companies.[18] This trend towards inter-departmental policy-making was sharpened by Britain's entry to the EC which added another layer of complexity to the whole policy process. The European Secretariat of the Cabinet Office is primarily responsible for co-ordinating activities related to the EC and is consulted about initiatives. The Treasury is also involved in any proposals with major spending implications, and as a result occupies a strategic position in policy-making. Inter-departmental negotiations at civil service level are an important source of bureaucratic power. Once the civil servants from two or three departments have worked out a plan acceptable to them all, it is a brave minister who says no and thereby unravels the entire ball of string.

In inter-departmental matters bureaucratic politics is another import-ant influence on policy content and quality. At ministerial and senior civil servant level, log-rolling, buck-passing and empire-building are endemic. No wonder Hann's discussion of the oil sector concluded that, whichever party was in office, government policy followed political and bureaucratic objectives as much as economic ones.

Table 4.2. *Career mobility of senior public servants*

	Percentage who have spent at least 25% or more of adult life outside national government	Percentage who have served in a ministry other than the present one
France	37	not ascertained
UK	12	51
USA	30	22

Source: From a sample reported in J. Aberbach, R. Putnam and B. Rockman, *Bureaucrats and Politicians in Western Democracies* (Cambridge, Mass.: Harvard University Press, 1981), table 3.7.

A distinctive feature of the British civil service is its generalist ethos. British civil servants typically have a humanities background, compared with a legal training in France and Japan and a technology or science background in the United States.[19] Although most top civil servants spend their entire career in the public service (see table 4.2), they usually serve in a range of departments on their upward journey. In 1977, less than one in six Permanent Secretaries had spent their entire career in the one department.[20] The pattern in Whitehall is for intelligent laypeople (senior civil servants) to pre-digest the advice of relative experts (lower-ranging civil servants) for the benefit of other intelligent laypeople (ministers).[21] This generalist spirit is reinforced by a civil service culture which regards policy advice to ministers as more exciting than either the efficient management of departments or the sound implementation of policy. This amateurish philosophy was criticised in the Fulton Report in 1968 but it has proved resistant to change. After all most Permanent Secretaries have spent more than twenty-five years in the service and are unlikely to be enthusiastic about a major change of approach.

One way around the problem of balancing policy advice against effective management is to hive off executive functions to agencies which are 'semi-detached' from their sponsoring department. An agency style of administration is already a familiar pattern in Britain. To adapt a nineteenth-century quotation about the Treasury, most departments are 'offices of superintendence and appeal rather than administration'.[22] In medical care, for example, the Department of Health has overall responsibility for the National Health Service but a major part of the service is delivered by general practitioners who are independent contractors.

Education shows a similar pattern. Only a few thousand civil servants work in the Department of Education and Science but over a million people are employed in education, most of them by local authorities. The Department of Social Security is one of the relatively small number of central ministries which delivers a service directly.

Agencies can be 'semi-detached' from their department in one of several ways. They may be non-ministerial departments: for example the Inland Revenue is separate from the Treasury but is responsible to Parliament through the Treasury for its tax collection work. Or agencies may be controlled by ministers but not staffed by civil servants: for example the armed forces. Or they may be other public bodies, such as local government, which provide services (such as the administration of student grants) for central government.[23] There is a dense network of these 'para-government organisations' in Britain, a network which survived attempts at pruning in the early years of Mrs Thatcher's administration and which then resumed its previous growth. This expansion was stimulated by a report from the Efficiency Unit in 1988 which argued that agencies have more flexibility than departments in responding to circumstances in a particular sector or region.[24] Britain may not be governed by agencies but it is substantially governed through them.

Parties

Britain's adversarial democracy is based on strong, distinctive parties. The governing party sets the political climate, dominates the legislature and controls what is, by international standards, a responsive bureaucracy. Particularly when a party wins two or three elections in a row, it has the opportunity to put its stamp on public policy. Conversely, governing parties pay the electoral price when policies fail. British parties are clearly much stronger than their United States counterparts. To know which party is in Number 10 tells us more about the direction of policy than does knowing which party occupies the White House, despite the fact that far fewer jobs change hands in Britain when a new government is formed.

One consequence of an adversarial democracy is that the opposition forms its policy in isolation from government. No party gains any competitive advantage by agreeing with its opponents. Hence opposition parties can be important sources of policy innovation (provided of course the party does eventually gain office). For example the radical style of Conservative governments in the 1980s owed much to new thinking on the right of the party when the Conservatives were in opposition. More specifically, most new taxes have come from proposals dreamed up by opposition parties.[25] Policy innovation is encouraged further because opposition parties are always under pressure to show how their policies differ from the government's.

Adversarial politics does not guarantee opposition parties will make good policies, only different ones. Indeed the system may encourage bad policy because oppositions work in ignorance and with inadequate resources. As Dick Taverne put it, opposition parties 'rely on pamphlets written on wet Sunday afternoons by people who don't really give all their devotion to it.'[26]

Although party competition encourages policy innovation, an implicit consensus is needed if the new policy is to stick. Long-term policy change in Britain depends on the opposition not reversing the policies of the preceding government when it arrives in office. Thus the long-run impact of a government should be judged by its effects on the opposition party. Once the opposition decides not to repeal a new policy, the reform is secure and the landscape is altered. Rose refers to this as 'the dynamics of a moving consensus'.[27] Without some such consensus, an adversarial system like Britain's is always prone to degenerate into ping-pong politics – as seen in the frequent nationalisation and privatisation of British Steel in the post-war period.

British parties are not unitary actors. To understand public policy, it is as important to know which wing of the party is in the ascendant as it is to know which party controls the government. Indeed competition within parties is the real source of fresh thinking. Within both parties, factional conflict reflects ideological as well as social divisions. In the Conservative Party, the contrasting perspectives of 'wets' and 'dries' reflect two strands in the party: upper-class paternalism against assertive middle-class values. In the Labour Party, the 'hard left' was based principally on middle-class public sector constituency activists. Within the party's trade union foundations there is a further battle between left and right. Hence British parties are battlegrounds as well as protagonists, arenas as well as actors. Under first past the post, control of the party is an essential stepping-stone on the path to control of the state.

Not all commentators accept the weight we have accorded to parties in policy-making. When Richard Rose raised the question, 'Do Parties Make A Difference?', his answer was a qualified no. He believes that when a party wins an election, the state takes over the party rather than vice versa. Parties say different things but behave similarly in office. The stock of legislation is created by many past governments and is only altered slightly by the current administration. In any case new legislation springs from the bureaucracy and the press of events, not manifestos. Little legislation enacted by previous governments is repealed. Further, governments (and hence the parties which form them) have little power to control events.

These are all sound points but they do not justify the thesis of the irrelevance of parties. What parties say is as important as what they do. For example Mrs Thatcher's government may have practised 'ideology in the general, pragmatism in the particular' but the ideology reshaped Britain's political climate.[28] Besides, over time her actions altered the economic and social structure. Even though the opposition may not reverse these changes, the Conservative Party – and Mrs Thatcher's faction in particular – still provided the initial momentum for change.

Pressure groups

Close consultation between the bureaucracy and organised interests is a characteristic of the policy process in Britain. Such negotiations are an integral part of the policy process in all contemporary liberal democracies. But there does seem to be a distinctive style of consultation in Britain: informal, pragmatic and non-partisan. The consequence is officially sanctioned self-regulation rather than legislation or administrative decrees. Writing from an American perspective, where formal regulation is more customary, Vogel says that 'British regulatory authorities rely more on persuasion and voluntary agreement and less on legal coercion than any other industrial democracy.'[29] Although the EC is encouraging a more formal style of regulation, policy on technical matters such as food labelling and industrial training still emerges from quiet negotiations between civil servants and pressure groups, not from parties, manifestos or ministers.

There is a long tradition of consultation in Britain. The British Rules Publications Act of 1893 required governments to allow forty days for written objections to proposed regulations. This requirement ended in 1946 not because governments wished to cease consultation but, significantly, because informal consultations rendered the law unnecessary. Closer co-ordination developed during the war and carried over into peacetime. Even today, some acts impose a condition of consultation with affected interests over implementation; and the courts have generally been sympathetic to consultation even when it is not mandatory. Consultation with producer groups is a norm of the system. In the past, cause groups such as the Consumers' Association and Friends of the Earth have been less welcome at table but even they are now gaining admission if they show they are prepared to play by the rules.

Although pressure groups in Britain are generally strong, the peak associations have limited authority over their members and restricted penetration through society. The CBI (Confederation of British Industry, the main organisation representing employers, especially in manufacturing) and the TUC (Trades Union Congress) are confederations with a limited capacity to deliver their members who themselves represent only a fraction of employers and workers. For example in 1986 only 37 per cent of the working population belonged to a trade union, higher than in the other countries in this study but a marked decline on the figure of 50 per cent recorded in 1977. (see p. 10). The TUC cannot 'deliver' the workforce and even at their height the 'peaks' were more effective at blocking change than implementing it. The failure of tripartite negotiations between government, employers and unions in the 1970s to develop into effective policy-making illustrates this.

Why should consultation leading to self-regulation be so common in Britain? One factor is the organisation of government itself, especially the system of departments (a factor which applies to most democracies) and the adversarial system (a factor more specific to Britain).

In a system of departments, ministries compete for money and legislative time. They therefore form alliances with their 'client' groups to strengthen their hand. Where would the Ministry of Agriculture (MAFF) be without the National Farmers Union (NFU)? Where would the NFU be without MAFF? Departments often encourage the formation of interest groups in their field for precisely this reason. The groups can supply information, legitimacy and some capacity to implement policy, all of which helps the sponsoring department in its Whitehall battles. Close links of this type are particularly likely where distributive policies predominate (see p. 16).

Adversarial politics adds to the influence of these communities of pressure groups and bureaucrats. Because party platitudes do not yield a formula for governing a complex society, detailed policy-making inevitably gravitates towards communities of experts which quietly work out details acceptable to all sides. Adversarial politics encourages ministers to seek agreements with pressure groups as a way of reducing political risk: how can the opposition benches object if all the interests accept? To get the work done, these communities of experts attempt to insulate themselves from the party battle: they are deliberately apolitical and operate in private, thus producing greater autonomy for themselves as long as they succeed in staying out of party politics. Ministers themselves encourage the specialists to sort it out among themselves in order to keep issues off an already crowded agenda.[30]

How did pressure group representation change under Mrs Thatcher's administration? There are two views here. Jordan and Richardson suggested that reality changed less than the rhetoric: 'despite Mrs. Thatcher's general antipathy towards quangos, the system of standing and ad hoc committees continues to operate'.[31] They noted that some new policy initiatives, such as the Manpower Services Commission, had strong involvement from the CBI and the TUC. They implied that the system's predilection for bargaining, compromise and consensus would reassert itself in due course. On the other hand, King attached more importance to Mrs Thatcher's reforms:

The Thatcher government has reduced the number of quangos and has resolutely refused to engage the peak organisations in corporatist discussions. In its insistence on limiting the role of intermediaries between the government and the people the Thatcher administration is at least mildly Gaullist ... corporatism is virtually at an end.[32]

All commentators are agreed that the corporatist tide receded in the 1980s and, more significantly, that the tide turned before Mrs Thatcher came to office. Yet it remains to be seen whether the Thatcher government was exceptional enough to establish a new pattern for the future.

Arenas

Government departments are the main arena within which policy is made. Routine policy is hammered out in detailed discussions among civil servants, often involving discussion with pressure groups. Politicised issues naturally have a stronger ministerial input and tend to spill over into wider arenas, involving backbenchers of the governing party, the floor of the House of Commons and the mass media. The most important issues of all may even involve the voters through election campaigns and referenda. At some stage issues which play on a wide canvas will decay into the 'standard' pattern of civil service/pressure groups consultation.

Governments cannot keep all issues within the Whitehall frame. The Gulf War, unemployment and funding of the NHS are examples of 'big' issues which encompassed all arenas. Governments can, however, choose to extend the arenas within which some issues are processed. Arenas such as public enquiries and Royal Commissions provide a thorough airing for problems and can contribute to the development of consensual solutions. They are one means of coping with controversial moral issues. But they are slow and they reduce the autonomy of government, even though government can, at a price, reject the recommendations. For these reasons, enquiries and commissions did not find favour with Mrs Thatcher. The ability of governments to choose the arena for processing is itself a form of power. For example politically difficult issues can be sidetracked to a commission. By the time the commission reports, the issue may have 'lost its legs' or another government may be in office.

Referendums are not an important policy arena in Britain. There were four in the 1970s – on the EEC, in Scotland and Wales on devolution and in Northern Ireland on secession – but more often than not these were attempts to legitimise decisions already taken by government. On EEC membership, for example, the government used its considerable powers of persuasion to ensure a substantial majority vote for continued membership. The voters became accomplices after the fact.

Parliament remains an important arena. This is for three reasons. First, the floor of the House witnesses a continuous debate between government and opposition which often results in subtle shifts in the policy agenda. Secondly, the law-making function is still significant. Parliament processes legislation even if it does not initiate it. Hence governments must be sure there is time to get a bill through, and little chance of a back-bench rebellion, before introducing it. Thirdly, the new system of fourteen select committees established in 1979 has enhanced the capacity of the Commons for policy scrutiny. These remain far less weighty than United States congressional committees but they contribute to, and depend on, some cross-party cohesion among MPs. As with Parliament as a whole, select committees react to policy even though they do not make it. In general, then, Parliament is still an important policy arena even though it is not a central policy actor. This arena role was strengthened by the decision to begin television coverage of the Commons in 1989.

However, Britain's entry to the EC has reduced the significance of the parliamentary arena. The coalition-building, log-rolling style which has so far characterised the EC means that Parliament has little control over a minister's negotiating position. A crowded parliamentary timetable leaves little time for detailed scrutiny of EC measures. In general Parliament has adapted less well to the EC than the executive has. On EC matters, Parliament is little more than a stage on which announcements are made about decisions reached in the more important European arena.

Although Britain is a unitary state, the political arenas outside London can not be dismissed as easily as they can in, say, Japan. Scotland, Wales and Northern Ireland have been governed through varying forms of administrative devolution. This means that a single department (such as the Scottish Office) is responsible for the implementation of all government functions in its territory. However, even in England, local authorities traditionally enjoyed considerable control over the administration of policy in such sectors as education, transport and social services. Local government spends about a quarter of all public funds.[33] Historically the relationship between central and local government was a partnership, albeit an unequal one. The power of the centre derived from its constitutional authority, from its provision of most local authority income through bloc grants, and from its willingness to specify in detail how policy should be carried out in politically sensitive areas.

In the 1980s, however, the partnership element declined and the relationship between central and local government became much more adversarial. Central–local relations became a major arena of political conflict, culminating in riots in England over the introduction of the poll tax in 1990. As with Ronald Reagan's administration in the United States, Mrs Thatcher's government was concerned about 'over-spending' by lower levels of government. Even before the poll tax, the Conservatives had set expenditure limits which councils could not exceed even by raising more funds through local property taxes ('the rates').

This dispute reflected the emergence of local government as one of the few sites of effective Labour-led opposition to a dominant Conservative government. Particularly in some inner cities, local government had been captured by factions on the left of the Labour Party, factions which welcomed open confrontation with the Conservative government. Conflict was intensified by the centralising tendencies of the Conservative government, a phenomenon which ran counter to the trend towards devolution in the other countries examined in this book. Some commentators saw the emergence of a 'dual state' in Britain, in which the priority of central government lay in improving national economic performance while local authorities were oriented to the provision of services, not least for those left out of economic prosperity.[34]

Instruments

Law is the most obvious instrument of public policy. But as Miller points out, 'the making of law is an expensive, difficult and time-consuming business. It is also increasingly pressured: the volume of legislation has increased from around 200 pages in 1900 to over 2000 pages a year today.'[35] Hence legislative proposals often involve core policies, such as manifesto commitments, or cases where existing law is to be changed, such as repeals. But the 'ongoing Whitehall process' is still the well from which most bills spring. Bills sourced in Whitehall generally go through the Commons without a division.[36]

In quantitative terms, Britain is governed by delegated or secondary legislation, not by acts. Most laws allow ministers to issue 'statutory instruments' about implementation. These are only given cursory, if any, attention by Parliament – not surprising, since over 2,000 are issued each year, totalling around 8,000 pages. Many instruments take effect automatically unless either House decides otherwise; and in most cases Parliament can only accept or reject the instrument in its entirety. Walkland describes secondary legislation as the 'characteristic regulating device' of a politically developed society.[37] They are generally non-controversial, drawn up by civil servants often after consultation with relevant interests. By giving effect to policy, they are substantive – detailed, technical and immensely important to those affected by them.

Besides secondary legislation, government can issue even more detailed statements and regulations. For example the Department of Environment frequently issues circulars about planning and housing law to local authorities. Indeed this is characteristic of policy instruments in Britain. Central government does not itself execute policy but in a unitary state exercises close control over those who do. Central government provides the money and carries the can when things go wrong. This means that, with the threat of legislation always in the background, it can often cajole the implementers into doing what it wants without any formal policy instruments at all.

Unlike France and Japan, the UK has no indicative planning. Its only recent effort in that direction – the expansionist National Plan introduced by the Labour government elected in 1964 – ended ignominiously, defeated by the weakness of the economy and opposition from the Treasury. Modest efforts in the 1970s at tripartite negotiations between government, business and the unions also failed to bite. This led to widespread fears that British governments lacked both the capacity and the instruments to modernise an ailing economy. After 1979, however, the Conservative government followed a philosophy of 'supply side' economics though this took the form of tough crisis-management rather than a strategic plan. Using a combination of instruments – exhortation, law and simple political determination – the Conservative government demonstrated that, at least in the context of a depressed economy and a divided opposition, Britain could still be governed.

Budget allocation is a crucial part of strategy-setting, representing as it does a public statement of priorities. Mrs Thatcher came to power determined to cut public expenditure and reallocate it towards defence and law and order. Her success, or otherwise, should therefore tell us something about the capacity of Prime Ministers (and indeed the government as a whole) to implement priorities. Experience in the 1980s showed that it was easier to spend than to cut and that changes to the balance of spending were easier to achieve in a growing economy. In the first Conservative administration of 1979–83, spending on defence and law and order grew but so did public expenditure as a whole. This was because the recession decreased revenue while also increasing spending on the demand-driven benefits of unemployment pay and social security. As the recession passed its peak, however, revenues became buoyant and public spending declined as a proportion of national income. Thus Mrs Thatcher at least accelerated substantial changes to public spending patterns (some were under way before 1979) but she had to invest considerable political capital to overcome opposition from client groups and those of her Cabinet ministers whose budgets were being cut. Indeed in the late 1980s political pressure to expand public spending increased again as the contrast between private affluence and public squalor intensified. Just as Mrs Thatcher found it difficult to cut the budget in hard times, so she found it difficult in better times to resist pressures for an increase in public spending in areas such as health and education.

The politics of allocation follow an annual budgetary cycle. Bilateral negotiations take place between the spending departments and the Treasury, with disputes and hard cases settled by the 'Star Chamber', a Cabinet committee which operates within a total public expenditure budget previously approved by the Cabinet. These negotiations are classic examples of government by department. The job of spending ministers is to get as much money as they can, not to take a broader view. Indeed ministers who ask for too little, perhaps on the grounds of the overall need for restraint, will just end up getting less money than their department needs, thus upsetting the precarious rationality of the whole system.

The Chancellor makes a traditional statement of changes in taxes and expenditure in the March budget. This remains an important piece of parliamentary theatre but its significance has been reduced by the further adjustments which Chancellors sometimes make in the summer or autumn.

The Conservative government operated a system of cash-planning: most departments were told their funding level and translated this into the services they could provide. However some open-ended commitments, such as unemployment pay, cannot be funded in this way. Cash planning, which itself modified a similar system of cash limits introduced by the Labour government in 1975/6, represented a retreat from attempts under previous governments to introduce more sophisticated planning systems, based on 'real' resources rather than cash. Finance-based cash planning indicates the continued pre-eminence of the Treasury in the process of allocation. It is a crude system but it does allow public expenditure to be controlled. Indeed if cash planning is based on optimistic estimates of inflation, as it usually is, public spending can be discretely cut.

Interpretation

There are a bewildering variety of perspectives on the British state. In the 1970s, many authors wrote of overloaded government, incapacitated by the power of big business and trade unions. In the 1980s, we heard accusations of a dominant, high-handed and authoritarian state. Marxist writers argue that whichever party is in office the underlying function of the state is to protect capitalism. Yet some non-Marxists suggest that the alternation of parties and policies positively damages economic performance. Britain has been called 'a much-governed nation' but many commentators bemoan the failure of successive governments to plan and direct, particularly on industrial matters.

Let us begin with the proposition that British government is neither state- nor group-dominated but party-dominated. The idea of adversary politics is that the alternation of two sovereign parties in office yields capricious instability of policy and, therefore, ineffective government. In contrast to the USA, neither parliament nor the courts nor federalism checks the power of the governing party. In contrast to France, it is not possible for power to be shared between a left-wing President and a right-wing Assembly. In contrast to Japan, policy continuity is not ensured by the long-term dominance of a single party. Instead the governing party changes at every other election, on average, and electoral competition forces each party to demonstrate the distinctiveness of its policies. So the advocates of adversary politics assume the state is an important actor (otherwise it would not matter which party controls it) but not an autonomous one (otherwise parties would not be able to control it).

Critics argue that parties are not so important. Rose notes that almost 90 per cent of legislation emerges from the bureaucracy or the press of events rather than party manifestos, and that most bills and standing orders are uncontested in the Commons.[38] Were British politics truly adversarial, argues Rose, a change of government would be an apocalyptic event – which it is not. Underlying these criticisms is the idea that the bureaucracy, in combination with interest groups, is the dominant force in policy-making in Britain. 'Party government' and 'government by the bureaucracy and interest groups' are two of the main interpretations of the policy-making process in Britain.

Which is right? The adversarial politics thesis certainly captures some characteristics of policy-making in Britain, though policy oscillations are perhaps the least important of them. As Wilks suggests, 'the real effect of ideological differences is not so much to create actual policy discontinuities as to force politicians into rigid doctrinal positions that preclude constructive discussion of practical solutions'.[39] Ministers develop an over-sensitive nose for the party politics of an issue and lose their sense of substance. They want a quick fix to cope with the opposition party, not a long-term solution to cope with the problem. Besides, a solution which fails attracts more criticism than a problem which is ignored and quietly dumped on the next minister's desk.

In reality, however, the adversary politics model and the bureaucracy/ interest group model are *both* valid images of policy-making in Britain. British policy-making runs on a dual track. The fast lane is for hot political issues. Here party politics predominates. Parliamentary and media scrutiny is intensive but short-term, ministers are directly involved and radical policy shifts are possible. By contrast, the slow lane is for routine policy. This is based on private detailed negotiations between civil servants and pressure groups. Here neither side has the capacity or the desire to innovate; the whole purpose is to reduce uncertainty. But there is considerable flexibility over detail. This is classic incrementalism: compromises are agreed even though objectives differ.

The problem is that these two tracks run parallel with insufficient contact between them. Professional expertise does not impinge sufficiently on the 'hot' issues while on routine matters there is a norm of avoiding public discussion lest negotiating flexibility is lost. Hot issues are overpoliticised; routine policy is depoliticised. In the fast lane, policies are changed too fast; in the slow lane, they are hardly changed at all. Neither mode is suited to strategic policy-making; the combination of the two is particularly ineffective. As the Webbs pointed out in the 1920s:

Government today is the work of an honest but secretive bureaucracy, tempered by the ever-present apprehension of the revolt of sectional interests, and mitigated by the spasmodic intervention of imperfectly comprehending ministers.[40]

The bureaucracy/interest group interpretation is helpful in characterising routine policy-making. But this leaves open many questions. Does the bureaucracy govern through the interest groups, do the interest groups 'capture' the relevant departments, or do both the public servants and the group representatives form a comfortable community of their own? The answer will vary from sector to sector but much current research favours the community interpretation. In day-to-day negotiations between government and interest groups, policy-making often has a communal feel. Shared expertise, reinforced by regular interaction, naturally leads to similar perspectives among civil servants and pressure group representatives. Both sides also have some autonomy from those they represent: interest groups from their members and, perhaps to a lesser extent, civil servants from their ministers. In Britain, these wheels are oiled by the normative value placed by government on consultation and voluntary agreement. Liberal values in British government, especially the bureaucracy, discourage a directive role.

Yet underlying these conventions lie competing interests and an awareness of the varying resources of the participants. Here there is a fundamental asymmetry: 'when push comes to shove the government can make policy on its own, and the implications of that point are seldom lost on either party to the negotiations'.[41] The structural power of the government exists but is often not fully utilised because of cultural inhibitions. This allows for variability across administrations and across departments in the nature of its interactions with groups.

For some writers, Britain's routine policy-making style has contributed to the process of relative decline which has shaped the agenda of British politics for so long. For example Olson suggested in the early 1980s that Britain's long-established interest-group system was over-powerful and, in consequence, a cause of the country's relative economic decline:

'Britain has precisely that powerful network of special interest organisations that we would expect in a country with its record of military security and democratic stability ... in short with age British society has acquired so many strong organisations and collusions that it suffers from an institutionalised sclerosis that slows its adaptation to changing circumstances and technologies.[42]

According to Olson, interest groups defend selective interests which are better represented than broader interests: doctors, teachers and food manufacturers are more powerful than patients, pupils and consumers. Interest groups represent established interests which do not support radical solutions: often indeed, they are the problem rather than the solution. In conjunction with departments, they shift the costs of inefficiency to the public charge: what would the NFU or MAFF gain from cheap food? A system of departments, each just concerned with its own part of the forest, encourages this sectional approach. Britain also lacks the powerful peak associations, capable of taking the broad view and of controlling their members, which are needed if strong interest groups are to prove compatible with a fast-growing economy.

Olson concentrated on the routine track of British policy-making. Since he wrote, the 'hot' track has seen more traffic. In the 1980s the Conservative government, motivated by a similar diagnosis of Britain's problems to Olson's, reduced the power of trade unions and introduced a measure of flexibility to selected industries and professions. This showed that the British state was not always a prisoner of special interests and it also confirmed the capacity of the state to act in a tough and decisive fashion. Yet the Conservative government followed a highly political – and very risky – strategy of offending established interests (whether miners or opticians) to benefit the general good. To be effective, this strategy must produce visible results to maintain electoral support. When it fails, or fades, and it will surely do one or the other, Britain will return to its former state: over-administered but under-governed.

NOTES

1. A. King, 'Networks, Ladders and National Purposes', in *Proceedings of the Three-University Conference* (Soka-shi: Dokkyo University, Japan, 1986), p. 189.
2. See the discussion of Gallup polls by M. Harrop and A. Shaw, *Can Labour Win?* (London: Unwin Hyman, 1988), p. 59.
3. D. Butler, *Governing without a Majority* (London: Macmillan, 1986).
4. The classic work is S. Finer, ed., *Adversary Politics and Electoral Reform* (London: Anthony Wigram, 1975).
5. P. Dunleavy and R. Rhodes, 'Core Executive Studies in Britain', *Public Administration*, 68 (1990), pp. 3–28.
6. B. Headey, *British Cabinet Ministers* (London: Allen and Unwin, 1974), p. 58.
7. J. Blondel, *Government Ministers in the Contemporary World* (London: Sage, 1985), p. 143.
8. Headey, *British Cabinet Ministers*, p. 62.
9. A. King, 'Who Cares about Policy?', *The Spectator*, 10 January 1970.
10. T. Mackie and B. Hogwood, 'Decision-making in Cabinet Government' in T. Mackie and B. Hogwood, eds., *Unlocking the Cabinet* (London: Sage, 1985), p. 9.
11. For example, an analysis of Harold Wilson's diary showed he had more informal appointments with ministers than Cabinet meetings and Cabinet committee meetings combined. See H. Wilson, 'A Prime Minister At Work', in A. King, ed., *The British Prime Minister*, 2nd ed. (London: Macmillan, 1985), p. 20.
12. Ibid., p. 12.
13. R. Emerson quoted in R. Rose, *Ministers and Ministries* (Oxford: Clarendon Press, 1987), p. 2.
14. R. Rose, ibid., p. 41.
15. J. Aberbach, R. Putnam and B. Rockman, *Bureaucrats and Politicians in Western Democracies* (Cambridge, Mass.: Harvard University Press, 1981).
16. Headey, *British Cabinet Ministers*, p. 143.
17. A. King, 'Introduction' in A. King, ed., *The British Prime Minister*, p. 8.
18. D. Hann, *Government and North Sea Oil* (NY: St Martin's Press, 1986).
19. Aberbach, Putnam and Rockman, *Bureaucrats and Politicians*, table 3.2.
20. R. Brown and D. Steel, *The Administrative Process in Britain*, 2nd ed. (London: Methuen, 1979), p. 91.
21. Headey, *British Cabinet Ministers*, p. 127.
22. Quoted in Rose, *Ministers and Ministries*, p. 25.
23. For a classification, see P. Dunleavy, 'The Architecture of the British Central State, Part I', *Public Administration*, 67 (1989), pp. 249–75.
24. *Improving Management in Government: The Next Steps* (London: HMSO,

1988). See also C. Hood, 'Para-government Organisations in Britain', in C. Hood and G. Schuppert, eds., *Delivering Public Services in Western Europe* (London: Sage, 1988), pp. 75–93.

25. B. Hogwood, *From Crisis to Complacency? Shaping Public Policy in Britain* (Oxford: Clarendon Press, 1987), p. 139.
26. Quoted in P. Hennessy, *Whitehall* (London: Fontana, 1990), p. 279.
27. R. Rose, *Do Parties Make A Difference?* (London: Macmillan, 1984).
28. The quotation is from A. King, 'Governmental Responses to Budget Scarcity: Great Britain', *Policy Studies Journal*, 113 (1985), pp. 476–93.
29. D. Vogel, 'Co-operative Regulation: Environmental Protection in Great Britain', *Public Interest*, 72 (1983), pp. 88–106.
30. J. Richardson, G. Gustafsson and G. Jordan, 'The Concept of Policy Style', in J. Richardson, ed., *Policy Styles in Western Europe* (London: Allen and Unwin, 1982), p. 10.
31. A. Jordan and J. Richardson, *British Politics and the Policy Process* (London: Unwin Hyman, 1987).
32. A. King, 'Governmental Responses to Budget Scarcity'.
33. R. Rose, *Politics in England*, 5th ed. (London: Macmillan, 1989), p. 320.
34. P. Dunleavy and R. Rhodes, 'Government Beyond Whitehall', in H. Drucker et al., eds., *Developments in British Politics 2* (London: Macmillan, 1988), pp. 107–43.
35. C. Miller, *Lobbying Government* (Oxford: Blackwell, 1987), p. 60.
36. R. Rose, *Do Parties Make A Difference?*, p. 71.
37. S. Walkland, *The Legislative Process in Britain* (London: Allen and Unwin, 1968), p. 17.
38. R. Rose, *Do Parties Make A Difference?*, p. xxvi.
39. S. Wilks, 'Has the State Abandoned British Industry?', *Parliamentary Affairs*, 39 (1986), pp. 31–46.
40. Quoted in Jordan and Richardson, *British Politics and the Policy Process*, p. 30.
41. R. Goodin, 'The Principle of Voluntary Agreement', *Public Administration*, 64 (1986), pp. 435–44.
42. M. Olson, *The Rise and Decline of Nations* (New Haven: Yale University Press, 1982).

FURTHER READING

Many general texts on British politics now include sections on the policy process. These include R. Rose, *Politics in England*, 5th ed. (London: Macmillan, 1989) and, at a more introductory level, B. Jones, ed., *Politics UK* (Hemel Hempstead: Philip Allan, 1991). Of the books concentrating exclusively on policy, an excellent starting point is M. Burch and B. Wood, *Public Policy in Britain*, 2nd ed. (Oxford: Basil Blackwell, 1990). More advanced alternatives are B. Hogwood, *From Crisis to Complacency? Shaping Public Policy in Britain* (Oxford: Clarendon Press, 1987) and A. Jordan and J. Richardson, *British Politics and the Policy Process* (London: Unwin Hyman, 1987).

5   The United States

Rod Hague

The National Situation

The 'American Century' has turned out to be no more than a few decades of international ascendancy for the United States. True, the war-shattered economies of Western Europe and Japan were successfully reconstructed after 1945 with American aid. But the major trading partners of the US inexorably became its major competitors. By the 1970s, the US was feeling the strain of leading the world economy; by the mid-1980s the world's largest creditor nation was rapidly becoming its largest debtor. American economic supremacy was thus eroded, as other major nations caught up (see table 5.1). In military terms, too, it was not long before US supremacy was strongly challenged. The Soviet Union established broad parity with the US as a nuclear superpower. Massive military capabilities did not save the US from serious reverses in Vietnam, Lebanon, Iran and Central America. Setbacks in the international standing of the US had major repercussions in domestic politics. The Gulf Crisis in 1990–91, in the wake of communist collapse in Eastern Europe, did produce a spectacular re-assertion of US international leadership and military power. This depended heavily, however, upon financial support from other nations: the military superpower now has economic feet of clay. Thus, the central trend underlying both foreign and domestic policy-making in the USA since the 1970s has been a weakening of US hegemony.[1]

From the 1930s onwards, the course of domestic American politics has largely been shaped by liberal-conservative conflict. The liberal view, typified in Franklin Roosevelt's New Deal administration, demanded not socialist ownership or planning but an expanded and active role for the federal government in managing the economy and tackling social prob-lems. In response to the crises of the Great Depression and World War II, the rudiments of a welfare state and a big government to manage vastly expanded commitments were built in Washington under Roosevelt in the 1930s and 1940s. Conservatives have remained unreconciled to a power-ful, heavily taxing and free-spending central government. They have

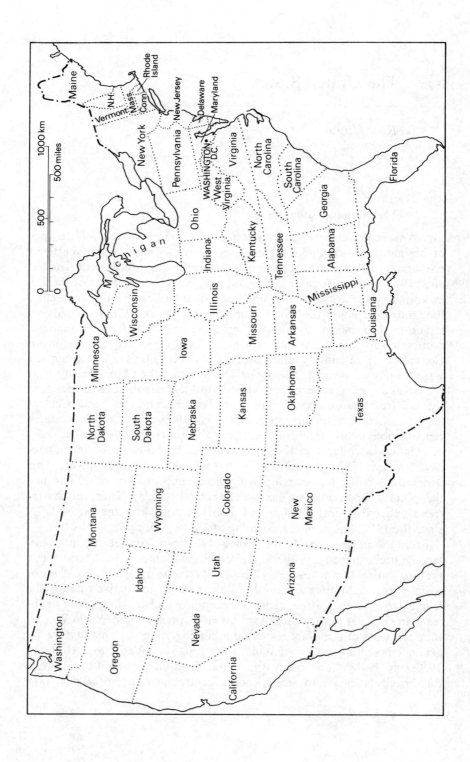

Table 5.1. *Gross Domestic Product, in total and per worker, relative to the United States (= 100), 1950–87*

	1950	1960	1970	1980	1987
Gross Domestic Product					
United States	100	100	100	100	100
France	12	13	16	17	16
Japan	9	15	28	34	36
United Kingdom	20	19	18	16	16
Gross Domestic Product, per worker					
United States	100	100	100	100	100
France	37	46	62	80	85
Japan	15	23	46	63	71
United Kingdom	54	54	58	66	72

Source: B. Bosworth and R. Lawrence, 'America in the World Economy', *Economic Impact*, 68 (1989), pp. 34–40.

continued to advocate minimum government and an economy of unfettered market forces. The scale of government must be held down to preserve individual liberty and the vitality of free enterprise. As Ronald Reagan declared on assuming the presidential office in 1981, 'Government is not the solution to the problem: government is the problem.' Though liberal–conservative conflict is rarely sharply drawn in party terms, the Republican and Democratic parties undoubtedly reflect different tendencies: the Democrats towards the liberal, the Republicans towards the conservative, end of the ideological spectrum.

Roosevelt's achievements in the New Deal era provided his party with a longstanding lead in electoral support. Until 1980 the Democrats lost control of Congress to the Republicans on only two occasions (1946 and 1952). In presidential elections, however, Democrat success has diminished. The New Deal coalition was an incongruous alliance: the unionised working class and liberal intellectuals from the Northern cities, alongside traditional Democrats from the rural South defending white racial supremacy. The coalition became increasingly strained. Post-war American electoral history is largely that of the decay of the New Deal coalition; whether it involved the wholesale rejection of the policies for which it stood, however, is less clear-cut.

Divided party control of executive and legislative branches has reduced coherent direction of public policy and led to stalemate. Big government, welfarism and what might be called 'military' Keynesianism continued largely intact under the conservative Eisenhower administration in the 1950s. Levels of public expenditure increased, but more controversially in the liberal-dominated 'Great Society' administration of Lyndon Johnson in the mid-1960s. Since the mid-1970s, American politics has been dominated by budgetary constraints, as conservatives and liberals, Republicans and Democrats, Presidents and Congress, bureaucrats and legislators, state politicians and Washingtonians, have fought bitter but mostly inconclusive battles for supremacy over the taxing, spending and borrowing powers of government. Under Ronald Reagan, serious fiscal and domestic social problems went unresolved while aspects of presidential foreign policy, particularly towards Central America, became bitterly contentious. Moreover, the underlying tendency towards declining hegemony, economic as well as political, was not halted, despite a massive military build-up.

The constitutional framework

The main structural characteristic of policy-making in the US is the 'weak state'. Government, especially the central authorities, is not as strong in relation to society as in the other democracies in this book. Indeed, the idea of the 'state' (in the European sense of the locus of sovereign power, an authoritative source of values and direction over society) seems but weakly held and is almost a misnomer in the context of American political culture.[2] Throughout their history, Americans have displayed suspicion and antagonism towards government, and asserted the rights of individuals against it. Government has, of necessity, grown in scope and capacity, but citizen consent has tended to be grudging and mindful of abuse. This is, of course, fully consonant with the cautionary attitude of the Founding Fathers. The constitution is designed, above all, to prevent over-concentration of power, methodically dispersing it through federalism and the separation of powers. Federalism entails a division of authority between the federal (or national) government and the states, while the separation of powers imposes an elaborate system of checks and balances between the branches of the national government. In the context of a nation of immense size, geographic extent and social diversity, the result is a decentralised and complex political system.

Rather than an arbiter imposing policies from above, government is thus much more an arena (or rather, many arenas) in which policy results from the interplay of numerous actors, institutions and interests. For all this, the American political system is deeply constitutional: the constitution is both supreme and revered, its authority binding on citizens and governments alike. But unlike the centralised states of Europe and Japan, it does not provide for a single, decisive locus of political will.

Public policy in the US has followed a distinctive course. The record in public policy is perceived as different from other democracies; slow in starting, little happening until the New Deal and with lower levels of taxation and welfare; health care and income maintenance policies are still less well developed than in Europe to this day. This is true, but the US has not simply been a laggard state in public policy terms. As Amenta and Skocpol have pointed out, US public policies have followed a zigzag course.[3] In the late nineteenth century, the US was in fact a leader among nations in the early development of pensions policies. Then came a period of retreat, until the next leap forward during the New Deal, when the US was again briefly a pioneer in public policy. By 1950 the New Deal had run its course and the US once more began to fall behind Europe, with only a short period of innovation in the 1960s. Amenta and Skocpol argue that the main factor behind this zigzag profile has been the decentralised institutions of the USA. These, together with early democratisation, meant that public policies were quick to develop, but politicians oriented them towards patronage and divisible benefits which could be directed at electorally important groups (such as civil war veterans) rather than general, collective benefits. Changes in the party system and the impact of crisis during the New Deal only partially overcame the effect of decentralised institutions; indeed, it can be argued that the pattern of nineteenth-century public policy has been reasserted in the late twentieth century. Public programmes for income support sharply distinguish between 'deserving' and 'undeserving' recipients, for instance. Contributory programmes such as social security (that is, old age pensions) are popular, politically well supported and virtually sacrosanct. Non-contributory programmes (such as income assistance or 'welfare' for the very poor) are much less generous and more vulnerable to budgetary attack.

American policy-making can be described as organised anarchy where no one, not even the President, is in overall charge.[4] Head of state and ceremonial leader he may be, but there is no guarantee that the president will be an effective chief executive. He is one major powerholder among many in Washington alone. But if policy-making is unco-ordinated overall, particular sectors may be well organised, a feature often referred to as sub-government. Each sub-government deals with a relatively narrow segment of governmental activity, such as agricultural support or military procurement, and can to some extent bridge the divisions created by the separation of powers and federalism. Thus, sub-governments, though not part of the constitution, are in a sense a response to it.[5]

Within a sub-government, policy-making may be carried on in a routine, predictable and efficacious way. Veterans' affairs is a good illustration. Veterans are ex-military personnel, who are numerous, politically well-organised and catered for by a range of services, covering pensions, medical needs, training and education, and a system of employment preference. These are provided by the Veterans' Administration, an independent executive agency of the US government; this is closely supervised by House and Senate Committees on Veterans' Affairs, and the appropriations committees which vote the funds for its operations. Finally the client groups of veterans' organisations, notably the American Legion and Veterans of Foreign Wars, liaise with and lobby both legislative and executive branches. Such three-way relationships between executive agencies, Congressional committees and pressure groups, are so strong and mutually supportive that they have been described as 'iron triangles', fairly impervious to presidential control or budgetary attack. Each sub-government acts independently of others; consequently there is little co-ordination or consistency across the policy-making system as a whole.

Within sub-governments, most policy-making activity consists of limited 'jiggling and poking' with existing government programmes.[6] 'Incremental' policy-making, as this approach has been termed, possesses considerable merit. Minor changes, rather than major ones, are likely to be more readily accepted by key actors and interests, and this may be vital to the successful implementation of a measure. By staying within the limits of what is acceptable, incrementalism fosters co-operative relationships among interest groups and decision-makers, greatly reducing the tensions that accompany decision-making. By sticking close to what is familiar, incrementalism has the further merit of involving limited risk, with less chance of serious failure.[7]

By contrast, major policy initiatives tear up the familiar. They invariably generate conflict, involving as they do sharp departure from established priorities or existing practice. Given the dispersal of power in the American system, non-incremental policy changes need a massive investment of political resources to overcome inbuilt inertia; to fail, they need fall at only one of numerous clearance points in Congress and elsewhere. Policy ideas must sometimes incubate for years or even decades before a combination of leadership and circumstances facilitates their adoption. Major policy breakthroughs (for example, the introduction of social security during the New Deal, or the passage of the Kennedy/Johnson Civil Rights bill in 1963/4) are therefore few and far between; they tend to be associated with situations of acknowledged crisis in which the President provides strong leadership while his party simultaneously has undisputed control of the legislature. There are exceptions to this: a skilful policy entrepreneur in Congress may be able to draw normally divergent elements behind a common cause. The Tax Reform Act of 1986 is a major case in point, in which Senator Bradley successfully assembled a coalition of liberals, wanting to close numerous tax loopholes favouring business interests and the rich, and conservatives (including the President) who wanted lower tax rates.

Domination of policy by sub-governments is not the whole picture, though. In recent decades, government by sub-government has increasingly yielded to more open, contentious and unpredictable patterns of decision-making. Heclo describes these looser arrangements as 'issue networks'. The root cause of this development has been the growth of government, especially of its regulatory activities, which has created a more complex, interdependent and conflictual pattern of policy-making.[8] Growing complexity of policy issues and tightness of resources now often blurs the boundaries between sub-governments. Compared with the closed and relatively cosy world of the sub-government, policy-making within issue networks reflects a wider and more variable cast of participants. In the modern climate of American politics, it is clear that 'iron triangles' can rust and disintegrate, as the tobacco industry discovered. For several decades, the tobacco industry enjoyed a cosy relationship with officials in the Agricultural Stabilization and Conservation Service, which operated the subsidy schemes, and the House Appropriations Sub-Committee (whose members invariably came from tobacco growing areas) which voted the money. But as public concern grew over the links between smoking and ill-health, policy toward the tobacco industry came under sustained attack from medical and anti-smoking lobbies; within eight years the tobacco sub-system was changed completely.[9] The experience of regulatory reform in several major industries (among them trucking, airlines and telecommunications) in the 1970s and early 1980s confirmed this trend. Once perceived as embodiments of the iron triangle and of 'agency capture' (regulators being dominated by the interests they were supposed to regulate), the regulatory environment of these industries was completely recast, as administrators and politicians responded to expert analysis and diffuse public sentiment favouring greater competition and less price-fixing.[10]

Actors and arenas

Presidency

Since Franklin Roosevelt established the contours of the modern office, the President has become the pivotal actor in contemporary American politics. But the American president operates within a capricious and often hostile institutional environment. He must compete for influence with other powerholders. Only rarely can Presidents achieve directive leadership. Far more often, Presidents are facilitators, articulating and amplifying a pre-existing disposition.[11] At any time, many policies are incubating in Washington, their sponsors hoping for presidential approval. The President would be wise, however, to make only a few selections from a long menu rather than dissipating support across a large number of measures.[12]

Congress is crucial to what is achievable, and thus to the fulfilment (or frustration) of presidential intentions. The constitutional framers ensured that the President has some means to influence Congress. He may coax and cajole it but cannot command it; conversation between President and Congress is the central dialogue of American politics. Legislative–executive relations vary from amicable co-operation to acrimonious stalemate. Weak and undisciplined parties mean that the stable congressional support necessary to turn presidential proposals into law is rarely available. Contemporary Presidents must assemble legislative coalitions as best they can. If the White House occupies centre-stage in the public life of the American nation, as far as Congress is concerned the occupant of the White House is sometimes little more than another lobbyist on Capitol Hill.

Though nominally subordinate to the President, the federal administration has permanent interests of its own. A major problem for every President is that no one other than himself has much interest in co-ordinating the executive branch. Various instruments have been developed to advise the president and aid him as chief executive officer, but none has had complete success.

The oldest of these devices is the Cabinet. By tradition, this comprises the heads of the thirteen major executive departments plus other individuals appointed at the President's discretion. But the US Cabinet is far different from its British namesake. The Cabinet has only the purpose and standing the President gives it, and most give it little. Under recent Presidents, 'inner' Cabinet members (the Secretaries of State, Defense, Treasury and Justice) have had frequent, often daily, contact with the President. 'Outer' Cabinet members (mostly the heads of the other executive departments) have sometimes had difficulty getting access to the President at all.

The failure of the Cabinet to develop a settled purpose has given rise to other agencies to aid and advise the President, notably the Executive Office of the President (EOP). Since its creation in 1939, the EOP has grown into a sizeable 'presidential branch', structurally complex and politically powerful, operating at the very heart of government (see table

Table 5.2. *Executive Office of the President, 1983*

Unit	Number of employees
Office of Management and Budget	567
White House Office	365
Office of US Trade Representative	132
Office of Administration	159
National Security Council	59
Office of Policy Development	50
Council of Economic Advisors	33
Office of Science & Technology Policy	20
Council on Environmental Quality	11

Source: Adapted from J. Hart, *The Presidential Branch* (Oxford and New York: Pergamon Press, 1987), p. 44.

5.2).[13] Placing the Bureau of the Budget (now the Office of Management and Budget) inside the EOP substantially augmented presidential control over formulation of the budget, at least until Congress begins to work his budgetary plans over, and to a lesser degree enhanced his managerial grip over the administration. The personal aides and assistants of the President in the White House Office (WHO), National Security Council (NSC) and Council of Economic Advisors (CEA) enable him to grapple with national and international commitments that have vastly expanded throughout this century. Without doubt, the EOP extends the President's reach and influence within Washington. At the same time, as the Watergate and Iran-Contra affairs have shown, the presidential branch and especially the senior staff of the WHO and NSC present serious problems of control for the President himself. While it does enlarge the President's policy-making capabilities, the presidential branch also functions to shield the President and protect him from risky or excessive involvement. The record suggests that it does not always do so wisely or successfully.

How does the US President get what he wants? The short answer is more by persuasion than by command: the President must bring others round to his point of view. Richard Rose identifies three main strategies of presidential influence: 'going Washington', 'going public' and 'going international'.[14] 'Going Washington' involves the President in wheeling and dealing with a Congress in which even individual senators or representatives may be able to block important measures desired by the President. 'Going Washington' has become harder, because of changes within Congress: the institutionalised pluralism of the early post-war period (when the President needed to bargain chiefly with committee chairmen) has given way to the individualised pluralism of the present (where every member of Congress is essentially an independent political entrepreneur). Coalitions are now far harder to construct.

Since the days of Woodrow Wilson and Roosevelt, Presidents have increasingly been 'going public' to persuade Washington indirectly by influencing the public. Ronald Reagan's reputation as a skilled communicator, exceptionally good at winning the hearts and minds of the American public, underpinned his standing within Washington itself.

'Going international' reflects increased US involvement in world affairs across this century; every President now spends more time on foreign relations and national security issues than anything else. But the world has shrunk in on the White House: the international environment is now far more complex and problematic for the United States than it was in the early post-war period of assured strength. The President is rarely in full control of events. Indeed, as the history of repeated conflict between the State Department and the President's National Security Adviser demonstrates, even presidential control of official US foreign policy is far from assured.

Congress

The legislative branch was intended by the framers to be the main policy-maker under the constitution, but now tends to be reactive, responding to policy initiatives from the executive and interest groups. Congress remains strongly autonomous, however.[15] It does not merely debate and legitimate decisions made elsewhere: it moulds and shapes policy through bargains struck in committees and choices made in legislative roll-calls. To a degree unparalleled in the other liberal democracies discussed in this book, public policy in the USA emerges from the politics of the legislature.

This is because congressional power is widely dispersed throughout its membership and across numerous committees and sub-committees, in which the real business of deliberating on policy proposals goes on. The specialised standing committees of Congress (16 in the Senate, 22 in the House plus a total of 227 subcommittees, in 1989–90) are the bedrock of its legislative autonomy. A bill which does not obtain solid backing from the committee which considered it has little chance of passing into law, because Congress as a whole is reluctant to overturn the judgement of its individual committees. If it were done to one committee, it might be done to others. Congressional committees, with their large supporting staffs, constitute a vast reservoir of expert knowledge on government operations, structure and finance. Scrutiny of government is, thus, probably deeper (though less co-ordinated) through the committee system in the US than in other liberal democracies.

The legislative parties are far removed from being monolithic voting blocs. Party leaders in Congress may work with the President but they definitely do not work for him. It may be that legislators like to go along with their party leaders (who have favours to trade and modest patronage at their disposal) but they face no compulsion to do so and often have solid reasons for doing otherwise. Thus, party membership bears only modestly upon legislators' voting decisions, and the extent of party cohesion in Congress varies from issue to issue and from time to time. Every member of Congress is, fundamentally, an independent entrepreneur, co-operating with other legislators as and when it suits. Compared with the looseness of party bonds, electoral imperatives for legislators are strong and pervasive. Given that members of Congress running for re-election are essentially running alone, rampant individualism means that the capacity of national elections to impose a programmatic vision upon Congress is very limited.

We can distinguish three main patterns of policy-making within the Congress, all involving coalitions: partisan, log-rolling and pork-barrel. *Partisan* policy-making implies coalitions based upon shared party values. While it is true that voting along party lines increased in the 1980s, particularly in the House of Representatives, the strength of partisanship remains changeable and often unpredictable. It seems useful, therefore, to extend the notion of 'partisan analysis' to cover situations where the proponents of legislation persuade other members of Congress that they also favour it, in virtue of shared values. *Log-rolling*, by contrast, involves legislators in the trading of mutual favours: the price of winning support for your own favoured measures is to vote for those of others, probably with scant regard to the intrinsic merits of the legislation concerned. *Pork-barrel* legislation is clearly intended to confer benefits upon a legislator's constituents, in the shape of government contracts, construction projects, or federal installations. Legislative coalitions are necessary to authorise such projects and appropriate the funds, so co-operation between legislators will clearly pay dividends until the pork-barrel is empty.[16]

The legislative process is complex and outcomes are uncertain. All bills are introduced by individual senators and representatives. There is no 'official' programme of government legislation, though many bills originate, of course, in the federal bureaucracy or have the backing of the White House. To enact a bill its sponsors must first steer it through the committee system. Most bills are fated to die in committee. If the committee reports it out favourably (and it remains recognisable), the bill is sent for debate on the floor of the chamber before its provisions (and probably also hostile amendments to them) are put to the vote. The House Rules Committee, which schedules these stages, was once a veritable roadblock and can still attach restrictive conditions. In the Senate, the possibilities of procedural delay and a filibuster by opponents are ever-present. A soundly argued case, procedural know-how, skill in face-to-face negotiation, a good sense of timing – and luck – are needed by sponsors of controversial legislation, in order to negotiate the congressional labyrinth. If approved by one chamber, the bill must then survive passage through the other chamber; any differences between the House and Senate versions then need to be reconciled (and sometimes in the process greatly altered) by a joint conference committee; it finally goes to the President to sign into law – unless, that is, he decides to veto it. Though a veto can be overridden by a two-thirds majority in the legislature, this is hard to achieve and most presidential vetoes succeed. Thus a bill's protagonists must achieve a majority at each of several 'clearance points', steering it through a process which offers antagonists many opportunities to block, mutilate beyond recognition or delay. Small wonder, then, that usually less than one in eight of all bills and resolutions introduced into Congress will be passed into law during an election year session (even-numbered years), while in the off-year session (odd-numbered years) when the pressure for results is lower, only about one in thirty measures will be enacted in some form.

For all the hazards of the legislative process, it is important for senators and representatives to put their mark on public policy. They want to matter. Few would be content (or feel electorally secure) as the relatively anonymous lobby fodder which still inhabits the bars and back-benches of the House of Commons. The most cogent explanation of the dynamics of congressional behaviour is that for most legislators the electoral imperative, the drive to be re-elected, is uppermost.[17] While it is the case that most incumbents are re-elected, this is taken by congressional politicians to mean that their unending efforts to secure re-election pay off, not that such efforts are unnecessary.

Bureaucracy

The federal bureaucracy is fragmented. In addition to the thirteen cabinet departments, there were fifty-seven independent executive agencies and government corporations in 1985–6, plus numerous other quasi-official agencies, boards, commissions and committees. Fragmentation is not simply a result of the number of agencies. Some Cabinet departments (such as Health and Human Services) are not internally cohesive, and more closely resemble a holding company for a large number of relatively autonomous sub-units. To take another example, over forty years after the creation of a unified Department of Defense, inter-service rivalries between army, navy and air force are still the staple of bureaucratic politics in the Pentagon.

The operational units of the federal government, whether established inside the major Cabinet departments or outside them, can use their links with Congress to maintain a degree of organisational autonomy. This may not be to the President's liking, but it does suit the legislature, allowing members of Congress opportunities for detailed intervention in remote corners of the bureaucracy. Moreover, the independent regulatory commissions, such as the Interstate Commerce Commission, were deliberately placed by Congress beyond direct presidential control. The consequences are far-reaching. For example, although the electoral buck for managing the economy stops with the President, in reality he shares that responsibility with the independent Federal Reserve Board. The President, therefore, has been provided with only some of the levers needed to control the federal administration and manage the national economy.[18]

Presidential control of the administration remains tenuous despite the fact that the entire echelon of senior officials is appointed by him. Presidents want federal executives who are competent in their area of responsibility but also responsive to presidential interests and objectives. In practice, they face considerable difficulty in satisfying these divergent requirements. Ideological zealots tend not to have much expertise in the nuts and bolts of government programmes. Experienced administrators do, but are less likely to feel commitment to the President.

The outcome can be uninspiring. Many federal executive appointees have little prior experience of government or even the specific area of operations to which they are appointed. They rarely know one another beforehand, and few stay in post longer than two years. Such a policy-making elite has aptly been called 'a government of strangers'.[19] Inevitably, day-to-day control of operations gravitates downwards, to the agencies and bureaus headed by career officials, which typically have close links with congressional committees and client groups. Bureaus can thus cultivate their own bases of political support, enabling them to sustain a considerable degree of autonomy against their nominal superiors. This has been described as a situation of 'bureaucratic egoism', in which agencies strive competitively to maintain or expand their funding, staff and programmes.[20] These tendencies are aggravated by the strongly technical and professional bias of recruitment to the career bureaucracy; officials are oriented towards the technical tasks performed by their agency, rather than infused with a common conception of public service.

All modern Presidents have seen the federal administration as over-complex, unwieldy and obstructive, and all have attempted to re-organise it, usually with scant result. In 1980, presidential candidate Ronald Reagan declared his intention to abolish the recently created Cabinet-level Department of Education (he saw no need for a federal role in education). But the department was still there when he retired from office nine years later. Government organisations are not immortal but they usually outlast Presidents.

Courts

A distinctive feature of policy-making in the USA is the major role of the courts. The fifty state court systems plus the federal courts are arenas in which all manner of rights, claims, issues and controversies are daily contested, and where judges make policy on matters which in other societies would be the province of elected policy-makers. Above all, the task of interpreting and adjudicating the constitution itself has fallen to the US Supreme Court, which stands at the apex of all these court systems. In the final analysis, the constitution is what the nine Justices of the Supreme Court say it is. Judicial review means that the Supreme Court can invalidate legislation or executive actions that are challenged in the courts and which do not, in the Court's view, conform with the constitution.[21]

Control of the constitutional rule-book thus lies with the Court, but it has also initiated many important policy changes in recent decades, among them the outlawing of racial segregation; the reform of electoral boundaries; police procedure and criminal rights; prison administration; and the reform of laws regarding abortion and capital punishment. These innovations were not only bitterly controversial, but raised major questions about the legitimacy of judicial activism. 'Strict constructionists' hold that the Supreme Court should adhere as far as possible to the original intent of the constitutional framers. Closely related is the view that the judges should practice 'self-restraint', respecting the constitutional authority of the elected branches, and not second-guessing the elected policy-makers. On the whole these views have not prevailed among the judges – the Supreme Court, in particular, became more conservative but no less interventionist in the 1970s and 1980s.

Inter-governmental relations

Few areas of policy-making are unaffected by the fifty states and eighty thousand local government jurisdictions in the United States. Despite centralising trends in the twentieth century, mostly achieved through

Washington's fiscal resources, the states still constitute major legal, political and administrative units. The dispersal of power in the USA remains underpinned by a weak party system, and strong territorially rooted representation in the Congress, as well as by fundamental respect for the autonomy of the states.

In the 1960s, under the 'creative federalism' of Lyndon Johnson's Great Society initiatives, Washington sought to deal directly with local governments and community groups, bypassing the states which were viewed as unresponsive and dominated by parochial and reactionary interests. The centralising and redistributive character of Johnson's programmes antagonised conservative politicians, and aroused traditional fears of endangered 'states rights'. Under the guise of 'New Federalism', Richard Nixon sought to reimpose the political and financial whip hand of the states over local government and (much less successfully) to restrain the growth of inter-governmental aid. Inter-governmental relations under Ronald Reagan can be described as 'coercive federalism'. The President was undoubtedly committed to cutting federal subsidies. But his administration also made increasing use of the powers of federal pre-emption accumulated over the previous forty years of co-operative federalism to override state and local authority and impose unfunded mandates. Policy under Reagan thus aimed at pushing lower-level governments into assuming fuller responsibilities for services, in the belief that citizens were much more sensitive to taxing and spending decisions made at local level. Between 1981 and 1986, federal grants to state and local government were reduced by 36 per cent in real terms, despite the efforts of the inter-governmental lobby. The central government was reducing its reliance on fiscal inducements, and employing regulatory power more freely in inter-governmental policy.

A diverse and decentralised political system has given proof of its continuing vitality, however. Throughout the 1980s, cutbacks and paralysis in federal policy-making transferred power, policy initiatives and financial burdens back to the states. The role of the states, always dominant in education, has been growing in health care, transport, economic development and the environment. Politically, moreover, federalism remains popular, with voters showing more faith in their state governments than in either Congress or the presidency.

It has never been realistic to describe intergovernmental relationships in the US simply as a 'layer cake', of one layer of government superimposed on top of another. At the operational level, to use Grodzin's metaphor, federalism is more like a marble cake, with a complex intermingling of federal, state and local powers, finance, laws and regulations.[22] One consequence has been the growth of 'picket fence' federalism, in which distinct professional communities of policy-makers (such as highway planners at federal, state and local levels) interact more with one another than with other policy-makers (such as health care administrators) at the same level. Picket fence federalism thus points to a pattern of vertical policy communities, overlapping different levels of government, while interaction and co-ordination between the various policy communities at the same level of government remains limited.

Over two centuries, federalism has altered from being a loose alliance of near-sovereign states to a fine-spun web of financial, legal, administrative and political interdependence between central, state and local governments. The forces of centralisation have clearly grown over the last half-century or so, but the constitutionally based and culturally rooted preference for the dispersal of power ensures the continuing political vitality of the states.

Parties and interest groups

American political parties are notable mainly for what they are not. They are neither disciplined nor programmatic nor well structured. Each party is electorally heterogeneous, and with the exception of blacks, no social category gives overwhelming allegiance to one party. Split-ticket voting between presidential and congressional elections is now also frequent. Although the Republicans and Democrats are associated with divergent ideological tendencies, compared with European parties, the American parties are relatively weak and incoherent when it comes to specific policies.

Recent decades have seen further decomposition of organisations that were ramshackle to begin with. Party identification has substantially weakened within the electorate. Traditional local party machines based on spoils and patronage have withered. The legislative parties in Congress, never very cohesive, have become less so over time. Electoral campaigning, once the domain of the party professionals, has been taken over by the candidates, who in effect create their own electoral organisations. Campaigning at every level has become candidate- rather than party-centred. With political individualism rampant, decaying parties are even less likely to present coherent policy programmes. Candidates may, of course, strike responsive electoral chords, as Reagan did in 1980, when he identified and amplified an anti-government, tax-cutting mood in the electorate. But this rapidly produced a bandwagon effect among other candidates in both parties. The incoherence of party plus the large number of elected personnel (in states and local government, as well as federally) diffuses responsibility, clouds accountability, and probably weakens citizen control.

Interests can be what the parties are not: well organised and highly specific in their aims. With a political system providing multiple points of access, interest group activity permeates all levels and sectors of policy-making. Some powerful interests are in effect veto groups. For example the National Rifle Association, which opposes gun control, was long able to block measures it disliked. Most interests, however, need to form coalitions for successful action; this may restrain extreme particularism to some degree.

Except when populist outrage is directed at the machinations of 'big business', the United States is unusual though not unique among the major democracies in that the supremacy of capitalist enterprise has never been seriously challenged.[23] To be sure, organised labour has developed an efficient political lobbying arm, mainly to compensate for its declining industrial muscle. Yet the peripheral status of the labour lobby is shown by its tendency to be more successful as a partner in liberally oriented coalitions than on union-only concerns.

The policy environment within which interest groups operate is both crowded and constantly changing. Producer groups do not have the field to themselves. Arguably the most momentous change in post-war America, the civil rights 'revolution', was led by organisations rich not in material resources but in charismatic leaders and mass commitment. A few years later, public interest groups like 'Nader's Raiders' and Common Cause, wanting honest and efficient government, safe products and a clean environment, were probably at the peak of their influence. And a striking development of the early 1980s was the spectacular rise of the new Christian Right, harnessing the technology of television evangelism and computerised direct-mail fund raising to a message of strident moral and cultural conservatism. It engaged liberal politicians and secular values in head-on electoral and ideological combat.

Groups employ a whole gamut of strategies and techniques for influencing policy. Consultative techniques include routine contacts between group spokesmen and bureaucrats; direct contacts between captains of industry and executive leaders; public testimony before congressional committees or quiet discussions with congressional research staff. Lobbying techniques include mobilising grass-root membership to pressurise legislators or hiring expensive professional lobbyists to persuade them. Electoral techniques include giving public endorsements (or opposition) to political candidates; financial donations through the PACs (Political Action Committees) which have transformed campaign financing since the 1970s; and practical assistance to favoured candidates. Publicity techniques include expensive public relations campaigns or coming up with good news stories to generate 'free' media coverage.

Despite a traditional cultural preference for voluntary association and an apparent maelstrom of interest group activity, social participation is far from equal or even. The interests of lower social strata are severely under-represented in the pressure group universe. Barriers to greater participation by the working class and social minorities are no longer legal or institutional. Poor Americans simply lack sufficient resources, confidence, experience, knowledge of government and allies to organise more often and more effectively on their own behalf.

Instruments

There are several types of policy-making instrument in the US, of which the main ones are legislation, budget-making, regulation and adjudication. Some kinds of policy instrument are not used. Despite widespread concern at the impact of Japan on America's world trading position and intense US interest in Japanese business methods, efforts at MITI-style economic planning would be futile amid the rampant individualism of American society.

Of the instruments that are used, *legislation* might be described as the classical, though not numerically the most important, form of policy-making. The annual output of the national legislature is modest. Moreover, although Congress deliberates and investigates extensively, much legislation is in fact of an outline character. This sometimes reflects insufficient expertise in Congress to draft the technicalities of the legislation but is more often, perhaps, a studied vagueness to avoid giving offence to potential supporters in Congress. Invidious choices are also thereby evaded, as the legislature passes responsibility for handling what may be hot and contentious problems to the bureaucrats. Detailed steps to realise legislative goals are thus often the responsibility of the executive branch. Since the Supreme Court declared that the legislative veto (through which Congress retained the final say over an administrative decision) infringed the separation of powers, the hands of the bureaucrats to devise and implement administrative procedures have been even freer.[24]

Budget-making in the USA is unusually fragmented; multiple points of leverage produce inconsistency, lack of co-ordination and weak overall control. At the heart of the presidential–congressional relationship is the annual struggle over the budget. Though it is rarely the creation of the executive branch, the President lacks full control over the budget, especially once he has submitted it to Congress. The legislature retains an unusual leverage but tends to employ it in a piecemeal and often negative manner.

After acquiescing for decades in the expanding presidential role in budgetary management and economic policy-making, Congress over-hauled its budgetary procedures in the 1970s. The 1974 Budgetary and Impoundment Control Act was a major attempt to re-assert Congressio-nal authority over the budget. A new budget committee was set up in each branch of Congress, together with a Congressional Budget Office to provide expert advice, rendering the legislators less dependent upon the executive branch. In outline, the process involves detailed scrutiny of spending proposals by 'programme specialists' in the appropriations sub-committees, together with overall consideration of spending totals and strategic objectives by 'putters-together' on the Budget Committee.

The new procedures worked reasonably well in the Carter presidency. Then, in 1981, President Reagan skilfully exploited the reconciliation procedures (which compel the legislature to consider the package as a whole) to force through large tax and spending cuts.[25] The remainder of Reagan's presidency was marked by protracted budgetary warfare between the White House and the Democrat-controlled House of Rep-resentatives. The result was stalemate, with budgetary procedures fre-quently remaining technically incomplete.

Swelling budget deficits began to undermine international confidence in the US economy, but agreement could not be reached on how to balance the books until Congress resorted to panic measures in December 1985. The Budget Deficit Reduction Control Act (usually known after its main sponsors, Gramm–Rudman–Hollings and memorably described by the first-named of these as 'a bad idea, whose time has come') provided for annual automatic across-the-board reductions in government spending to reduce the deficit, in the absence of congressionally determined cuts. The intention was to shift the odious task of cutting expenditures on to an obscure government official, the Comptroller-General (though this aspect of the legislation was then ruled unconstitutional by the Supreme Court). In practice, Gramm–Rudman–Hollings has been a weapon of last resort, the threat of which has compelled White House and Capitol Hill to reach temporary accommodations and if necessary to fudge their budgetary differences. But Gramm–Rudman–Hollings has not so far succeeded in its primary aim of eliminating the budgetary deficit.

Although Congress expends many thousands of hours on the budget each year, most budgetary changes are incremental in character. The expenditure of nine federal dollars out of ten is uncontrollable from year to year. In consequence the range of discretionary programmes, facing the possibility of major changes, is narrow. Those which are politically more

controversial and vulnerable (such as the main public assistance programmes for the poor) are likely to bear the burden of fiscal adjustment.
Federal funding for these programmes was cut by over a quarter in the
early 1980s. It is not just difficult to create programmes with redistributive
aims in the first place: they are difficult to sustain in the face of budgetary
pressures.

Administrative *regulation* is a major mode of contemporary policy-
making. Regulation is a form of delegated legislation, by which legislative
statute confers upon executive agencies the authority to make rules with
the sanction of law. Delegated legislation was slow to develop in the
United States, not least because of the suspicion in which it used to be held
by both Congress and courts. But the growing scope and technical
complexity of government since the New Deal has engendered extensive
regulatory activity. Major policy initiatives, particularly in the field of civil
rights, have sometimes come in the form of executive orders or other
regulatory instruments, rather than as congressional legislation: the
decision, for example, to integrate the armed services or to require
affirmative action towards minority groups in the hiring policies of
companies accepting federally awarded contracts. Growing concern for
the environment and consumer product safety in the 1960s and 1970s
spawned new regulatory agencies (often with a more adversarial style
towards the industries they regulated) and led to a burgeoning of
regulation.

Despite Reagan's de-regulatory drive, the volume of federal regulation
remains enormous, with thousands of pages added to the Federal Register
each year. Under the 1946 Administrative Procedures Act, the regulatory
process allows representations from the public and consultation with
affected interests before a proposed regulation is published in its final
version and takes effect.[26] Consultation helps to generate consent from
those affected and so legitimises the process of regulation. In a society so
sceptical of power and so conscious of democratic values as the USA, this
is a practical necessity. But the process of consultation enables administrators to draw upon information from actual practitioners (or their representatives) and thus improve the quality of the rules made. The process
of consultation can be so effective that administrative agencies can be
'captured' by the very interests they are supposed to regulate. For a
democratic society, the main danger posed by the growth of governmental
regulation is the discretion it places in the hands of non-elected
bureaucrats.

The striking role of the judiciary in *adjudicating* American public policy
has already been noted. Litigation is a commonplace form of pressure
group activity. Business corporations subject legislation and regulations

to routine challenge in the courts. As the highest appeal court in the land, however, the Supreme Court largely controls its own agenda; all appeals are sifted but the vast majority are rejected as either frivolous or not involving a substantial federal question. Others are summarily decided. Only a minority of appeals are permitted oral argument and full review (for example, in the 1981 term, 48 cases were granted full consideration out of the 5,311 cases on the docket).[27]

A landmark ruling like *Roe v. Wade* (1973) in effect prescribed policy guidelines for abortion laws in every state, but the impact of Court decisions is usually less dramatic. Every judgement relates to an individual case: it is open to the Justices to stress how general or specific they consider the ruling to be. The Opinions which accompany rulings are frequently obscure, and sometimes appear to be deliberately vague or ambiguous. This may arise from the necessity of building a majority within the Court, or reflect uncertainty and confusion among the Justices. Since so many cases involve balancing competing interests, a degree of ambiguity in a ruling allows the Court to observe the effect of decisions, with possible future modification in mind.

For implementation of its rulings, the Supreme Court has to rely on the lower courts, and other branches and levels of government respecting its decisions. Outright defiance (by federal authorities) is rare, but foot-dragging and non-compliance is common. The Court has no enforcement agencies of its own. This can produce a major gap in implementation. Ten years after the Brown case declared educational segregation unconstitutional, only 2.4 per cent of black children were attending integrated schools in the South (see chapter 7). The impact of the Court's decisions depend upon the recognition of its authority. This is linked in turn with the Court's public standing, which will diminish if it embroils itself too often in controversy or strays too far from the mainstream values of American society. The irony, then, is that although it is a non-elective institution, the Supreme Court needs to have some regard for public opinion in order to maintain its credibility as constitutional arbiter.

Interpretation

The complexity and variability of American politics and policy-making mean that no single model is likely to capture all its characteristics. Sub-government with its tendencies towards 'iron triangles' and agency capture, can result in policy sectors dominated by tightly knit interests. Some sectors may still be dominated in this manner, but the policy-making process in other instances is more like a confused fight than a conspiracy. The reasons for this change in policy style include greater technical complexity; more intensive lobbying; and heightened public interest across a greater range of issues (such as environmentalism). Statutory developments (such as requirements for mandatory public hearings and the impact of the Freedom of Information Act) have also contributed. Though sub-government tendencies remain strong in the more routine phases of policy-making, the climate of policy-making has been changing, with settled patterns of interaction being disrupted by a new range of participants and by increasing interdependence between once distinct sectors of policy-making.

If this thesis of growing complexity is valid, it implies no easy answer to the question: who rules? The pluralist conception of American politics emphasises the dispersal of power, the openness of the political system, and portrays the policy-making process as a competitive struggle to mobilise resources and marshall majorities in a complex institutional setting. The pluralist view emphasises the variability of outcomes, reflecting the skill, luck and opportunities of the proximate policy-makers as well as the broader societal forces at work. Arguably, the policy-making process has become more pluralist, not less so, as once tidy sub-governments have disintegrated into more open but less stable issue networks. The pluralist view need not imply equality of resources, or access or outcomes. With this proviso, it surely offers a fairly realistic conception of policy-making in the USA.

The US constitution was once characterised as 'a government against government'. Can a political system with such institutional arrangements govern effectively, particularly against a background of hegemonic decline? McKay identifies three major critiques of US policy-making, concentrating on problems of economic efficiency, overall effectiveness and social justice.[28]

The first view, concerned with economic efficiency, regards the US political system as excessively pluralistic.[29] Every social interest has some access and must be taken into account, to some degree. In an increasingly harsh and competitive international economic environment, the US political system is simply too clogged to redirect resources and re-order national priorities in a timely manner.

The second view, concerned with overall effectiveness, concentrates on the problem of the declining capacity of government, as marked by the gap between promise and performance. The American ideology raises high expectations, which the system over the last two decades has been less successful in meeting. This is reflected, writers such as Samuel Huntington argue, in symptoms such as disintegrating parties, presidential failure, and declining public trust in government institutions.[30]

The third view, by contrast, is concerned less with the declining legitimacy of the political system than with deepening social and political inequality, and especially with the plight of America's social minorities whose fortunes worsened substantially in the 1980s, partly as a result of structural changes in society and economy, but mainly because of cuts across a whole range of programmes which were largely directed at them.[31] Those who were already among the most vulnerable groups in society, lacking effective access to decision-makers or sufficient electoral clout – the poor, the unemployed, the homeless, single parent families – were the main losers in the policy struggles of the 1980s. At one level, American politics concentrates on single issues, or on bland, non-divisive themes, or the purely personal attributes of politicians. At another level, as the worsening plight of the minorities reveals, the American policy-making process continues to reflect sharply conflicting ideological preferences.

NOTES

1. See P. Kennedy, *The Rise and Fall of the Great Powers* (New York and London: Allen and Unwin, 1988), pp. 514–35. For a contrary view, see S. Gill, 'The Rise and Decline of the Great Powers: The American Case', *Politics*, 8, 2 (1988), pp. 3–9.
2. T. Skocpol, 'A Society Without a "State"? Political Organization, Social Conflict and Welfare Provision in the US', *Journal of Public Policy*, 7, 4 (1987), pp. 349–71.
3. E. Amenta and T. Skocpol, 'Taking Exception: Explaining the Distinctiveness of American Public Policies in the Last Century', in F. G. Castles, ed., *The Comparative History of Public Policy*, (Oxford: Polity, 1989), pp. 292–333.
4. This phrase, used by R. Rose, *The Postmodern President: The White House Meets the World* (Chatham, N.J.: Chatham House Publishers, 1988), p. 182, was coined by M. D. Cohen and J. G. March in a study of American university presidents.
5. Sub-governments are well described in R. B. Ripley and G. E. Franklin, *Congress, the Bureaucracy and Public Policy*, rev. ed. (Homewood, Ill.: Dorsey, 1980).
6. A phrase used by B. Guy Peters, *American Public Policy: Promise and Performance*, 2nd ed. (London: Macmillan, 1986), p. 13.
7. The classic text on incrementalism is C. E. Lindblom, *The Policy Making Process* (Englewood Cliffs, N.J.: Prentice Hall, 1968).
8. H. Heclo, 'Issue Networks and The Executive Establishment', in A. King, ed., *The New American Political System* (Washington, D.C.: American Enterprise Institute, 1978), pp. 87–124.
9. See A. L. Fritschler, *Smoking and Politics*, 4th ed. (Englewood Cliffs, N.J.: Prentice Hall, 1988).
10. M. Derthick and P. Quirk, *The Politics of Regulation* (Washington, D.C.: Brookings Institution, 1985), pp. 238–46.

11. G. C. Edwards III, *At the Margins: Presidential Leadership of Congress* (New Haven: Yale University Press, 1989), pp. 4–5.
12. R. Rose, *The Postmodern Presidency*, pp. 176–8.
13. J. Hart, *The Presidential Branch* (Oxford and New York: Pergamon Press, 1987).
14. R. Rose, *The Postmodern Presidency*, pp. 31ff.
15. A good collection of essays on presidential–congressional relations is A. King, ed., *Both Ends of the Avenue* (Washington, D.C.: American Enterprise Institute, 1983). A recent general treatment of Congress is C. J. Bailey, *The US Congress* (Oxford: Blackwell, 1989).
16. Pork-barrel activity is, of course, as old as Congress. For an informative survey, see 'The Perpetual Porkbarrel', *Congressional Quarterly*, 45, 3, 24 October 1987.
17. D. Mayhew, *Congress: The Electoral Connection* (New Haven: Yale University Press, 1974).
18. R. Rose, *The Postmodern Presidency*, pp. 189ff.
19. H. Heclo, *A Government of Strangers* (Washington, D.C.: Brookings Institution, 1977).
20. A. Downs, *Inside Bureaucracy* (Boston: Little Brown, 1967).
21. For a good introduction written for non-American students, see R. Hodder-Williams, *The Politics of the US Supreme Court* (London: Allen and Unwin, 1980). Also highly readable is D. M. O'Brien, *Storm Center: The Supreme Court in American Politics* (New York and London: Norton, 1986).
22. M. Grodzins, *The American System* (Chicago: Rand McNally, 1966).
23. Elite and mass attitudes in the US towards the close but potentially conflictual values of capitalism and democracy are explored by H. McClosky and J. Zaller, *The American Ethos: Public Attitudes towards Capitalism and Democracy* (Cambridge, Mass.: Harvard University Press, 1985).
24. *Immigration and Naturalization Service v. Chadha* (103 S. Ct. 2764, 1983).
25. D. McKay, p. 204.
26. G. C. Bryner, *Bureaucratic Discretion: Law and Policy in Federal Regulatory Agencies* (Oxford and New York: Pergamon Press, 1987), pp. 19–30.
27. D. O'Brien, *Storm Center*, p. 200.
28. D. McKay, *American Politics and Society*, 2nd ed. (Oxford: Blackwell, 1989), pp. 295–9.
29. For example, L. Thurow, *The Zero Sum Society* (Harmondsworth: Penguin, 1981); See also P. Duignan and A. Rabushka, *The United States in the 1980s* (Stanford, Cal.: Hoover Institution, 1980).
30. S. Huntington, *American Politics: The Promise of Disharmony* (Cambridge, Mass.: Harvard University Press, 1981).
31. For example, F. F. Piven and R. Cloward, *The New Class War: Reagan's Attack on the Welfare State and its Consequences* (New York: Pantheon, 1982); also M. Harrington, *The New American Poverty* (London: Firethorn, 1984).

FURTHER READING

Established texts on American public policy include *American Public Policy*, 2nd ed. (London: Macmillan, 1986) by B. Guy Peters and *Understanding Public Policy*, 6th ed. (Englewood Cliffs, N.J.: Prentice Hall, 1987) by Thomas Dye. The distinctive evolution of American public policy is illuminated in the chapter by Amenta and Skocpol in *The Comparative History of Public Policy*, ed. F. G. Castles (Oxford: Polity, 1989). Policy-making aspects are extensively considered in the textbook by D. McKay, *American Politics and Society*, 2nd ed. (Oxford: Blackwell, 1989). *The Postmodern Presidency* by Richard Rose (Chatham, N.J.: Chatham House Publishers, 1988) is an outstanding discussion of the presidency in the contemporary policy-making environment.

Part 2

Sectors

6   Industrial policy

Philip Daniels

Industrial policy is a broad category. At its most general it embraces all the activities of government which, intentionally or unintentionally, impinge upon national industrial development. A narrower, more operational definition of industrial policy refers to the myriad of government actions intended to promote or protect specific firms, industries or sectors. In this sense industrial policy refers to the policies and mechanisms (for example, public procurement and state subsidies) used by governments to influence the investment decisions of industries. According to this definition, industrial policy implies active intervention by government. This chapter uses this narrower interpretation.

State involvement

Governments in all advanced industrial states pursue policies designed to promote industrial growth and manage industrial change. The political benefits of economic success ensure that no government can be indifferent to the nation's industrial performance.

Governments pursue a variety of economic and social objectives through industrial policies. These include fostering national economic growth and development, encouraging the development of new technologies and industries, improving the international competitiveness of national industries, alleviating the contraction of 'sunset industries', facilitating the restructuring and rationalisation of ailing industrial sectors, safeguarding domestic employment and smoothing regional imbalances.

The scope, form and objectives of industrial policy have changed over the post-war years. In France, Japan and the UK the goals of intervention have been quite similar: in the late 1940s and 1950s, industrial policies concentrated on the strengthening of basic industries; in the 1960s, as tariff barriers were removed and world markets opened up, the main focus of industrial policy was the promotion of large national corporations able to compete internationally; in the 1970s attention turned to crisis indus-

Table 6.1. *Principal forms of industrial policy*

	France	Japan	United Kingdom	United States
Regional policy	Yes	Very limited	Yes – declining	Very limited
Competition policy	Relatively mild	Very limited	Relatively mild	Relatively strong
Protectionist measures	Significant	Significant	Moderately significant	Significant
Defence industrial policies	Important	Minor importance	Somewhat important	Very important
Assistance for small firms	Yes	Yes	Yes	Yes
Public ownership of industries	Very substantial	Limited	Diminishing	Not important
General (non-defence) R & D assistance	Yes	Yes	Yes	Yes
Export assistance	Yes	Yes	Yes	Yes
Attraction of inward investment	Very limited	Very limited	Yes	At state level
Aid schemes for declining sectors	Yes	Yes	Phased out	Under Carter (not continued)

Source: Table adapted from W. Grant, *Government and Industry* (Aldershot: Edward Elgar, 1989); UK and USA information from the same source.

tries hit by the onset of a world recession; and in the 1980s the accent was on the development of the new high-technology industries of the 'Third Industrial Revolution'. These similarities arise in part because each of the four countries is deeply enmeshed in the world trading system and is therefore subject to similar pressures to remain competitive.

Governments in each country have used a variety of policy tools to intervene in industry in the post-war period. These are summarised in table 6.1. Nonetheless, the four countries vary considerably in the nature, scope and success of their industrial policies. Government intervention in industry in the United States has been characterised by the absence of a co-ordinated strategy. British industrial policy has often been designed to help industries survive rather than to promote competitiveness and new industries. In contrast, the Japanese state has actively promoted industry and has largely succeeded in helping it to adapt to changing international markets. The French state has likewise played a strategic role in industrial development although, as in the UK, defensive policies have also been prominent and attempts to 'pick winners' have not always succeeded.

It is customary to portray France and Japan as strongly interventionist states with comprehensive and integrated industrial policies, while the United States and Britain are typically viewed as states in which government intervention in industry is more limited. Recent research, focusing on single industrial sectors, has challenged some of these traditional descriptions. These studies show that general national patterns of state involvement disguise significant variations in the extent and form of intervention from sector to sector in a given country.[1] In addition, subnational levels of government or local agencies may be responsible for industrial policies which differ from predominant national styles. For example, many American states have developed strategies for industrial development and in the UK the Scottish Development Agency, among others, has promoted industry. However, it is still useful to refer to predominant national styles and state traditions in industrial policy.

For both Britain and France, membership of the European Community impinges significantly on national industrial policies. In recent years, the EC has become more active in co-ordinating policies designed to promote high-technology industries and it has developed Community-wide strategies to deal with declining industrial sectors. In addition, EC competition policies place severe constraints on government assistance to national industries: for example, in 1990 the European Commission demanded that the French motor company Renault repay subsidies received from the state and British Aerospace was told to pay back government 'sweeteners' received when it took over Rover. While Japan and the USA must also bear in mind the importance of the European market, the EC does not influence national policy as directly or extensively in these countries as in Britain and France.

The next section describes the pattern of state involvement in industry in each of the four countries. The remainder of the chapter then examines the major issues on the agenda of industrial policy, the institutional structures and policy communities, and concludes with an appraisal of policy outcomes.

France

France has experienced a rapid economic transformation in the post-war period. By 1990 France had become the fourth richest Western nation in terms of GNP. The French state has a deeply rooted tradition of intervention and has been extensively involved in post-war industrial development. The principal objectives of industrial policy have been to promote new industries so that France remains at the leading edge of technological development (including prestige projects and national champions); to assist ailing and crisis industries (for example, steel and shipbuilding); and to encourage regional development.

French industrial policies fall into two broad categories: firstly, those which target specific sectors or companies (for example, government funding for aerospace, nuclear energy and data processing; trade barriers; government procurement); and secondly, horizontal measures aimed at stimulating general industrial growth (for example, tax measures to encourage investment, indicative planning, research funding and export assistance). In addition, nationalisation has been an important element of industrial policy; about 25 per cent of French manufacturing industry is in the nationalised sector, including most basic industries (steel, chemicals, metals, etc.) and most high-technology industries (aircraft, electronics, telecommunications).

The focus of industrial policy in post-war France has passed through several broad phases.[2] From 1945 to 1958 the main objective was to rebuild France following the ravages of war. Industrial policy focused on the sectors considered vital to sustained economic development; coal, electricity, steel, cement, agricultural machinery and transport. From 1958 to 1976, the principal goal of industrial policy was to create large, industrial corporations able to compete in international markets and to withstand the challenge of emerging multinational corporations; for example, in the chemicals, electronics, textiles and aeronautics industries. From 1976 to 1981, industrial policy focused on industrial adjustment in the wake of the recession induced by the 1973 oil crisis. The main accent of policy was to target industries with growth potential and to support 'sunrise' industries such as consumer electronics, biotechnology and office-automation equipment.

Since 1981, the period of the Mitterrand presidency, industrial policy has varied again.[3] From 1981 to early 1983, the Socialist government pursued a comprehensive industrial policy involving modernisation projects for specific industries (for example, machine tools, textiles, paper industries and electronics) and an extensive programme of nationalisation which took twelve industrial groups, thirty-six banks, and two finance companies into the public sector. However, many of the newly nationalised groups and existing nationalised firms required the injection of extensive state funds. At the same time the government's reflationary strategy (*relance*) worsened the trade balance and weakened the franc. In March 1983, the government adopted austerity measures to deal with the deteriorating economic situation. Industrial policy also changed direction: industry-specific policies were abandoned or scaled down and the government froze the level of state subsidies to nationalised firms. Greater emphasis was placed on private investment as the motor for economic recovery and the government relied mainly on reducing business taxes to stimulate industrial modernisation. Industrial policy continued broadly in this direction from March 1986 to April 1988, the period of *cohabitation* between the Socialist President Mitterrand and the Gaullist Prime Minister Chirac. The major innovation in industrial policy during this period was the right's programme of privatisation of public industries. However, the privatisation policy came to a halt in October 1987 when the stock market crash undermined investor confidence.

Japan

The remarkable success of the Japanese economy in the post-war period and the leading international position of many of its companies have focused attention, both critical and admiring, on its industrial policies. State involvement in industry is extensive and the close co-operation between government and industry has been a key factor in post-war success. In contrast to the UK, for example, state intervention and guidance in Japan have been 'market-conforming' in the sense that they have shifted with market trends and generally avoided the rescue of 'lame duck' industries.

In the post-war period the principal instrument of industrial development has been the administrative guidance emanating from MITI and the other ministries with industrial responsibilities. Administrative guidance is not legally binding but officials can use incentives (such as subsidies) to obtain compliance. However, the goals and instruments of industrial policy have shifted in the post-war period as Japan recovered from wartime destruction to achieve its present status as the world's second-ranking industrial nation.[4]

During the reconstruction period from 1945 to 1960, policy focused on modernising the industrial base and promoting exports. The government played an active role, providing tax incentives and government financing, encouraging mergers and the rationalisation of industry, directing loans to targeted industries (such as steel, machinery, petrochemicals, shipbuilding, automobiles and electronics), granting export subsidies, protecting national industry by trade barriers, and promoting the import of foreign technology and essential industrial materials.

From 1960 to 1970, the era of rapid growth, the tempo of modernisation accelerated and Japanese export industries became increasingly competitive on the international market. The government again played an active role in promoting international competitiveness, providing various forms of support (subsidies, low-interest loans etc.) to private corporations and encouraging firms to specialise, co-operate in production, merge and invest in targeted industries. In addition, governments attempted to promote specific industries such as computers and electronics.

The upheavals in the world trading and financial systems in the early 1970s, and the first oil shock of 1973, posed new problems for a Japanese economy highly dependent on trade and by now extensively integrated into the world economy. In response to the changing economic environment (which included the growing friction caused by Japan's trade surplus), industrial policy objectives shifted to assisting declining industries, promoting technological innovation (including alternative energy sources) and encouraging new, knowledge-intensive industries (for example, integrated circuits, computers, and robotics). Broadly speaking, this latter period has seen greater reliance on the market mechanism and less targeting of particular industries for promotion or protection. At the same time the 'vision' has become an increasingly important tool of industrial policy. The 'visions' contain policy targets and furnish information about the evolution of the industrial structure to facilitate long-term strategic planning by firms and to induce them to move in a given direction.

The United Kingdom

All post-war British governments have had to contend with the problem of underlying and persistent weaknesses in the economy. Britain's relative industrial decline dates from at least the late nineteenth century and can be seen in its diminishing share of world trade in manufactures and generally slower rates of productivity growth than its principal industrial competitors.

The British approach to industrial policy in the post-war period has been characterised by a general preference for market solutions coupled with periodic, and largely unsuccessful, attempts at government intervention. In contrast to Japan, UK government involvement in industry has been marked by policy discontinuity, ad hoc measures and a reactive, defensive style. Although British governments have used a wide variety of industrial policy instruments (including regional aid, export assistance, general research and development funding, public ownership of industries and public procurement), industrial policy has generally lacked clear and consistent objectives.

In response to growing international competition, British governments have developed industrial policies targeted at specific sectors or firms. From around the mid-1960s government intervention in industry placed increasing emphasis on the creation of large national corporations able to compete effectively in international markets. In the 1970s, with the onset of world recession, industrial policy was largely defensive, concerned principally with the support and rescue of ailing industries. Since the latter half of the 1970s the emphasis of industrial policy has shifted towards 'positive adjustment' and the promotion of new 'sunrise' industries.

The period of Conservative government since 1979 has been marked by a disengagement from industry and a greater reliance on the market mechanism. Privatisation has greatly reduced the nationalised sector of industry and the government has refused to rescue ailing industries. The Conservative's 'hands off' industrial strategy has focused on creating conditions within which industry can flourish; the means include the deregulation of industry, encouragement of small businesses, incentives in the form of personal tax cuts and attempts to foster an 'enterprise culture'. In addition, the Conservative government has succeeded in its efforts to attract inward investment, particularly from Japanese companies.

The United States

Of the four nations in this study, the United States has generally been regarded as the one whose government has played the most limited role in promoting the development of national industry. Indeed, the recession and America's declining international competitiveness in the 1980s have stimulated a debate in academic, business and government circles about the desirability of a comprehensive and integrated industrial policy comparable to that of Japan.[5] While it is true that the United States government has not made widespread use of policies to promote the international competitiveness of targeted industries, it has nonetheless affected industrial development through an extensive and developed set of policies at both federal and state level. In addition to public procurement and research and development funding, the federal government has channelled funds to assist ailing industries, provided export financing, granted tax concessions and erected trade barriers to safeguard threatened industries.

These policies may be less visible, more indirect, and less openly acknowledged than French or Japanese industrial policies, for example, but many American government policies 'have been as successful as the more explicit interventions of the governments of other nations'.[6] Many of the policies affecting industry have been 'both the unintended and unanticipated consequences of policies to achieve other objectives'.[7] This is strikingly apparent in the arena of government procurement; for example, large military budgets, justified on the grounds of safeguarding national security, have given important competitive advantages to the domestic armaments, aerospace, semi-conductor and computer industries.

Military spending has also helped to keep several industrial sectors at the leading edge of high-technology developments. In 1986, Department of Defense procurement expenditure accounted for 6.6 per cent of American GNP.[8] Likewise, government research and development expenditure has had an important commercial impact; for example, the civil aviation, telecommunications and electronic component industries have benefited greatly from direct government support. In addition, the Department of Defense is heavily involved in financing research for advanced computers, large-scale integrated circuits and fibre optics. Substantial government assistance has also been available to the pharmaceutical and biotechnology industries and the US government's space programme has produced a number of commercial spin-offs for the civilian sector.

Since the late 1970s state governments have become more active in promoting industrial development. Offering a variety of locational incentives, including tax concessions, the states have sought to attract national and foreign firms to their region. Although some states have benefited from these local policy initiatives, critics contend that the competition between states hinders the development of a coherent national industrial strategy.

Anti-trust or competition policies have been a significant instrument of state intervention in industry. In contrast to Japan (and to some extent France and the United Kingdom), the United States has enforced competition laws which are designed to prevent monopolistic control of markets and unfair trading practices. American corporations often complain that the stringent enforcement of anti-trust legislation puts them at a competitive disadvantage compared with their international rivals.

Policy agenda

Since the early 1980s the industrial policy agenda has been dominated by issues relating to international competitiveness. In France, Japan and the UK governments have tended to shift from protectionist policies towards 'positive adjustment' policies to promote national firms which can compete effectively in world markets. In the United States, the large trade deficits and a declining share of world markets have provoked a concerted campaign for government support for targeted industries.

The pressures for international competitiveness have highlighted divergencies in national approaches to industrial policy. It has also brought to the fore fundamental divisions regarding the desirability, feasibility and effectiveness of industrial policy. Ideological and partisan differences over state intervention in industry are most apparent in the United States and the UK. In both countries, the state has generally maintained an 'arm's length' relationship with industry. Industrial policy is highly politicised and there are fundamental disagreements about the relative merits of the market mechanism and state intervention. Such disputes are much less prominent in France and Japan where traditions of state intervention in industry are well developed and government–industry relations are more co-operative.

The industrial policy debate in the 1980s has focused on two major issues. First, should governments intervene with positive industrial policies in order to promote the development of new technologies and the growth of sunrise industries? Or should governments adopt a 'hands off', *laissez faire* approach and attempt to create the economic climate within which business can flourish? In the 1980s the ascendancy of neo-liberal approaches to economic management placed this issue at the heart of the political agenda. Secondly, should governments use defensive industrial policies to bail out ailing industries or leave them to go to the wall? These debates have taken place in each of the four countries, most prominently in the United States and the UK. In examining these debates, however, it is necessary to separate the rhetoric from the reality. In practice, all four states, faced with intensifying international competition, have intervened to promote industry. Their rates of success, however, differ quite markedly.

Policy community and policy-making institutions

There is not a single, stable national industrial policy community in any of the four countries. Policy-making in this area tends to be characterised by a proliferation of governmental and non-governmental actors and a fragmentation of interests. Broadly speaking, the leading actors are government departments and state agencies (both national and local), firms and business groups, and trade unions. The relationships among these actors are complex and there is considerable potential for conflict between competing interests. The actors often have different goals and priorities, and competition for the allocation of resources may be intense. An effective industrial policy is inherently distributive since it requires the targeting of particular sectors or industries. For example, a government decision to target resources towards new sunrise industries at the expense of declining industrial sectors might provoke considerable opposition from sunset industries and from regional lobbies adversely affected by industrial decline.

The pattern of government–industry relationships is quite distinctive in Japan, France, the UK and the United States, and the institutions responsible for industrial policy are equally variable. For some scholars, these differing institutional arrangements are the key to explaining the relative success of national industrial policies. Thus, British and American advocates of a more comprehensive, integrated industrial policy often argue that this requires Japanese or French-style institutional arrangements. However, critics contend that this would not be feasible since national institutions are the product of a distinctive national political, economic and social development and therefore not readily exportable.

In order to assist cross-national comparisons, it is helpful to consider policy communities and policy-making institutions along the following dimensions: (1) the organisation of the state; (2) the organisation of capital and labour; and (3) relationships among policy actors.

Organisation of the state

In each of the four countries the conduct of industrial policy is principally the responsibility of central government ministries and bureaucracies. It is in these institutions that the core of the industrial policy communities is typically located.

France has developed an elaborate institutional apparatus for intervening in industry. In many respects, the French institutions responsible for industrial policy closely resemble those of Japan. In both countries the central ministries and their personnel play an important role in formulating and implementing industrial strategy. However, industrial policy-making is more dispersed in France, with no single coordinating and strategic ministry equivalent to the Japanese MITI. Responsibility for French industrial sectors resides with the appropriate sponsoring ministry; for example, the ties between the Ministry of Defence and the armaments industries are very close, as are the links between the Ministry of Post and Telecommunications and the telecommunications and electronics industries. 'Policy networks' of this kind enable firms and industries to exert significant influence on policy. As a result, the decision-making autonomy of the ministries is constrained and government efforts to develop coherent industrial policies are undermined.[9]

The French Ministry of Finance, like its Japanese counterpart, is a key actor in industrial policy. The Treasury (*Trésor*), located in the Ministry of Finance and staffed by *corps* trained in the *Ecole Nationale d'Administration*, closely monitors the allocation of credit, the financial markets, the debt strategy of public industries and investments in general. It also distributes long-term government loans or capital endowments to private and public industry. Through its control or ownership of the major banks, the *Trésor* has been able to 'influence industrial policies without appearing to be in command'.[10] The Budget and the Foreign Trade Departments of the Ministry of Finance control various subsidies and export promotion loans to industry, extending the administration's influence in industrial policy. Thus, the state's pervasive influence in the financial system serves as an important lever for intervention in industry.

Indicative planning has also played a part in post-war French industrial policy, although it is much less important today. During the late 1940s and early 1950s the plan set the priorities for industrial development and the allocation of scarce resources. However, the Planning Commission (*Commissariat Général au Plan* – CGP), comprising experts and representatives from business, labour and government, saw a diminution of what power it had as French integration into the world economy increased the number of uncontrollable economic variables and made forecasting much more hazardous. Today the Planning Commission 'should be seen as not much more than a place where substantive actors meet for non-substantive discussions'.[11]

In *Japan* the Ministry of International Trade and Industry (MITI) oversees the majority of industries and has an extensive range of functions. It guides the development of targeted industries using the allocation of capital as its lever; it draws up recovery or adjustment plans for depressed industries; it manages Japanese foreign trade and external commercial relations; it is responsible for ensuring an adequate supply of energy and raw materials; and it oversees policy for small business and regional development.[12]

MITI is also responsible for the 'visions' which, like the French indicative plans of the early post-war years, set out the long-term priorities for industrial development. The visions are drawn up by MITI and the Industrial Structure Council (one of the many so-called deliberation councils, *shingi kai*, attached to MITI) which brings together leading industrialists, government figures, academic experts, journalists and representatives of labour, consumer groups and local interest groups. This wide representation is designed to establish a consensus on the development of Japan's industrial structure and to provide continuity in industrial policy.

Industrial policy is not, however, the exclusive domain of MITI. Its pre-eminence in industrial policy has declined since its heyday of the 1950s and early 1960s and today it is constrained by the autonomous power of big business and the rival claims of other ministries with responsibilities for industrial sectors (for example, the Ministry of Agriculture is responsible for the chemicals industry).

As in France, the Ministry of Finance (MOF) is also a key governmental actor in Japanese industrial policy. It supervises the Bank of Japan and has responsibility for credit control, monetary policy, foreign exchange policy, banking regulations, tariff and customs policies, government loans and selective tax incentives – all significant instruments for industrial policy. In addition, the MOF oversees the Fiscal Investment and Loan Plan, a budget for government investments and loans for targeted industries. The source of funds is the nationwide postal savings system which commands large resources – equivalent to about 6 per cent of GNP. These funds are used to finance the many public corporations 'as well as the innumerable foundations, associations, and promotional organisations that serve as intermediaries between the government and the private sector'.[13] Many of these funded institutions act as instruments of industrial policy. One of the most significant is the Japanese Development Bank (JDB) which provides loans to promote government development policies (for example, for new energy sources and fifth generation computers).[14] JDB loans also serve as a signal to the financial and business communities that a particular sector has been targeted by the government.

At first glance the *British* state appears well endowed with institutions for the conduct of a coherent and effective industrial policy. However, in practice, the institutional arrangements for carrying out industrial policy have been characterised by a dispersal of functions and the lack of a co-ordinating central ministry. This fragmentation is evident in the number of government departments with responsibility for some part of industry. These include the departments of Trade and Industry (DTI), Transport, Employment, Energy, Defence, Agriculture, and the Northern Ireland, Scottish and Welsh Offices. The problems inherent in these arrangements have been well summarised by Grant:

With so many departments involved in policies affecting industry, there is a danger that policies may be pursued which duplicate one another or which are contradictory. One does not have to believe in some kind of grand, highly centralized industrial strategy to believe that arrangements for the central co-ordination of policy affecting industry in the UK are inadequate.[15]

The Treasury, which has overall responsibility for economic policy, has also taken an interest in industrial policy. However, it does not promote industrial policies in the same way as the French and Japanese ministries of finance. Critics contend that the Treasury's traditional policy priorities (the control of public expenditure and the defence of sterling's value on the international currency markets) have undermined British industrial competitiveness. Britain's relative industrial decline has prompted calls from both left and right for a strengthened DTI with general responsibility for co-ordinating government policy towards industry.[16]

The political and administrative structures of the *United States* are the least conducive to the development of a comprehensive and integrated industrial policy. As noted in chapter 5, the American policy-making process is highly fragmented, with many actors and decision points. Effective policy co-ordination is undermined by the existence at federal level of 'functionally-defined sub-governments'[17] (comprising congressional sub-committees, interest groups and bureaus); by the separation of the three branches of government; and by the division of powers between the federal and state levels of government.[18]

The fragmented nature of American government is evident in the area of industrial policy. As in the UK, no single organisation within the federal government is able to formulate and implement a co-ordinated industrial strategy. A large number of federal departments and agencies have responsibility for various industries: they are key actors, able to use public procurement, research and development funding, and government regulation to shape the structure of industry. As Vogel has observed, 'the Department of Defense, the National Aeronautics and Space Administration, the National Institute of Health, and the Department of Agriculture have proven no less – or more – capable of picking winners than has MITI'.[19] The result, however, is an ad hoc approach to industry with 'too many programs and too little policy'.[20] Advocates of a more comprehensive and co-ordinated American industrial policy, like their counterparts in the UK, argue that this requires the creation of new central co-ordinating institutions comparable to those in Japan. However, critics contend that such institutional engineering would be futile since the American policy-making process is inherently fragmented.

For many commentators, the degree of state leverage over the financial system is a crucial factor in explaining cross-national variations in industrial policy.[21] Both France and Japan have 'bank-based' financial systems in which there is a close relationship between banks and industry. In France, the partially nationalised financial system enables the state to play a significant role in the provision of finance to industry. In Japan, the special state credit institutions for industrial investment are an important policy instrument which enable bureaucrats to intervene pervasively in industrial activities. By contrast, in the 'market-based' financial systems of the UK and the United States, industrial investment tends to be financed from retained profits and equity capital.[22] This gives firms considerable autonomy and limits the state's direct leverage over their investment decisions. The relationship between banks and industry is much less developed in Britain than, for example, in France. In Britain, bank lending to firms has not been a major source of industrial finance and loans have tended to be small and short-term. This disjunction between finance capital and industry is often regarded as a fundamental element of the British industrial problem:

As short-term lenders, the banks never acquired the interest or influence over industry necessary to lead them to orchestrate its periodic organization. This is important because it reduced the number of 'visible hands' in Britain. Initiatives for the rationalization of industrial sectors would have to come spontaneously from the firms themselves or from the state, if they came at all.[23]

In addition, the greater reliance on internally generated funds and equity issues for industrial finance gives British (and American) firms an incentive to seek short-term profitability rather than long-term success. The vulnerability to takeover bids also encourages firms to concentrate on short-term profits to keep shareholders happy.

Organisation of business and labour

Business and labour groups are potentially important non-governmental actors in the industrial policy community. The co-operation of these groups at the planning and implementation stages of industrial policy is often vital if the policy's objectives are to be realised.

In France, business is far more influential than labour in the industrial policy process. The close bilateral relationships which exist between specific industries and government ministries, and the shared backgrounds of administrative and industrial elites, give business an important input into decision-making. The trade unions, fragmented along ideological lines and organizing less than 20 per cent of the workforce, have less to bargain with and are effectively excluded from the policy process.

The key feature of the Japanese policy community is the co-operative relationship which exists between government and business. Business is organised into a number of peak associations (see p. 55).[24] These associations, which group together powerful industries, maintain close contact with central ministries and wield significant political influence as a result of their special relationship with the Liberal Democratic Party. In addition, business interests are represented on the deliberation councils. The close links between the bureaucracy and industry 'give Japanese government a power of consultation and co-ordination with the private sector that is smooth, continuously in operation, and much more easily controlled than the lobbying and political action committees that the American government–business relationship generates'.[25]

National labour organisations in Japan have a more limited influence than business although they do have representation on the deliberation councils. Japanese unions have limited industrial and political strength: the system of enterprise-based unions and the intense company loyalties of workers encourage consensual forms of labour-management decision-making.

In Britain, both the Confederation of British Industry (CBI) and the trade union movement have been concerned with questions of industrial policy. The CBI has generally close contacts with government, particularly with the Department of Trade and Industry, although in the 1980s its relations with the Conservative administrations were strained as a result of frequent disagreements over economic policy. The CBI functions as a general representative of business interests but the diversity of its membership undermines its efforts to speak with one voice.[26] The representative function of the CBI has also been undermined by the growth in importance in recent years of two rival business associations, the Institute of Directors and the Association of British Chambers of Commerce. British business is also organised into a large number of sectoral and product associations which 'have regular contacts on both a formal and an informal level with civil servants'.[27]

The trade union movement in the UK has generally had less influence on industrial policy. The peak association of labour, the Trades Union Congress (TUC), has had its greatest input into policy-making during periods of Labour government. During the 1980s the TUC's access to government declined as successive Conservative governments relegated trades unions to the sidelines of the policy-making process. In many respects labour organisations in the UK have greater industrial and political strength than their counterparts in France, Japan and the United States. This strength derives from two sources: first, the trade union movement has strong institutionalised links with the Labour Party; secondly, despite a recent decline, levels of union membership are higher in the UK than in the other countries covered (see table 6.2).

The strength of British trade unions, however, has not been translated into consistent influence on government policy. Trade union policy objectives have often been defensive, giving priority to safeguarding traditional industries and employment, thus hindering industrial change. The rather limited input into the policy process is also due to the decentralised structure of the trade union movement. The central organization, the TUC, is weaker than its constituent parts and it is unable to control them. Even within single unions central direction is often weak. This lack of vertical control hinders efforts to influence industrial policy since the TUC cannot bargain effectively for labour as an entity nor can it guarantee any bargain struck with government.[28]

The fragmented nature of business and labour organisation in Britain has hindered efforts to develop integrated industrial policies. Since the early 1960s British governments have made periodic attempts to create tripartite institutions bringing together representatives from government, employers and the unions. In 1962, the Conservative government established the National Economic Development Council (NEDC) as a tripartite forum for discussion between government, industry and the trade union movement. The NEDC, designed to emulate French-style indicative planning, set up Economic Development Committees (EDCs) and Sectoral Working Parties to study problems of particular industries and make policy recommendations. In practice, however, 'the EDCs were almost exclusively consultative bodies for the exchange of information within the industry rather than agents for the implementation of reform'.[29] For many critics, the form and functioning of the NEDC was emblematic of the 'pluralistic stagnation' or 'negotiated inertia' which bedevilled British politics in the post-war period. According to this perspective, the state, hemmed in by powerful interest groups, was unable to implement optimum policies and relied almost exclusively on accommodating conflicting demands. The NEDC's elaborate network of tripartite bodies provided the framework for consultation between government and industrial interests but 'perpetuated a voluntaristic tradition according to which the state left matters of industrial reorganization largely up to the private sector rather than try to impose its own plans'.[30] Efforts by government to develop a consensual approach to questions of industrial policy have been thwarted in two ways: first, by the CBI's reluctance to submit to government direction in industrial planning; and secondly, by the absence of an effective working relationship between the CBI and the TUC.[31] In 1987, the Conservative government, in keeping with its market-oriented approach to industrial adjustment, downgraded the role of the NEDC and disbanded many of the sector-specific bodies.

Business and labour are less well-organised at the national level in the USA than in the UK. It is customary to refer to business resistance to government intervention in the United States, yet in practice many private corporations maintain close and direct links with individual federal agencies. The defence, agriculture, aircraft and aerospace industries, for example, have benefited greatly from federal resources. Indeed, Vogel has argued that the links between officials in the Defense and Agriculture departments and their counterparts in the private sector are 'every bit as extensive and co-operative as those between MITI and Japanese individuals, and French Civil Servants and big business in France'.[32] Although American business has achieved significant political influence and has had an impact on a variety of public policies, it lacks organisational cohesion. It remains fragmented, with no peak organisation capable of representing the business community's divergent views and interests in negotiations with government. For some observers, the absence of a general national business organisation precludes the possibility of developing a comprehensive American industrial policy. As Heclo has observed, 'Executive branch policy makers have frequently turned to consult with American industry and found no one there, or more accurately found a jumble of agents who cannot commit the groups they represent.'[33]

A similar pattern of decentralisation and fragmentation characterises the organisation of American labour. The national federations of trade unions, such as the AFL-CIO, have traditionally been weak and do not include some of the largest and most powerful unions. Once again, the lack of a peak-level organisation for labour is viewed as a major obstacle to the development of a comprehensive industrial policy. Heclo argues that the process of industrial adjustment involves human costs, such as the closure of traditional industries, and if it is to be sustained politically it must be acceptable to the unions: 'Hence labor is crucial for industrial policy. No reliable bargaining units exist to incorporate in the process, however.'[34]

Relationships among policy actors

The comparative analysis of formal government institutions and industrial interest organisations provides only a partial picture of industrial policy communities. The informal relationships among governmental and non-governmental actors, often outside formal institutional settings, are also crucial to an understanding of how industrial policy is formulated and implemented.

The close co-operation between professional civil servants and industry is a key feature of industrial policy in *France*. The civil servants responsible for industrial policy are mainly drawn from the technical *corps* trained in the scientific and engineering schools: for example, the *Ecole des Mines* and the *Corps des Mines* provide the technical officials of the Ministry of Industry.[35] The *corps* officials enjoy a high degree of career stability and significant influence on policy. The French ministries are able to exert a good deal of influence over industrial sectors which are dependent upon them. The close co-operation and trust between administrators and industry is facilitated by the practice of *pantouflage* ('putting on the slippers'). This describes the movement by civil servants, either on a temporary or permanent basis, into key positions in nationalised industries, private enterprises, financial companies, government research centres and trade associations. The practice of *pantouflage* gives corporations the possibility to influence the ministries which control them and has resulted in a significant interpenetration of private management and the civil service: for example, by 1973 43 per cent of the heads of the hundred largest corporations in France came from a civil service background.[36] As Cawson et al. note:

The pattern that emerges is one of closely interconnected, indeed interlocking elites: administrative, industrial, financial, and political ... It is vital to recognize that this does not necessarily imply similar stances on any issue; but it may imply rather similar styles and language, and a degree of intermixing far greater than that to be found, for example, between the political and administrative milieux in Britain.[37]

The key feature of the *Japanese* policy community is the interdependent and co-operative relationship that exists between government and business. In many respects the Japanese pattern of informal government–industry links resembles that of France. Senior officials in the Japanese state bureaucracy (for example, MITI and the MOF) are selected primarily from among the best law graduates of Tokyo University, a pattern of recruitment similar to the French *corps* structure based on the *grandes écoles*. The close links between administrative and business elites are bolstered by the practice of *amakudari*, the Japanese equivalent to the French *pantouflage*. *Amakudari* means literally 'descent from heaven' and refers to the movement of retired officials into top positions in politics and business. Many officials who have retired from the bureaucracy move into senior political posts in government (including, on occasions, the premiership) and the Diet; and a large number secure key positions in public corporations, banks, trade and industry associations and private enterprises. The 'legendary old-boy connections'[38] ensure that Japanese industry has access to decision points in government and the bureaucracy and that it can exert pressure outside the formal channels of political institutions.

The pattern of circulating administrative and business elites produced by the practices of *pantouflage* and *amakudari* has no equivalent in the UK and the USA. In the UK, as Shepherd has observed, 'Senior civil servants are generalists, rather than technicians, and tend to belong to a different elite from the industrialists (and prevalent social values afford lower status to industrial than 'professional' occupations). It is not surprising that there is little career movement between industry and the civil service.'[39] Indeed, there is often open criticism or considerable disquiet on those occasions when senior British officials do retire into top posts in the business world.

In the *United States*, only a limited number of government officials embark upon post-retirement careers in industry; former military personnel, for example, often take up careers in the armaments industry. The 'discontinuities of executive personnel',[40] however, militate against the development of a close and consistent relationship between government officials and industry. With each change of administration, two or three thousand top executive officials are replaced, resulting in a considerable loss of experience and a 'government of strangers'.[41] In addition, the short tenure of non-career executive officials (averaging less than two years) gives them incentives to pursue short-term policy goals rather than worry about long-term planning and objectives. The movement of senior personnel between the bureaucracy and industry in the USA tends to occur in the opposite direction to that in France and Japan, namely 'from the boardrooms of private corporations *to* the government'.[42] The effects are summarised by Peters:

There is a tendency to assume that people brought into government from the private sector, especially from business, will be wiser and more capable than career officials, but a good deal of evidence indicates that they frequently fail to understand the complexity of their tasks.[43]

The differing relationships among administrative, political and business elites in the four countries partly reflect national differences in the legitimacy of state intervention in industry. Both France and Japan have long traditions of *dirigisme* or state intervention in industry. The legitimacy accorded to such intervention is attributable to the relatively late industrialisation in the two countries and their reliance upon governmental leadership to advance economic growth and modernisation. In Japan, in particular, there is broad national consensus on the legitimacy of state intervention in industry and a number of observers have noted the depoliticisation of the industrial policy-making process.[44]

By contrast, industrial policy debates in Britain and the United States are characterised by a lack of consensus about both the legitimacy and nature of intervention. In Britain, the adversarial style of politics is very evident in industrial policy debates and divisions over industrial policy occur both within and between the two major parties. In contrast to France and Japan, there is no consensual tradition in Britain that the state should play a leading role in fostering industrial change. Governments have tended to maintain an 'arm's length' relationship with industry. As Shepherd has noted, 'However much dirigisme has entered the British system, it is accepted with difficulty: industry and government still do not see each other as natural partners.'[45]

Much the same is true of government–industry relations in the United States. As in Britain, the absence of an ideological consensus in favour of government intervention in industry thwarts the development of a comprehensive industrial policy.[46]

Table 6.2. *Comparative economic performance by country, 1954–87*

	Real GDP (Average annual growth – %)	Consumer prices (Average annual rise – %)	Unemployment (Average annual rate – %)
1954–73			
France	5.3	4.5	1.6
Japan	9.3	4.7	1.2
United Kingdom	3.0	4.2	2.1
United States	3.5	2.6	5.0
1974–87			
France	2.1	9.4	7.1
Japan	3.8	5.9	2.3
United Kingdom	1.7	11.1	7.7
United States	2.4	7.0	7.3

Source: W. Rand Smith, '"We Can Make the Ariane, But We Can't Make Washing Machines": The State and Industrial Performance in Post-War France', in J. Howorth and G. Ross, eds., *Contemporary France*, vol. 3 (London: Pinter, 1989), p. 179. Figures derived from *OECD Outlook* (various issues); *OECD Historical Statistics, 1960–1980.*

Table. 6.3. *Growth of GDP, by country, selected periods, 1950–85*
Percent increase in GDP

Period	France	Japan	United Kingdom	United States
1950–58	41	89	20	27
1958–73	123	352	63	81
1973–85	28	56	17	30
1950–85	306	1233	129	200

Source: Adapted from W. J. Adams, *Restructuring The French Economy* (Washington, D.C.: The Brookings Institution, 1989), p. 4.

Policy outcomes

Evaluating the outcomes of industrial policies is fraught with difficulties. As Gerard Adams notes,

it is not always clear to what extent the degree of success is a reflection of the particular target chosen, the mechanism used, or even to what extent it reflects a fortunate combination of circumstances. In many cases it is difficult even to determine whether the policy *was* a success. The evidence of the failure of policy is frequently more clear than is the evidence of success.[47]

Table 6.4. *Percentage of world exports of manufactures originating in each country in 1913, 1937, 1973 and 1984*

Year	France	Japan	United Kingdom	United States
1913	12.9	2.4	29.9	12.6
1937	6.4	7.2	22.4	19.6
1973	7.5	10.0	7.4	12.9
1984	6.1	14.4	5.5	12.5

Note: Includes intra-EEC trade.
Source: Adapted from Duchêne and Shepherd, eds., *Managing Industrial Change in Western Europe* (London: Pinter, 1987), p. 24.

Disagreements over industrial policies revolve around two basic questions: first, does government intervention deliver industrial success or is reliance on the market mechanism more effective? Secondly, if interventionist policies can work, what mix of policies delivers success? Advocates of industrial policy usually cite Japan as the model to be replicated; the French approach to industrial policy has also been influential, particularly during the late 1950s and early 1960s. Japan's remarkable economic success in the post-war period is evident from the comparative statistics on economic performance (see tables 6.2, 6.3 and 6.4). France too has enjoyed notable economic success, transforming itself from a rather backward economy to a modern industrial state.

For supporters of industrial policy these examples demonstrate the link between economic success and state intervention. Critics however refute the claim that industrial policies have been the key to industrial success in post-war France and Japan. In their view, the operation of the market has been primarily responsible for French and Japanese industrial success – a process of catching up that would have been even more marked if state intervention in industry had been more limited.

These disputes about the effectiveness of industrial policy are not easily resolved since 'the chains of cause and effect in this field are notoriously full of uncertainties and virtually incomputable'.[48] A frequent lack of clear policy goals or the use of industrial policies to pursue non-economic objectives compound the difficulties. Policies are frequently devised to achieve social objectives (such as safeguarding employment and preserving regional economies) or other non-economic goals such as national security or national prestige. In these cases, an economic evaluation alone will not suffice to gauge the policy's effectiveness. For many critics of industrial policy, it is precisely the non-economic objectives and the opportunities that they provide to politicians and bureaucrats to meddle in industry which make government intervention undesirable.

Industrial policy is frequently the source of ideological and partisan disagreement. These divisions revolve around the questions of the relative merits and demerits of state intervention versus the market mechanism. For proponents of industrial policy, state intervention compensates for market failure by promoting industrial change and adaptation (for example, by providing investment and research and development assistance). However, critics contend that intervention in industry frequently diverts resources away from more promising uses; in their view, a 'hands off' approach to industrial change and adaptation ensures an optimal allocation of resources.[49]

The ideological and partisan nature of these debates obscures a pragmatic consensus which ascribes a role to both the market and the state in promoting industrial change. In all advanced industrial states, government intervention in industry is a fact of modern economic life. In France and Japan a co-operative government–industry relationship and state intervention is widely accepted. No such consensus exists in Britain and the United States, although even in these countries there is considerable backing for government involvement in industry.

Japanese industrial policy epitomises this balance between market forces and state intervention. The partnership between government and industry and the market-conforming industrial policies are an essential ingredient in the Japanese recipe for industrial success. Industrial policy complements rather than usurps the functions of the market. As Ozaki notes:

The Japanese approach is indicative, indirect, soft-handed, small-scale, and market-oriented. It fully recognizes the efficiency and the effectiveness of the private market as the primary agent of economic activity; the state, at best, is merely to serve as a catalyst of industrial growth by supplementing or complementing (but not substituting for) the private sector.[50]

The market-conforming characteristics of Japanese industrial policy are evident in the government's attempts to promote economic efficiency and the consistent efforts to build internationally competitive manufacturing industries. In contrast to Japan, industrial policies in Britain and France have frequently ignored market signals. Britain in particular has an unenviable record of defensive, ad hoc policies devised to rescue ailing industries, coupled with periodic, and largely unsuccessful, attempts to 'pick winners'. According to Grant, 'the available evidence suggests that industrial policies in the UK have, to put it generously, had a rather patchy record in terms of cost-effectiveness and policy success'.[51]

The Japanese formula for industrial policy has undoubtedly contributed to the nation's industrial success, while the records of state intervention in industry in France, the United Kingdom and the United States are more mixed. This raises the key question of why some states are more successful than others in their interventions to promote industrial change and adaptation. The comparative examination of industrial policies in each of the countries suggest that four factors are central to an effective industrial policy:

1. *State tradition and industrial culture*: State intervention in industry is more readily accepted in France and Japan than in the United Kingdom and the United States. A basic consensus on the legitimacy and goals of industrial policy is important for the success of state intervention.

2. *The institutional and bureaucratic capacity of the state*: The four states differ markedly in their capacity to devise and implement policies affecting industry. A comprehensive national industrial policy requires an effective co-ordinating ministry. Once again Japan, and to a lesser extent France, have created institutions with the bureaucratic capability, organisational resources and policy tools for effective government intervention. British attempts at industrial policy have been hindered by the lack of both effective co-ordination at the centre and a limited set of policy tools. The delivery capacity of the American political system is even more limited due to the fragmented nature of political organisation and the policy process.

3. *Government–industry relationships*: Good channels of communication among politicians, officials and economic actors, and co-operative government–industry relationships are important for developing effective industrial policies. In broad national terms, the French and Japanese industrial policy communities exhibit closer administrative, political and economic links than those in Britain and the United States.

4. *The organisation of business and labour groups*: The possibilities of an integrated industrial policy are enhanced if government is able to negotiate with peak industrial interest organisations. In Britain and the United States the fragmented nature of labour and business organisations undermines governmental efforts to formulate and carry out industrial policy. In Japan, peak business associations have well-developed, co-operative links with government ministries and agencies, while in France large industrial groups enjoy close relationships with sponsoring departments. In these latter countries labour organisations are relatively weak and therefore relegated to the sidelines of the policy-making processes.

Conclusion

Although there are significant cross-national variations in the scope and form of industrial policy, governments in France, Japan, the United Kingdom and the United States are inextricably involved in industry. The growing interdependence of advanced industrial economies and the pressures of international competition encourage all governments to pursue policies to promote industrial change and adaptation. The national responses to this competitive challenge vary from greater state intervention to a 'hands-off' approach to industry. Japan's market-conforming industrial policy, emphasising economic efficiency and comparative advantage in international markets, is frequently regarded as a model of state–industry partnership. However, attempts to emulate the Japanese approach are likely to prove futile. The distinctive national policy styles, the differences in the legitimacy of state intervention in industry, the varying patterns of government–industry relationships, and the contrasts in political structure and institutional capacity make it very difficult to replicate particular national approaches. Thus, the pressures towards convergence arising from international competition are unlikely to result in uniform industrial policies.

NOTES

1. S. Wilks and M. Wright, 'Conclusion: Comparing Government–Industry Relations: States, Sectors, Networks', in S. Wilks and M. Wright, eds., *Comparative Government–Industry Relations* (Oxford: Clarendon Press, 1987), pp. 274–313.
2. On post-war French industrial policy see C. Stoffaës, 'Industrial Policy and the State: From Industry to Enterprise', in P. Godt, ed., *Policy Making in France* (London: Pinter, 1989), pp. 105–26.
3. On this period see W. Rand Smith, ' "We Can Make the Ariane, but We Can't Make Washing Machines": The State and Industrial Performance in Post-war France' in J. Howorth and G. Ross, eds., *Contemporary France*, vol. 3 (London: Pinter, 1989), pp. 175–202.
4. See R. Komiya, M. Okuno and K. Suzumura, eds., *Industrial Policy of Japan* (London: Academic Press, 1988).
5. See for example C. Johnson, ed., *The Industrial Policy Debate* (San Francisco: ICS Press, 1984).
6. D. Vogel, 'Government–Industry Relations in the United States: An Overview', in Wilks and Wright, eds., *Comparative Government–Industry Relations*, p. 92.
7. Ibid., p. 94.
8. Some commentators argue that the concentration on defence expenditure has an overall negative impact on American industrial performance. For a summary of the arguments see B. Guy Peters, 'The Politics of Industrial Policy

in the United States', in S. A. Shull and J. E. Cohen, eds., *Economics and Politics of Industrial Policy: The United States and Western Europe* (Boulder: Westview Press, 1986), pp. 53–4.

9. See J. Hayward, *The State and the Market Economy* (Brighton: Wheatsheaf, 1986).

10. S. S. Cohen, S. Halimi and J. Zysman, 'Institutions, Politics, and Industrial Policy in France' in C. E. Barfield and W. A. Schambra, eds., *The Politics of Industrial Policy* (Washington, D.C.: American Enterprise Institute, 1986), p. 114.

11. A. Cawson, P. Holmes and A. Stevens, 'The Interaction between Firms and the State in France: The Telecommunications and Consumer Electronics Sector', in Wilks and Wright, eds., *Comparative Government–Industry Relations*, p. 14.

12. R. S. Ozaki, 'How Japanese Industrial Policy Works', in C. Johnson, ed., *The Industrial Policy Debate*, pp. 47–70.

13. C. Johnson, 'The Institutional Foundations of Japanese Industrial Policy', in C. E. Barfield and W. A. Schambra, eds., *The Politics of Industrial Policy*, p. 191.

14. Ibid., p. 191.

15. Grant, *Government and Industry*, p. 93.

16. The Labour Party's 1989 policy review contains proposals for a strengthened DTI. Michael Heseltine, a prominent Conservative, also advocates the creation of a new strategic, industry ministry: see M. Heseltine, *Where There's A Will* (London: Hutchinson, 1987).

17. Guy Peters, 'The Politics of Industrial Policy in the United States', p. 61.

18. On the fragmentation of American government see W. Grant, *Government and Industry*, chapter 5 and H. Heclo, 'Industrial Policy and the Executive Capacities of Government', in C. E. Barfield and W. A. Schambra, eds., *The Politics of Industrial Policy*, pp. 292–317.

19. Vogel, 'Government–Industry Relations in the United States: An Overview', p. 95.

20. Heclo, 'Industrial Policy and the Executive Capacities of Government', p. 300.

21. See for example J. Zysman, *Governments, Markets and Growth: Financial Systems and the Politics of Industrial Change* (Oxford: Martin Robertson, 1983). Also see A. Cox, ed., *The State, Finance and Industry* (Brighton: Wheatsheaf, 1986).

22. P. Hall, *Governing the Economy* (Cambridge: Polity, 1986), pp. 38–40.

23. Ibid., p. 39.

24. On the organisation and influence of the business groups see R. Boyd, 'Government–Industry Relations in Japan: Access, Communication, and Competitive Collaboration', in S. Wilks and M. Wright, eds., *Comparative Government–Industry Relations*, pp. 71–6.

25. Johnson, 'The Institutional Foundations of Japanese Industrial Policy', p. 193.

26. W. Grant with J. Sargent, *Business and Politics in Britain* (London: Macmillan, 1987), pp. 123–7.

27. W. Grant, *The Political Economy of Industrial Policy* (London: Butterworths, 1982), p. 41.

28. Ibid., pp. 41–2.
29. Hall, *Governing the Economy*, p. 87.
30. Ibid., p. 87.
31. W. Grant with J. Sargent, *Business and Politics in Britain*, pp. 134–8.
32. Vogel, 'Government–Industry Relations in the United States: An Overview', p. 104.
33. Heclo, 'Industrial Policy and the Executive Capacities of Government', p. 308. Also see B. Guy Peters, 'The Politics of Industrial Policy in the United States', pp. 63–6.
34. Heclo, ibid., pp. 308–9.
35. Cawson et al., 'The Interaction between Firms and the State in France', pp. 64–5.
36. Hall, *Governing the Economy*, p. 168.
37. Cawson et al., 'The Interaction between Firms and the State in France', p. 15.
38. Johnson, 'The Institutional Foundations of Japanese Industrial Policy', p. 188. On the practice of *amakudari* see K. E. Calder, 'Elites in an Equalizing Role: Ex-Bureaucrats as Coordinators and Intermediaries in the Japanese Government–Business Relationship', *Comparative Politics*, 21 (1989), pp. 379–403.
39. G. Shepherd, 'United Kingdom: A Resistance to Change' in F. Duchêne and G. Shepherd, eds., *Managing Industrial Change in Western Europe* (London: Pinter, 1987).
40. Heclo, 'Industrial Policy and the Executive Capacities of Government', pp. 304–5.
41. H. Heclo, *A Government of Strangers* (Washington, D.C.: The Brookings Institution, 1978).
42. Johnson, 'The Institutional Foundations of Japanese Industrial Policy', pp. 187–8 (emphasis in original).
43. B. Guy Peters, 'The Politics of Industrial Policy in the United States', pp. 59–60.
44. See, for example, R. Boyd, 'Government–Industry Relations in Japan', p. 70.
45. Shepherd, 'United Kingdom: A Resistance to Change', p. 152.
46. Heclo, 'Industrial Policy and the Executive Capacities of Government', p. 309.
47. F. Gerard Adams, 'Criteria for U.S. Industrial-Policy Strategies', in F. Gerard Adams and L. R. Klein, eds., *Industrial Policies for Growth and Competitiveness*, p. 405 (emphasis in original).
48. See F. Duchêne and G. Shepherd, 'Sources of Industrial Policy', in *Managing Industrial Change in Western Europe*, p. 19.
49. Grant, *Government and Industry*, chapter 2, provides an admirably clear analysis of the state/market dispute.
50. Ozaki, 'How Japanese Industrial Policy Works', pp. 60–1.
51. Grant, *Government and Industry*, p. 33.

FURTHER READING

Useful comparative introductions to industrial policy include C. E. Barfield and W. A. Schambra, eds., *The Politics of Industrial Policy* (Washington, D.C.: American Enterprise Institute, 1986); W. Grant, *Government and Industry: A*

Comparative Analysis of the US, Canada and the UK (Aldershot: Edward Elgar, 1989), F. Gerard Adams and L. R. Klein, *Industrial Policies for Growth and Competitiveness* (Lexington, Mass.: D.C. Heath, 1983). For factual information see OECD, *Industrial Policy In OECD Countries: Annual Review 1989* (Paris: OECD, 1989). On France, see W. J. Adams, *Restructuring the French Economy: Government and the Rise of Market Competition since World War II* (Washington, D.C.: The Brookings Institution, 1989). On Japan, see C. Johnson, *MITI and the Japanese Miracle: The Growth of Industrial Policy, 1925–1975* (Stanford University Press, 1982). On the United Kingdom and the United States see W. Grant, *Government and Industry*.

7   Health policy

Martin Harrop

The traditional medical definition of health is the absence of abnormalities caused by specific diseases. This definition is narrow and negative, focusing on lack of symptoms rather than on positive well-being. However, the narrow medical definition does accord well with the emphasis of the state within the health sector on ensuring the provision of treatment for the sick. By and large, health policy has been a policy for dealing with illness. More positive definitions of health, such as the World Health Organisation's interpretation of health as a 'state of optimal physical, mental and social well-being', have hardly impinged on how the state has gone about its business. This chapter reflects this agenda, concentrating on the organisation of treatment for the sick.

State involvement

The constitutional position of governments in relation to health care varies between countries. In Japan and France, the constitution explicitly refers to health. The Japanese constitution provides that 'the state shall use its endeavours for the promotion and extension of social welfare and security, and public health'. The French constitution, too, guarantees 'protection of health' to all. By contrast the American constitution does not mention health. In consequence the federal government restricts its direct provision of health care to special groups such as military personnel. For the general population, the federal government seeks not to provide health care but rather to influence the services provided by the fifty states and the private sector. Britain lacks a written constitution but the principle of direct state provision of health care has been widely accepted at least since the Beveridge Report of 1942. This report, and the principles it embodied, acquired some of the aura of unimpeachable authority for the next forty years.

Whatever the constitutional position, governments in all four countries accept that they must ensure the provision of decent medical care to most of their citizens. The form this takes varies, and encompasses the range of systems found in liberal democracies:

National health service	National health insurance	Voluntary private insurance
(The Beveridge model)	(The Bismarck model)	(The market model)
UK	France, Japan	USA
Universal coverage funded out of general taxation with provision administered by the state.	Compulsory health insurance funded by employers and individuals, largely through state schemes. Substantial private provision on a fee-for-service basis.	Voluntary private insurance and provision with a safety net of Medicare (for the old) and Medicaid (for some of the poor).

France

Like most liberal democracies, France operates a system of national health insurance (NHI). Under NHI people pay premiums to insurers who reimburse patients (or providers of care) for the cost of treatment. The insurer is typically the state or a public body. Primary care is usually private though the state is more involved in hospital care and medical education.

The national health insurance scheme in France forms part of a social security system which also covers pensions and other benefits. The starting point for the system was the 1930 Social Insurance Act, which covered low-paid workers in commerce and industry, and for which organised labour was the driving force. After the war the system developed incrementally until it covered virtually the whole population by 1978. There is a safety net of free health care through the Social Aid programme.

Employers contribute 13.5 per cent of employees' taxable salary to the social security system and employees add in 6.5 per cent. This ratio favours the employee compared to the more equal contributions in Japan. In both countries health care is funded primarily from contributions earmarked for social insurance, not as in Britain from general taxation. However, the French government, like the Japanese, does subsidise the social security system directly. This contribution amounts to about a quarter of the system's total revenue.

The health section of the scheme is administered by CNAMTS (Caisse Nationale d'Assurance Maladie des Travailleurs Salariés – National Health Insurance Scheme for Salaried Workers). Unusually for France, this is a quasi-public body rather than an organ of the state. It is composed of representatives of employers, the unions (traditionally divided among themselves) and the state. The consumer pays the doctor according to a national fee schedule agreed each year, then reclaims about 70 per cent of the cost of consultation, treatment and drugs from CNAMTS. The remaining 30 per cent, known as the co-payment, is paid by the consumer. Treatment for twenty-five serious illnesses which require expensive or prolonged treatment, such as cancer and diabetes, attracts no co-payments.

In theory co-payments should discourage over-use of medical resources. However, to cover co-payments, about half the population takes out private insurance with one of 7,000 insurance funds known as *mutuelles*. Premiums here average about 2.5 per cent of income. Co-payments notwithstanding, the French are among the heaviest users of prescription and non-prescription medicines in the world. In 1975 they averaged ten prescription items per person, compared to six in England and Wales.[1] For physicians, a prescription offers a quick, easy and costless way of gaining the patient's confidence. Heavy prescribing by doctors is combined with excessive self-treatment by consumers. This reflects the deterrent of co-payments and the simple inconvenience of obtaining refunds for prescriptions, as well as a cultural hangover from an earlier era when many poor people did not have, or could not afford, access to a physician.

Primary care is provided by private physicians operating largely in solo practice. These physicians are committed to the principles of 'liberal medicine'. That is, they have jealously guarded their freedom to practise where they like, to treat who they like and to prescribe what they like. 'Liberal medicine' also means the patient has free choice of physician, though in under-doctored rural areas there may be no choice. However, physicians can no longer charge what they like. In 1960, after a bitter struggle which split the medical profession, physicians agreed with government to provide treatment under a national fee schedule – that is, a set fee for each type of treatment. Over 90 per cent of physicians now participate in this scheme. More recently physicians have successfully resisted further inroads into their traditions. In the 1980s they saw off proposals by the socialists to encourage integrated health centres bringing together groups of doctors and nurses in a format already familiar in Britain and the United States.[2]

French hospitals are a mixture of public and private. This has led to tensions and poor co-ordination between sectors though the existence of private hospitals has never been seriously threatened. In 1980 there were 1,038 public hospitals with 400,000 beds and 2,445 private, and generally smaller, hospitals with 175,000 beds. Public hospitals are large, general-purpose institutions offering emergency care and staffed by salaried doctors. Since 1983, French public hospitals have been reimbursed on the basis of fixed annual budgets, as in the UK. This gives hospitals an incentive to get patients out, rather than keep them in. There is now a nominal daily co-payment paid by the patient for hospital care. Private hospitals are a mixture of for-profit *cliniques* (1,622 in 1980) and non-profit hospitals (823). Though more numerous than private hospitals in Britain, *cliniques* are of similar character. They are small, concentrate on profitable scheduled surgery and serve more affluent patients who dislike the thought of a stay in a public hospital. *Cliniques* are reimbursed through CNAMTS on a fee-for-service basis.

Japan

Japan was the first Asian country to introduce health insurance. Its employee health insurance law, passed in 1922, covered industrial employees. The law was designed to defuse industrial unrest and improve labour productivity. Employee health insurance (EHI) was gradually extended to other employment-based groups and now, including cover for dependants, it covers about half the population. The scheme is funded by a pay-roll tax of about 4 per cent on both employers and employees, plus a government subsidy. EHI covers 90 per cent of the insured person's medical costs and 70 to 80 per cent of the dependants' costs, with maximum limits on patients' contributions.

Extension of health insurance to those not covered under EHI began in 1938 in response to the poor health of military recruits. However, it was not until implementation in 1961 of the National Health Insurance (NaHI) Law that Japan's system became comprehensive and compulsory. NaHI is organised by local government and funded by taxes on house-holds plus a subsidy from central government. NaHI pays 70 to 80 per cent of patients' costs, again with a maximum contribution from the patient. Because NaHI covers more old people than the employment-based EHI, its finances are shakier and its reimbursements less generous.

Table 7.1. *Outpatient consultations per head per year, 1975–86*

	1975	1980	1986
France	3.1	4.1	5.2
Japan	13.6	14.4	12.8
UK	3.8	4.2	4.5
USA	4.6	4.8	5.3

Source: OECD, *Health Care Systems in Transition* (Paris: OECD, 1990).

Attempts have been made to reduce these anomalies, though without progress towards combining the schemes, and the overall system receives public support. The Japanese are well supplied with medical care at limited direct cost to the patient, with the provider, not the patient, responsible for claiming back the fee from the insurer.

In any fee-for-service system, decisions on the fee to be charged for a given test or treatment are crucial. These decisions influence physicians' income, the overall cost of medical care and the frequency with which specific services are performed. In Japan these decisions are made by a committee containing an equal number of providers and insurers, plus a few public interest representatives. Each service attracts a certain number of points. These points are then multiplied by a unit cost (e.g. 10 yen) to determine the fee the insurer will pay to the provider for that service.

Private practitioners provide over 90 per cent of primary care clinics in Japan. In contrast to Britain, Japanese physicians present themselves as specialists though in reality most are engaged in general practice. The Japanese are heavy consumers of primary care; they are three times as likely to consult a physician as the stoical British (see table 7.1). Consultations are brief; physicians may see 40 to 50 patients in a morning. On the demand side, this reflects Japanese sensitivities to their physical state and a cultural desire among some Japanese people for injections as well as pills. On the supply side, physicians in any fee-for-service system have an incentive to maximise treatments. In addition, and unique to Japan, physicians also dispense the medicines they prescribe, giving them an additional reason to over-treat.

Many physicians own 'clinics' – mini-hospitals with less than twenty beds which perform minor surgery and also provide long-term care for the chronically ill (there are few special long-term care facilities such as nursing homes in Japan). In 1980 there were 78,000 clinics compared to 8,000 hospitals. Physicians have an incentive to treat in these clinics since

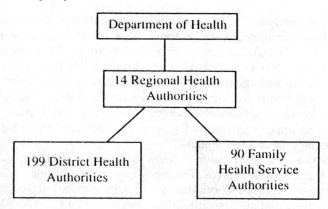

Figure 7.1 Structure of England's National Health Service, 1990.

Note: The structure differs in the rest of the United Kingdom.

in hospitals salaried doctors take responsibility for treatment and also, therefore, for the income generated as a result of the treatment. About half of all Japan's physicians are salaried hospital employees though about 80 per cent of hospitals are themselves privately owned.[3]

The United Kingdom

Britain's National Health Service, established in 1948, provides medical care funded principally out of general taxation. Initially provision was free at the point of service but charges were soon introduced for appliances (e.g. dentures) and prescriptions. However, charges have never contributed more than 6 per cent of the NHS budget. In 1984 they made up only 3 per cent of the total budget.

The service is overseen by the Department of Health (figure 7.1). Major reorganisations occurred in 1974, 1982 and 1991. The purpose of the most recent reforms was to encourage the introduction of an internal market into the NHS. The Conservative government hoped that establishing a contractual relationship between hospital 'providers' and health authority 'purchasers' would encourage detailed costings of treatment, competition between providers and more effective use of resources. The reforms did not increase direct charges to patients. The internal market was grafted on to the existing structure of the NHS. It involved a change in how these institutions operated, rather than a change in the institutions themselves.

Fourteen Regional Health Authorities (RHAs) interpret national policy to fit regional needs. The Department of Health and the RHAs are mutually dependent. The Department has ultimate power to direct RHAs but, as Brown comments, this is about as usable as nuclear weapons.[4]

Beneath the RHAs sit 199 District Health Authorities (DHAs). Their relationship to RHAs is similar to that between RHAs and the Department of Health with the significant exception that the department, and not the RHA, appoints the chair of the DHA. The DHAs oversee service delivery, ensure collaboration between the NHS and related services, interpret national and regional guidelines, and develop five-year programmes as well as annual plans.[5]

In addition Family Health Services Authorities (FHSAs) administer general practice in their areas. These pay general practitioners (GPs) from central funds, obtain information about GPs' prescribing patterns and provide advice and guidance to GPs. However, in contrast to RHAs and DHAs, FHSAs only acquired management responsibilities under reforms introduced in 1990. GPs remain independent contractors, not salaried employees, and they have retained substantial autonomy in their work. Under a contract introduced in 1989, 60 per cent of a doctor's payment is determined by the number of patients on his or her list. This high proportion is designed to encourage GPs to attract patients. GPs provide the initial point of contact for nine out of ten patients. (The average person visits a GP four times a year but is only admitted to hospital once every ten years.) GPs provide primary care and make referrals to specialist care in hospitals. In the internal market, GPs can become budget holders, able to purchase services from hospitals. This is designed to provide another arena of competition for hospitals and to encourage cost awareness among GPs so that unnecessary referrals are reduced.

As in other countries hospitals take the lion's share of the health budget – about 70 per cent in Britain. Hospitals are funded through annual prospective budgets. The integration of virtually all public hospitals into the NHS was not achieved without a price. Consultants retained their pre-eminent position and a right to private practice not just in NHS 'pay beds' (now declining) but also outside the NHS. Changes to consultants' contracts in 1980 made it easier for consultants to combine NHS work with private practice and contributed to a supply-led expansion of private medicine in the 1980s.

By 1990 over 10 per cent of the population had private health insurance, approximately twice the proportion of ten years earlier. However, private insurance does not mean people leave the NHS altogether. More than half the inpatient stays made by privately insured people are to NHS hospitals.[6] The major insurers are non-profit provident associations; most subscribers participate in group schemes funded by employers or arranged by professional associations or unions. One trend in the private market in the 1980s was the expansion of commercial operators at the expense of traditional religious and charitable organisations. Between 1979 and 1990, the proportion of private hospital beds in commercial hands doubled from 28 per cent to 60 per cent.[7] In 1988 the independent sector as a whole supported 203 hospitals with 10,400 beds, less than 3 per cent of the total. The private sector concentrates on non-emergency surgery; for example it performs about half of all abortions.

The United States

Unlike Britain, Japan and France – indeed unlike nearly all liberal democracies – the United States has neither a national health service nor national health insurance. Instead it relies largely on private health insurance. This currently covers about 80 per cent of the population, mainly through employment-based schemes. Private health insurance expanded rapidly after the war, reflecting the cost and improved effectiveness of hospital treatment. By 1965 75 per cent of Americans were covered. This expansion was helped by labour unions who pressed employers for a valuable benefit; contributions are usually paid by employers. Tax relief on contributions gave a further incentive to take out insurance. This relief meant it was cheaper, and not just safer, for people to buy medical care through insurance than to pay cash. (Tax relief was reduced under the Reagan administration but still amounted to more than $40 billion a year.) This expansion of private insurance to cover virtually the whole of middle America prevented any steam building up behind the periodic demands by liberals for national health insurance. Many unions were also reluctant to accept a collective scheme because it would mean giving up the valuable selective benefit they had negotiated for their members.

Private health insurance does not usually cover all medical costs. Most schemes (indeed a growing number) involve co-payments and 'deductibles' – amounts which are deducted from payments so as to preclude claims for, say, standard medicines. Many schemes do not cover long-term care or the most expensive treatments. About one in two private insurance policies are with non-profit organisations.

To help meet the health costs of the elderly and the poor, the United States introduced Medicare and Medicaid in 1965. These formed part of Lyndon Johnson's 'war on poverty'. Medicare offers federally administered insurance for the over-65s, a group which is unattractive to private insurers. It insures against most hospital costs and is funded as part of the social security system through a pay-roll tax on employers and employees. In addition 95 per cent of those eligible for Medicare take out Supplementary Medical Insurance, a scheme which subsidises the cost of insuring against non-hospital medical expenses. Even though co-payments have been increased, Medicare's annual expenditure was approaching $100 billion by the end of the 1980s.

About one in ten Americans are covered by neither private insurance nor Medicare. Some of these will be eligible for Medicaid. This programme for the poor is funded 50:50 by federal and state governments; payments are smaller, and eligibility rules tighter, in poorer and meaner states. In 1981 20 million Americans received benefits through Medicare though eligibility has since been tightened; fewer than two-fifths of America's poor now qualify. Uninsured people who do not qualify for Medicaid either pay for their own treatment until they have 'spent down' to the Medicaid level; or obtain free treatment from non-profit hospitals; or do not pay their bills; or go without treatment altogether.

Hospitals cannot legally deny emergency treatment to the uninsured though about 250,000 patients were denied treatment for that reason in 1988. The cost of treating the uninsured is met by higher bills to the insured, a hidden redistribution which is becoming harder to sustain as hospitals become more cost-conscious.

Primary care is provided by private physicians. Reimbursement is to the physician; with a multiplicity of insurers, there is no national fee schedule. However, in an effort to contain costs, the federal government simply froze physicians' fees for Medicare patients in the early 1980s and many states did the same for Medicaid patients.

The general hospital is the centre-piece of the American health care system. American hospitals are predominantly private non-profit institutions. Hospitals used to be reimbursed retrospectively on an agreed cost basis but Medicare now requires some co-payments and pays the hospital on the basis of a set fee for each of 467 Diagnostic Groups to which the patient is allocated. This should give the hospital an incentive to treat economically but in practice it has had only limited success in reducing costs.

Policy agenda

In the post-war era, the main shift in the health policy agenda has been from access to cost containment. For twenty-five years after the war, the priority was to ensure access to advanced medical care for all citizens. Health insurance schemes were extended or, in Britain, replaced; new hospitals were built and old ones modernised; and the supply of medical personnel expanded. But when escalating costs hit the recession of the 1970s, the emphasis shifted to capping health expenditure. Far from building more hospitals to put people in, the objective now was to get patients out of existing hospitals. Efforts at cost containment were partly successful and stimulated the current concern with the efficiency of health care. Policy-makers want to improve efficiency by incorporating cost into the calculus of whether and how to treat, but physicians resist this threat to their autonomy and their established source of income. Patients, too, have grown accustomed to expensive care at low direct cost. This conflict between the administrative drive for efficiency and physicians' claim to autonomy is at the heart of contemporary health policy; how it is resolved will influence the provision of health care into the next century.

Access

In France and Japan, improved access took the form of a gradual extension of NHI from core industrial workers to virtually the whole population. In the USA, with its cultural bias against public solutions, employment-based insurance expanded to the point where the state could merely fill the main gaps with welfare-oriented safety nets.

The British decision to replace patchy NHI with a universal NHS was by far the most radical solution to the problem of access. Quite why Britain took this step has never been explained satisfactorily. The election of a Labour government in 1945 was clearly important but support for the NHS principle had developed well before the end of the war. One factor seems to have been the war itself. The Emergency Medical Service (EMS) exposed many senior doctors and middle-class patients to 'dark, over-crowded, ill-equipped infirmary blocks in which the chronic sick drag out the last days of their existence with few amenities of civilised life'.[8] The EMS also showed that hospital provision could in fact be co-ordinated on a national basis.

Whatever the explanation for the introduction of the NHS, the result was a system based on the popular principle of access according to need. In reality the NHS has never fully implemented this principle. Queues for non-urgent treatment soon developed and have remained. The waiting list has usually been around the half million mark. Queues are probably inherent in a cash-limited service; when demand exceeds supply, rationing is the only solution once the price mechanism is rejected. But establishing a universal right to care which is free at point of treatment was itself important. As Klein notes, in the early years rationing and queues were symbols not of inadequacy but of fairness.[9]

As citizens in liberal democracies gained low-cost access to medical care so demand increased. This led to measures to improve supply. For twenty years after the war, hospitals were the focus of this expansion.

Table 7.2. *Inpatient beds per 1,000 population,*
1960–1980s and occupancy rate, 1980s

	1960	1970	1980s	Occupancy rate, 1980s
France	9.6	10.4	11.6	73%
Japan	7.4	10.2	12.1	84%
UK	10.3	9.4	8.1	81%
USA	9.2	7.9	5.9	79%

Source: OECD, *Financing and Delivering Health Care* (Paris:
OECD, 1987).

Technical developments – antibiotics, respirators, x-rays, bloodbanks –
had improved the effectiveness of hospitals, particularly for emergencies,
transforming their image from charitable dumping-grounds for the dying
to high-tech miracle workers.

But how this expansion was achieved varied between countries, reflecting national policy styles. For example, France launched a massive
hospital building programme in 1958 as part of its national plan. New
public hospitals were built, administered directly by the Ministry of
Health. With the continuation of private hospitals, this led to over-supply
and poor distribution of beds. Hospital beds were still increasing in
France when a shift away from hospital-based care had already begun in
the UK (table 7.2). In 1970 a new hospital act gave provincial governments more control over where new hospitals, even private ones, could be
sited.

Characteristically, the United States government proceeded indirectly.
The Hill-Burton Act of 1946 stimulated local activity by giving a federal
subsidy for hospital construction and renovation. This led to many small
hospitals in rural areas. Britain launched its own plan for District General
Hospitals somewhat belatedly in 1962. The existence of the NHS enabled
the British government both to delay the hospital programme initially and
to produce a coherent plan once funds were committed. Only in Japan,
where small private clinics remain important, do question marks remain
over the extent of access to high quality hospital care for acute cases.[10]

Hospital expansion produced a large increase in the proportion of
physicians working in the public sector or at least in salaried posts. This
has weakened the power of national medical associations which remain
oriented to the interests of physicians in private practice.

While the overall health agenda has now switched from access to
containment, concern has increased over the specific issues of access in

rural and inner-city areas. The problem here is to alleviate the inherent tendency to under-doctoring in poor areas. Here Britain's NHS does have advantages. Although the health service cannot direct GPs to work in particular areas, it can prevent doctors from setting up in well-provided areas. Capitation payments also provide an incentive to set up in poorly served areas. However, financial inducements to attract GPs to less-favoured areas and grants for improving inner-city practices have not overcome the problem.

The major British attempt to redress geographical inequalities in access to health care was made by the Resource Allocation Working Party (RAWP), a government committee which in 1976 recommended a gradual reallocation of resources between regions so that funds would reflect population size, type (e.g. age distribution) and morbidity. This policy was followed until 1989 and did in fact redistribute resources away from the South-East of England. But formula-based allocations are inherently crude; for example they need to take account of the many high-cost teaching hospitals in London and a host of other special factors. In addition the RAWP formula led to politically sensitive pressures on facilities in the over-resourced regions, particularly the South-East. This is the Conservative heartland and RAWP was abolished by the Conservative government in 1989. In Britain as elsewhere, it is politically easier for governments to accept a maldistribution of resources than to seek a correction, even if the correction simply means more limited growth in the over-provided regions. This nicely illustrates the dictum that political addition is easier than political subtraction.

In other countries financial incentives have been the main, and generally unsuccessful, mechanism for correcting the maldistribution of physicians. Doctors do not decide where to live on economic grounds alone because their income is comfortable enough wherever they live. In France, for instance, there are three or four times as many physicians per head in urban as in rural areas. This ratio has worsened and its consequences intensified as rural depopulation left an older, sicker constituency in the countryside. Rural doctors in France have a lower income, experience more difficulty in keeping up-to-date, are further away from emergency hospital care and are less satisfied with their work than their city counterparts.[11]

Cost containment

In the 1980s cost containment rose to the top of the health policy agenda. The reason why is apparent from table 7.3; between 1960 and 1987 the proportion of gross domestic product devoted to health care doubled in

Table 7.3. *Health expenditure as a percentage of*
gross domestic product, 1960–87

	1960	1970	1975	1980	1985	1987
France	4.3	6.1	6.8	7.6	8.6	8.6
Japan	3.0	4.4	5.5	6.4	6.6	6.8
UK	3.9	4.5	5.5	5.8	6.0	6.1
USA	5.3	7.6	8.4	9.2	10.6	11.2

Source: OECD, *Health Care Systems in Transition* (Paris:
OECD, 1990).

France, Japan and the USA (The increase was much smaller in the UK).
By 1985 Americans were spending well over $1 billion a day on health
care. The growing cost of health insurance contributions became a major
concern to American employers who feared loss of international competitiveness. By the 1980s these contributions made up more of the cost of a
General Motors car than the steel used in its manufacture. As Tresnowski
comments, 'employers used to be an absentee host who paid the bill but
never showed up at the table. Now they want to be involved in planning
the menu'.[12]

Why has spending on health care risen so fast? One reason is growing
affluence. As income rises, a higher proportion of it is devoted to services
such as health care. In that sense health care is a luxury good rather than a
necessity.[13] Other reasons for growth include the cost of new high-tech
treatments, post-war hospital expansion and an over-supply of physicians.
In the United States another factor has been growing fear among
physicians of litigation by patients. This leads to defensive medicine which
bases treatment 'not on the good that it will do, but that nothing may be
left undone'.

However, the underlying reason for cost explosion has been the 'third
party pays' basis of health insurance. Physicians over-treat in a fee-for-
service system and patients, once insured, have no incentive to limit
consumption. Chiropodists in Michigan, USA, grew rich treating the
ingrowing toenails of insured workers – one toe per visit! By contrast
Britain's NHS (which has never paid doctors by piecework) has controlled
costs more successfully than any of the countries with health insurance.

Three main strategies of cost containment have been tried. The first is to
dampen demand, principally through consumer co-payments. These have
been introduced or increased in France, Japan and the United States,
particularly for drugs and inpatient treatment. In the United States the
proportion of employer-funded health insurance schemes involving 'sub-

Table 7.4. *Average length of stay in hospital (in days), 1960–87*

	1960	1970	1980	1987
France	23	18	14	13
Japan	57	55	56	53
UK	36	26	19	15
USA	21	15	10	—

Note: The Japanese figure is high because long-term care facilities are not separated from hospitals.
Source: OECD *Health Care Systems in Transition* (Paris: OECD, 1990).

stantial cost-sharing' rose from 11 per cent in 1979 to 50 per cent in 1984.[14] An American experiment by the Rand Corporation suggests that co-payments do decrease use without damaging people's health in most cases.[15] But governments will find it hard to shift the bulk of the cost burden back onto consumers. Even if governments do succeed in this, patients might simply take out additional insurance, so defeating the object. In practice cost-sharing seems to be a symbolic reminder by payers to patients about the real cost of their treatment.

The second strategy of cost containment is to tighten control over reimbursement. The system of diagnosis-based fees used for Medicare in the United States is an example of this strategy. France has moved to the British system of funding hospitals through annual budgets set in advance. These cap expenditure effectively; indeed the whole history of Britain's NHS is a demonstration that cash limits work provided there is a political will to enforce them. However they provide no rewards for good or economical treatment. Indeed tight cash limits lead to rationing.

The third strategy of cost containment is to provide less expensive delivery arrangements. Outpatients cost less than inpatients; nursing homes less than hospitals. The main thrust here has been to reduce the over-supply of acute (and expensive) hospital beds. Average length of stay in hospitals fell dramatically as evidence accumulated that patients did no worse at home (table 7.4). As a result, occupancy rates are falling throughout the West and the number of beds per capita has been reduced in Britain and the USA.

As a result of these measures, the rate of increase of health expenditure certainly slowed and in some countries stabilised in the mid-1980s. However, policy-makers remain concerned about the future health costs of ageing populations. This problem will arise first in Japan, where the age profile is still adjusting to late industrialisation. Old people require not only more medical attention but different attention: they suffer from many more chronic complaints which require long-term support, the costs of which are often not covered by insurance. Coping with an ageing population became a national problem in Japan in the 1970s. Initially Japan's response was to exempt the elderly from all direct charges for health care. Then, as hospitals turned into rest homes for the aged, the government reintroduced cost-sharing in the bold Health and Medical Services for the Aged law of 1982. This sought to incorporate prevention, treatment and rehabilitation services for the elderly within general welfare services. It is unclear whether this radical new departure will succeed.

From cost control to cost effectiveness

As policy-makers attempted to limit the growth of health expenditure, so attention naturally turned to the effectiveness of existing expenditure. Could medical interventions be performed more economically? How effective is treatment? How many interventions are necessary at all? What quality of care is provided? How is the performance of physicians' measured? The fact is that policy-makers are unable to evaluate the effectiveness of health spending. They suspect, though they do not know, that the marginal cost of extra expenditure exceeds the marginal benefit. Certainly policy-makers no longer accept the 1950s equation, 'more is better'. They want to be more involved in setting medical priorities and monitoring quality.

One way in which NHI systems can help policy-makers is through the bills sent to insurers by doctors or patients. These invoices give detailed information about the practices and costs of individual medical providers. Computers can then spot over- and under-providers. In 1978 the French government proposed to use such information to penalise doctors who over-prescribed but this and other proposals led to three one-day strikes and the proposal was dropped. However, the United States has had more success in monitoring medical practice.[16] With Medicare, the government has had a lever to encourage peer review and peer review organisations are now a significant force in health policy-making. These examples suggest that the medical profession may yet rue the day when it accepted payment from third parties. Although clinical autonomy was guaranteed at the time, ultimately those who pay the piper call the tune. Funding agencies, whether public or private, are becoming more restive as costs increase with little apparent benefit to health.

In Britain's NHS, costs have been controlled directly by the government and so there has been less need to interfere with clinical practice. As

Harrison and Schulz comment, 'clinical autonomy in Britain involves a tight budget within which physicians exercise almost total freedom'.[17] Yet even in Britain attempts have been made to render physicians more aware of the cost-effectiveness of treatment. In 1988 the Conservative government proposed to make GPs budget-holders who would then buy hospital services for their patients on an internal NHS market. These reforms would give incentives for quality (who would want to go to a hospital with an above-average death rate?) and economy (GPs would save money by finding a cheap hospital). However, precisely because the NHS budget was already tightly controlled, the proposals were fiercely attacked. So despite the gradual introduction of professional managers into the NHS, the cost and effectiveness of treatment still go unmeasured – and therefore neither economy nor quality can be systematically encouraged.

In the United States the 'competitive option' has made more headway. The advance was led, with federal encouragement, by Health Maintenance Organisations (HMOs). These are fixed fee, pre-paid health plans which reimburse providers per enrollment rather than per treatment. Hence the provider, rather than a third-party insurer, carries the risk. This gives physicians an incentive to keep enrollees well, to treat less, to limit hospitalisation and to shop around an increasingly competitive hospital sector. Estimates suggests HMOs are about 10 to 40 per cent cheaper than orthodox insurance schemes, largely as a result of reduced hospital admissions. Yet, as one cynic remarked, 'No-one in Washington who advocates HMOs actually belongs to one. HMOs are great – for the other guy.'[18]

A more recent development is preferred provider organisations (PPOs). Here the insurer contracts with various groups of physicians to provide services to the insured. PPOs give the patient some choice of provider but the insurer can still negotiate a wholesale rate in exchange for volume business. PPOs are expanding rapidly; they had achieved 6 million enrollments by 1986 and some estimates suggest that by the mid-1990s PPOs and HMOs will together cover most privately insured people.[19]

Developments such as HMOs and PPOs do offer the prospect of eliminating much wasteful treatment. Competition between providers may be more successful at this than the administered prices associated with NHI in France and Japan, or with DRGs in the United States. As Easthaugh comments, 'the price system may soon prove more effective at closing beds than any system of health planning regulations'.[20] But whether competition gives sufficient incentives for quality as well as cost containment is more doubtful. Certainly peer review is still needed.

Policy community

Physicians and administrators are the leading figures in the health policy community. Physicians, like all professionals, seek to protect their income, their monopoly and, above all, their clinical autonomy. Administrators, like all managers, want to control resources, set priorities and improve overall efficiency. The main resources of physicians are specialist knowledge and public sympathy; by contrast administrators occupy a strategic position in organisations and seek additional influence through control of the budget. Traditionally physicians have played the leading role but, as the agenda has moved on from improving access to containing costs and increasing efficiency, so the administrators have moved towards the centre of the stage.

The historic basis of physician power has been the state's acceptance of medical autonomy. National medical associations (NMAs) came to play an essential role in recruiting, training, licensing, assessing and disciplining physicians. In several countries the state has helped to institutionalise the dominant position of physicians within the health care professions. For example, Japanese law requires hospital directors to be physicians and requires technicians to work under a physician's direction. Membership of the Japanese Medical Association (JMA) is virtually a precondition of setting up a practice.

This strong position has been well tended by national medical associations which are among the best-organised and most influential of all pressure groups. The tightly organised and pugnaciously led JMA has been particularly aggressive in defence of its members' interests, organising 'holidays' (short strikes) by physicians and making large financial contributions to the LDP.

A central object of NMAs has been to maintain the autonomy of physicians – and especially of the self-employed physician in private practice. Thus medical associations have invariably opposed the introduction (and subsequent reform) of NHI in France and Japan, of the NHS in Britain and of Medicare/Medicaid in the USA – even though these schemes have increased demand for medical care and usually improved doctors' incomes. In France the medical profession split in 1960 over the introduction of binding fees for NHI patients. Several organisations split off from the CSMF (Confédération des Syndicats Médicaux). These new organisations later coalesced in the new FMF (Médecins de France). Hence in contemporary France a divided medical profession confronts a strong state. This is the opposite of the situation in the United States, where the profession is as strong as the state is weak.[21]

In all four countries, the power of medical associations, and indeed of the physicians they represent, has passed its peak. This reflects some public loss of faith in orthodox medicine, the rise of self-help groups such as Alcoholics Anonymous, the emergence of new hospital-based technologists such as medical physicists and the rise of the salaried hospital doctor, whether working in the public or private sector. The interests of these salaried physicians differ from those of the private practitioner to which NMAs are oriented. Indeed in Japan only a third of employed doctors belong to the JMA, compared to 95 per cent of the self-employed.

But the fundamental reason for the declining strength of physicians has been the rise of administrators and managers in the health care sector. This can be seen both at operational level and at the level of national policy making. At operational level, such as a hospital, the managerial culture of the administrator conflicts with the clinical orientation of the physician. But salaried doctors need to be managed in a way that the private practitioner does not. As Freddi notes, 'the history of the modern hospital is the history of the steady decline of the physician's power to control his work environment'.[22] Hence the hospital manager, a well-established figure in the United States, is now gaining authority in Britain – and the role of the manager is changing from being an agent of medicine to an agent of government.[23] In the United States, managerial control has been further strengthened by the recent 'corporatisation' of medicine. Large companies which own hospitals and/or run health insurance schemes demand a level of knowledge about their physician's activities which would be unacceptable in Britain's NHS, for example. In France, managers and accountants came to the fore in the 1980s as the emphasis within the state health care sector switched from public service to public enterprise.[24] Freddi comments that the physician used to be a soloist but is now just a member of the orchestra – and not necessarily the conductor.[25]

The challenge from administrators can also be seen at national level. Finance ministers are concerned about rising costs, health ministers are responsible for at least some hospitals and, in France and Japan, NHI administration is a major public task. Whatever guarantees of clinical autonomy physicians may have been given in the past, these public bodies are not averse to flexing their considerable muscle. In fact major reforms have always come from the bureaucracy and the politicians, with NMAs adopting a reactive and defensive role. The strategy of NMAs has been to welcome the principle, oppose the legislation and control the implementation. While effective in the short term, this has itself led to some irritation and a further loss of influence. For example, here is Senator Robert Dole speaking at a Congressional hearing in the United States:

Our problem is that Medicare is going to sink altogether if everybody comes up here and tells us not to do anything this year, do it next year, or don't do it at all. We have a heavy responsibility on this committee to get a handle on health care costs. We would hope that those who are directly involved would do more than suggest we delay it for another year. We can't delay it for many more years. We won't be around. Medicare won't be around.[26]

Although governments have become more active in health care, this is more at an administrative than party political level. Once NHI/NHS systems developed, consumers were broadly satisfied with health care, so the sector stayed on the slow track of policy-making, detached from the hurly-burly of party politics. Britain, again, is the exception. Labour's creation of the NHS after the war linked the party with the service for ever more; the Conservatives, by contrast, are seen as the party most sympathetic to private medicine. Thus health care policy has always been more partisan in Britain than elsewhere.

France has also seen some politicisation of the health sector. When the left came to power in 1981, it proposed radical policies such as phasing out private beds in public hospitals. This provoked street demonstrations by physicians and other professionals whose traditional privileges were under attack. Few Socialist reforms were implemented. But this episode does not represent the normal French mode of policy-making in the health sector. In general, as Godt notes, 'consensus has served over the past three decades as a formidable constraint on policy-making, precluding radical change and guiding both left and right towards consensual policies'.[27]

The pharmaceutical industry has an obvious interest in the health policy arena. Drugs are a significant component of health costs: in the 1980s, they stood at 39 per cent of all medical expenditure in Japan, 19 per cent in France, 11 per cent in the UK and 9 per cent in the USA.[28] Furthermore, the industry is economically important, giving companies clout with government. However, the pharmaceutical industry is not a dominant active player in the health policy arena. (Some would argue this is just because its interests have not been threatened, allowing the industry to appear passive). Influence over the Industry Ministry does not always extend to the Health Ministry. Even in Japan, where over-prescription is rife, the pharmaceutical industry is 'very weak as a political force'.[29] Drugs companies have allowed NMAs to make the running in defending the right of physicians to prescribe expensive medicines. Over-prescription owes more to the fee-for-service system, the marketing of drugs by manufacturers and, in Britain, to the government's open-ended commitment to meeting the cost of prescriptions, at least until the limited list was introduced in 1984.

Although the policy network in health care is somewhat removed from the partisan battle, it cannot be portrayed as just a cozy cartel. Members of the network share specialist knowledge and perhaps even a common understanding of what needs to be done. But different interests may prevent them from reaching a solution which, off the record, all the players would accept as sensible. Interests, in other words, matter more than opinions. And this implies that forces outside the network intrude upon it: the likely reactions of physicians, taxpayers, patients, and legislators to a policy shift must all be considered by participants in the policy network. Thus the intimacy of the network does not mean all is sweetness and light. This description of the network in Japan illustrates the point:

The health insurance sub-arena is the best example in Japan of the point that subgovernments are not always harmonious 'iron triangles' of specialised actors working against the rest of the world. It has been so conflict-ridden for so long that the battle lines have become institutionalised. One important cleavage is between NHI and EHI institutions. The dominant cleavage, however, is between the JMA and the Ministry of Health and Welfare.[30]

Policy outcomes

Providing professional medical care to virtually the whole population is a major achievement of the liberal democratic state in the post-war period. A few gaps remain: non-insured Americans who do not qualify for Medicaid, Britons waiting for non-urgent hospital treatment, French country-dwellers living far from the nearest hospital and Japanese patients who find that emergency treatment at small local hospitals is far from state-of-the-art. But most people in most democracies most of the time get prompt treatment at little direct cost.

This extension of medical care to the whole population forms part of a more general expansion of the state's activities in the welfare field over the course of the century.[31] Other examples of this expansion are education, pensions and income support. Although the proposition is difficult to prove, it seems likely that this overall programme of welfare provision has added to the legitimacy of the liberal democratic state. It may even have helped a sense of common citizenship diffuse more widely through the populations of liberal democracies. This is particularly so in Britain and France, which exemplify the West European pattern of a welfare state based on social insurance. In Japan and the United States, where social security spending by the state is lower and health insurance is still partly employment based, this legitimising effect may be smaller.

But in health care, as in most sectors, there is a price to be paid. Particularly in the USA and France, medical care has become a financial

Table 7.5. *Life expectancy at birth, 1900–87 (in years)*

	Females				Males			
	1900	1930	1960	1987	1900	1930	1960	1987
France	49	59	74	80	45	54	67	72
Japan	45	46	70	81	44	45	65	76
England and Wales	52	63	74	78	48	59	68	72
USA	51	61	73	78	48	58	68	72

Source: OECD, *Health Care Systems in Transition* (Paris: OECD, 1990).

black hole. More and more resources pour in but less and less comes out in terms of longer or better lives. Health insurance schemes fall ever deeper into the red. Yet it is not politically feasible for governments to withdraw from their commitment to ensure the provision of professional care at little direct cost to the patient. It remains to be seen how this dilemma is resolved, if at all. Perhaps the most likely outcome is a combination of cost containment, cost efficiency and cost sharing. This may decelerate cost increases to a rate which is sustainable in a growing economy. However, the proportion of national income devoted to health care is set to continue to increase.

What effect has this extension of medical care had on the health of populations? At first sight the record seems impressive. As Table 7.5 shows, life expectancy has improved enormously in each of the four countries over the twentieth century, with Japan moving from the bottom to the top of the league. Most people now live close to their biological lives; they die of chronic, not acute, diseases. But these trends are attributable to prevention as much as medical treatment. The control of infectious diseases such as measles and tuberculosis was important in extending life expectancy earlier in the century. Lifestyle changes, such as reduced obesity and smoking, have contributed to the cut in heart attacks and strokes which has been the main cause of the decline in adult mortality observed in many countries (though not so much in Britain) since the early 1970s.

Future improvements in longevity are also likely to spring from prevention. A reduction in fatal accidents and suicides would save most years of life.[32] Among the general population, healthier lifestyles – no tobacco, less alcohol, more exercise, improved diet, less obesity – can still yield significant benefits.

Public health programmes lay behind the improvements in life expectancy earlier in the century. But since then governments have been slow to cross the barrier from health protection (creating a healthier environment through, say, safety at work regulations) to health promotion (changing individual behaviour through, say, anti-smoking campaigns). Indeed governments with a strong interest in and record on health protection are often weak at health promotion. Britain is a clear example. The public environment is highly regulated but private life-styles are just that – private. The United States, by contrast, has a much stronger record in reducing heart disease through public health campaigns. The death rate from coronary heart disease has been cut by a third since the mid-1960s. American success reflects the efforts not just of the state but also of pressure groups such as the American Heart Association. These have been much quicker than their British counterparts to switch their emphasis from research to education – and Americans have been quicker on the uptake in responding to health promotion campaigns.

Unfortunately health promotion is not a cost-saving strategy for governments. Preventing premature deaths among the young and the middle-aged simply means more must be spent looking after them when they are old and sick. For a Finance Minister, tobacco is the perfect drug, causing people to drop dead around retirement age after a lifetime paying tobacco tax. Perhaps, then, we should be grateful that governments have entertained the promotion option at all.

NOTES

1. B. Abel-Smith, *Cost Containment in Health Care* (London: Bedford Square Press, 1984).
2. J. Ardagh, *France Today* (Harmondsworth: Penguin, 1987), pp. 423–7.
3. W. Steslicke, 'Health Care and the Japanese State', in *Success and Crisis in National Health Systems*, ed. M. Field (New York: Routledge, 1989), pp. 101–28.
4. R. Brown, *Reorganising the National Health Service* (Oxford: Martin Robertson, 1976), pp. 10–11.
5. C. Ham, *Health Policy in Britain*, 2nd ed. (London: Macmillan, 1985), p. 141.
6. R. Klein, *The Politics of the National Health Service*, 2nd ed. (Harlow: Longman, 1989), p. 216.
7. Community Hospitals Group PLC, *Report and Accounts 1990*, p. 3. On private health care in Britain generally, see J. Higgins, *The Business of Medicine* (London: Macmillan, 1988).
8. An official report quoted in J. Allsop, *Health Policy and the NHS* (Harlow: Longman, 1984), p. 26.
9. Klein, *The Politics of the National Health Service*, p. 196.
10. Steslicke, 'Health Care and the Japanese State', p. 118.
11. D. Levy, 'A Prospective View of the Provision of Health Services in French Rural Areas', in *The Future of Health and Health Care Systems in the Industrialised Societies*, ed. B. Doan (New York: Praeger, 1988), pp. 159–81.

12. Quoted in S. Easthaugh, *Financing Health Care* (Dover, Mass.: Auburn Press, 1987), p. 69.
13. A 1 per cent increase in GDP in OECD countries between 1975 and 1987 was associated with an average increase of 1.3 per cent in expenditure on health. See OECD, *Health Care Systems in Transition* (Paris: OECD, 1987), p. 56.
14. Easthaugh, *Financing Health Care*, p. 59.
15. F. Keeler and I. Rolph, 'Cost Sharing in the Health Insurance Experiment', *Journal of the American Medical Association*, 249 (1983), pp. 583–9.
16. J. Bjorkman, 'Politicising Medicine and Medicalising Politics', in G. Freddi and J. Bjorkman, eds., *Controlling Medical Professionals* (London: Sage, 1989), pp. 28–73.
17. S. Harrison and R. Schulz, 'Clinical Autonomy in the United Kingdom and the United States', in G. Freddi and J. Bjorkman, eds. *Controlling Medical Professionals*, pp. 198–209.
18. H. Schwarz quoted in T. Cooper, 'A US View', in *Health Care Provision under Financial Constraint*, ed. T. Binns and M. Firth (London: Royal Society of Medicine, 1988), p. 13.
19. Cooper, 'A US View', p. 9.
20. Easthaugh, *Financing Health Care*, p. 79.
21. D. Wilsford, 'Physicians and the State in France', in *Controlling Medical Professionals*, ed. Freddi and Bjorkman, pp. 130–56.
22. G. Freddi, 'Problems of Organisational Rationality in Health Systems', in *Controlling Medical Professionals*, ed. Freddi and Bjorkman, p. 8.
23. S. Harrison, *Managing the National Health Service* (London: Chapman and Hall, 1988).
24. Godt, 'Health Care', p. 205.
25. Freddi, 'Problems of Organisational Rationality in Health Systems', in *Controlling Medical Professionals*, ed. Freddi and Bjorkman, p. 8.
26. Quoted in Bjorkman, 'Politicising Medicine and Medicalising Politics', p. 61.
27. Godt, 'Health Care', p. 206.
28. K. Calder, *Crisis and Compromise* (Princeton, N.J.: Princeton University Press, 1988).
29. I. Neary, *Japan's Pharmaceutical Industry in the Postwar Period* (Newcastle upon Tyne: Newcastle University Microbial Technology Group, 1988), p. 57.
30. J. Campbell, 'Policy Change in Japan', typescript.
31. On which, see P. Flora and A. Heidenheimer, eds., *The Development of Welfare States in Europe and America* (New Brunswick, N.J.: Transaction Books, 1981).
32. J. Last, 'The Future of Health and Health Services', in *The Future of Health and Health Care Systems in the Industrialised Societies*, ed. B. Doan, pp. 20–34.

FURTHER READING

Useful comparative introductions to health policy include M. Raffel, ed., *Comparative Health Systems* (University Park, Pa.: Pennsylvania State University Press, 1984); M. Field, ed., *Success and Crisis in National Health Systems* (New York: Routledge, 1989) and for factual information OECD, *Health Care Systems in*

Transition (Paris: OECD, 1990). On Britain, R. Klein, *The Politics of the National Health Service*, 2nd ed. (London: Longman, 1989) is excellent. On France, see P. Godt, 'Health Care', in *Policy Making in France*, ed. P. Godt (London: Pinter, 1989) pp. 191–210. On Japan, see E. Norbeck and M. Lock, eds., *Health, Illness and Medical Care in Japan* (Honolulu: University of Hawaii Press, 1987). On the United States, see R. Alford, *Health Care Politics* (Chicago: University of Chicago Press, 1975) for a classic political analysis and V. Fuchs, *The Health Economy* (Cambridge, Mass.: Harvard University Press, 1986) for an economist's perspective.

8   Ethnic minorities

Ian Neary

In each of our four countries what the state has done or should do about the condition of 'problem' minorities within its borders has concerned the leading policy-makers. The definition of these minorities is something that has troubled the implementers of policy but it has been of less concern to the elected policy-makers. Their definition has largely followed that of public recognition – those groups which for social or historical reasons are considered to be a 'problem' even if it might be practically difficult to distinguish them from their neighbours. In what follows then I shall not use any sophisticated definition of ethnic minority to guide or justify my concentration on particular groups but simply follow the common usage in the country being considered.

In the United Kingdom it was usual well in the 1980s to refer to the racial minorities as 'immigrants'. However, most of the people resident in the UK who were not born there are white and over 40 per cent of the black 'immigrant' population were born there.[1] The presence in Britain of large groups of immigrants who came from Eire or from the 'white' countries of the Old Commonwealth is not defined as a problem by the host society. Thus when we speak of the ethnic minorities of the UK it is to these 2.3 million 'black Britons' – 4.3 per cent of the total population in the mid 1980s – to which we refer. Moreover, it is important to be aware that the term 'black Britons' suggests a good deal more homogeneity than actually exists. They are migrants (or descendants of migrants) from the islands of the Caribbean, from India, Pakistan and Bangladesh who have quite different racial origins, social structures and religious traditions. They are as different from each other as they are from the majority white population.

Similarly there is a long tradition of immigration into France. In 1982 about 7.2 per cent of the population were foreign citizens resident in France – about 4 million legal migrants and another million 'illegals'. Of these the largest group (and the most easily identifiable one) consists of those who came from Africa, either Algeria or west Africa. These are the 2 million strong *Maghrebi* community. It is this section of the population which in popular opinion makes up the 'immigrant population'.[2]

There is a great difference between the state's response to the arrival of migrant groups in the UK or France and state policy towards minorities which have lived in Japan and the USA for several hundred years. For most commentators the issue of 'civil rights' connotes the place of African-Americans in American society. Throughout this chapter it is this, the former slave group, which will be the focus of my attention. Out of a total population of 240 million the black population is estimated to be around 11.5 per cent of the total, a minority considerably larger than in any of the other societies considered here.

Japan is a country of about 122 million people which is usually regarded as racially homogeneous. But, apart from the presence of over 650,000 Koreans and a small population of perhaps 15,000 Ainu, there are between 3 and 5 million Burakumin who are treated in a way comparable to that endured by minorities in the UK and blacks in the USA. Though physically indistinguishable from the majority, most Japanese will avoid social contact with them if possible.

State involvement

Unlike law and order it is not given that the state should concern itself with social minorities. Thus a neo-liberal politician might argue that in this area, as perhaps in industrial policy, it is either unnecessary or improper for the state to intervene on behalf of social or ethnic minorities. A form of this argument can be found in the discourse about minority groups in each of the four states considered here throughout the twentieth century. It was only in the late 1950s that a consensus emerged that government should take a positive interest in the issue.

In *France* the dominant ideology has supported the myth of French culture as the epitome of civilisation open to all those who accept civilised values. Thus, as a French official testifying before a UN committee said, his government has difficulty admitting the existence of ethnic groups and devising policies for minority religions or languages: 'The government limits its role to assuring [the citizens] of the full and free use [of these liberties] within the framework defined by the law.'[3] Similarly, the UK government was partially constrained by the ideology of empire to ensure that the mother country was open to all citizens and reluctant to admit that any non-white citizens faced difficulties within the mother country.

Such a laissez-faire stance did not constitute the starting point for minority policy in Japan or the United States. In both countries the state was directly involved with the position of minorities through structures of laws and institutions which adversely affected their social position. So, in Japan and the US the first moves towards improving the lot of ethnic minorities consisted in dismantling the state's own discriminatory laws and institutions.

In *Japan* the origins of the group now usually referred to as *Burakumin* lie in the strict status system which was erected by the Tokugawa rulers (1600–1868). All members of society were assigned to one of four social classes – samurai, peasant, artisan and merchant – in descending order of status. But outside this system, and not regarded as full members of it, were groups who were thought to be hopelessly polluted and therefore dangerous for others to approach.

Regulations were first introduced to formalise the distinction between 'unclean' groups and the rest of society in the 1720s though there is no doubt that customary discrimination preceded this. In many parts of Japan they were permitted to wear only certain types of clothes and to live only in simple housing; they were not allowed to enter the castle town after dusk or to engage in certain trades. Despite this their numbers increased.[4] All feudal status restrictions were removed in the early 1870s. However, no similar dilution of social prejudice took place in the relations between the majority society and the descendants of the outcasts.

In the 1920s the *Burakumin* attempted to organise a mass movement to fight for their civil rights and the government was persuaded to provide limited funds to improve their lifestyle, but little change in their circumstances had occurred by 1950. It was still hard to persuade the government to do anything to assist them. It was argued that the post-war constitution included prohibitions against discrimination of all kinds. There was no more that the state could or should do. It was not the role of the state to interfere in what essentially were matters of the heart.

The situation in the *United States* is better known. Despite the attempts by some radical Republicans between 1865 and 1877 to introduce desegregation, white supremacy in the southern states of the USA was not significantly altered following the victory of the north in the Civil War. The Supreme Court accepted that segregation was constitutional as long as each of the protected races was protected equally. However, in 1954 the case of Brown *v.* The Board of Education, Topeka, was selected by the National Association for the Advancement of Coloured People (NAACP) as an instance of two segregated schools where there was as near equal provision of facilities as possible. The Supreme Court was persuaded that despite the equal facilities such segregation deprived black children of 'some of the benefits they would receive in a racially integrated school system'. Many states resisted decisions which they saw as coming from central government and ten years after the court ruling only 2 per cent of black school children in the eleven southern states were attending integrated schools.

In *Britain* until the late 1950s and in France until the late 1960s there were few restrictions on immigration and no attempts to reduce discrimination or to improve the lot of immigrants. Since the 1960s, however, these states have found themselves involved in a debate over what measures they should adopt to combat discrimination, a debate which has echoed in Japan and the USA as well. For the foreseeable future complete disengagement from specific concern with minorities is not an option.

Policy agenda

The principal issue that has dominated minorities policy has been the attempt to reduce the inequality experienced by minorities. However, there is one question which is logically prior to the issue of achieving equality between groups and that concerns the make-up of the society itself. How far can the ethnic make-up of a society, itself, be governed by public policy? How far have governments sought to shape the composition of the populations they govern?

Immigration

Immigration controls have been a significant element of minorities policy in the UK, France and many other Western countries since the start of the twentieth century. Often these have been defended as attempts to contain the size of the total population, but in reality they have been motivated by a desire to control the ethnic mix of the society.

The earliest measures to control unwanted immigrants into *Britain* came in 1905 when an Aliens Act was introduced to keep out Jewish refugees who were fleeing from the pogroms of eastern Europe. During the Second World War some colonial labour was recruited to work in forestry and munitions. Following the British Nationality Act of 1948, both those who had British citizenship and those who were citizens of independent Commonwealth countries had the right to enter the UK freely, to settle and find work, and to enjoy full political and social rights. The labour shortage continued into the 1950s and immigrants from the Caribbean and the Indian sub-continent found work in such sectors as textiles, metal manufacturing and transport as well as the National Health Service.

Civil servants in the immediate post-war years and a Royal Commission in 1949 expressed doubts about the ability of British society to absorb aliens of a different race or religion but the British government was reluctant to complicate the delicate decolonisation process by preventing the free entry of coloured Commonwealth citizens. During the 1950s the number of non-white persons resident in the UK increased from 1.7 per thousand to 7.3 per thousand. The coloured communities became visible and the issue of race became identified with immigration.

By the early 1960s concern about the growing number of non-white immigrants resulted in the 1962 Commonwealth Immigrants Act which only allowed into the country Commonwealth citizens who had 'employment vouchers'. This system was largely a sham as the issue of the vouchers was not in practice linked to any economic need for a certain number or a certain type of workers; it was simply a way of keeping out black immigrants. As William Deedes was to say in 1968: 'The bill's real purpose was to restrict the influx of coloured immigrants. We were reluctant to say as much openly.'[5] At this time the basic premises which were to structure the debate on the immigration problem were established. It was assumed that British society had only a limited ability to assimilate coloured foreigners. The problem was located in the immigrant communities. It was their presence which constituted the problem – not white intolerance, nor poor housing stock, nor inadequate social services.

For three years the scheme operated quite liberally until in August 1965 severe restrictions were imposed on the number of vouchers. Then, in 1968, when it seemed possible that thousands of Kenyan Asians (the figure of 250,000 was mentioned by Conservative party politicians) might take up their right to move to Britain, an act was passed through Parliament in just three days to prevent the immigration of UK passport holders without a substantial connection with the UK. 'Substantial connection' was defined as birth in the UK or 'patriality' – descent from a parent or grandparent born there. Only 1,500 of those without such a connection would be allowed into the country each year. The Immigration Act of 1971 which was introduced to replace the Acts of 1962 and 1968 gave 'right of abode' to patrials and those resident in the country for five years or more, those born to or adopted by those born in the UK, and spouses. Still no controls were imposed (nor were possible) on Irish or other EC citizens.

By 1981 primary immigration had slowed to a trickle and the law on nationality was brought into line with that on immigration. The 1981 British Nationality Act created three categories of citizenship: British citizens with full rights of entry, British Overseas Citizens (New Commonwealth) and Citizens of the British Dependent Territories (mainly Hong Kong and Bermuda). Those in the two latter categories have restricted nationality and immigration rights. Although this tidied things up it was not the final chapter in the story. Following the agreement to return Hong Kong to Chinese control, it has been proposed that at least some of these 'citizens of British Dependent Territories' should be permitted to have a right of residence in the UK. These concessions offered by the Conservative government in 1990 evoked fears of a new wave of 225,000 Chinese immigrants.

The tradition in *France* of using migrant labour to augment an insufficient supply of workers or to avoid the cost of employing servants from the domestic workforce can be traced back to the nineteenth century. Until 1914 immigrants came mainly from Italy, Spain and Belgium; between the wars the sources were southern Italy, east Europe and north Africa; since 1945 those moving into France in search of work have come chiefly from Iberia, Algeria and west Africa.[6]

After World War II there was a particularly acute labour shortage in France and a policy was needed to ensure there were enough workers to keep industry going. In 1945 the Office National d'Immigration (ONI) was set up with a monopoly over the supply of foreign labour for industry.[7] However, this institution proved to be incapable of processing sufficient numbers to meet the requirements of industry. Moreover 'spontaneous' (illegal) immigrants could find work quite easily while the economy was expanding and they had little difficulty in regularising their status. In the 1950s, when the bulk of the immigrants were Italians, immigration was not identified with race but by the 1960s increasing numbers of Algerians and west Africans had settled in visible communities.

By 1968 the labour shortages were no longer acute and the French government felt its position was secure enough to be able to risk the displeasure of its former colonies. Moreover, emerging arguments suggested that cheap migrant labour was holding back the modernisation of industry. The following year a plan was announced which, while recognising the need for immigrant labour, argued for the adoption of selectivity. Persons from European countries were to be encouraged to settle while others were to be used simply as temporary labour. Preparations were then made for the imposition of immigration controls.

In 1972 two decrees sought to place stricter controls on those who had entered illegally and to prevent future illegal immigration. These created considerable insecurity among foreign workers and provoked protests which had the backing of many intellectuals. Then, in 1974 official immigration was stopped. The declared aim of policy was to keep the migrant population at 3 million. Not even the members of the families of workers already there would be allowed into France. Bilateral agreements were made with African countries by which single male workers would be allowed to enter France for a period of three to five years during which time they would acquire useful industrial skills and have the opportunity to save cash to take back with them after their visit was over. This was an attempt to establish a source of cheap non-permanent labour for French industry in the guise of an aid package. But it proved hard to eliminate illegal immigration since many peasants in Francophone Africa still believed jobs were to be found in France.

By this time the notion had developed that there existed a 'threshold of tolerance'. Any French community could cope with migrant inhabitants as long as they accounted for no more than 15–20 per cent of the population; more than this and trouble would inevitably ensue. This remained the dominant view but following the election of a Socialist government in 1981 the policy on the reuniting of families was revised to make immigration easier. Changes were also made in order to reduce migrants' eligibility for deportation and the policy based on bilateral agreements was ended.

Only five years later, following the growth in support for the *Front National*, the mainstream parties of the right adopted harsher policies. This resulted in a law of September 1986 which made it harder to enter France and easier for illegal immigrants and legal migrants convicted of certain crimes to be deported.[8]

Nevertheless the number of new arrivals has remained at an annual rate of 120,000, mainly family members joining individuals already with a right of residence in France. As recently as December 1989 the government declared that 'The economic situation of France no longer allows it to be a land of immigration.' By this time the number of legal immigrants was around 4 million with about 1 million more 'illegals'. Exactly how many of this total number were *Maghrebis* is unclear but a 1988 estimate put the number at 2 million.

Both the *USA* and *Japan* have operated immigration policies since the start of this century and they continue to be controversial. In the USA the most important immigration problem is the illegal migration into the country across the border with Mexico. This is just one part of a complex immigration policy now operated in the USA which, like that of the UK and France, is designed to ensure a certain racial and ethnic balance.

One could argue that since 1945 Japan has operated an extreme variant of this in that the immigration regulations have strongly discouraged any settlement in Japan by non-Japanese. This policy was uncontroversial until 1988 when Japanese industry encountered a chronic labour shortage. The Ministry of Labour estimates the worker shortage at 2.06 million and indicates that the problem is particularly acute in the construction industry. Already there are as many as 150,000 foreigners working illegally in Japan, most in heavy manufacturing and construction. A high proportion of them come from the Philippines, Thailand, Pakistan or

Bangladesh. While industry demands a more liberal policy which will legalise some kind of work schemes the government worries that the presence of foreign guest workers will generate racial problems of the kind experienced in Europe. No decision has yet been made but there are signs that something like the French strategy of 'economic insertion' is the favoured option.

The governments in the four states now have to accept the ethnic mix of the populations that they govern. For the most part, the separate identities of minorities remain a 'given' which governments can do little to effect. The problem is how to respect diversity and encourage equality of opportunity while at the same time promoting the interests of the disadvantaged minority groups.

Anti-discrimination legislation

America, Britain and France all passed anti-discrimination legislation in the 1960s or 1970s. In Japan demands for laws which would make discrimination against the Burakumin an offence have gone unheeded by the LDP.

In the *USA*, Supreme Court decisions stimulated African-American hopes and expectations of the political system. One activist has remarked that the civil rights movement 'would probably not have existed at all were it not for the 1954 school desegregation decision'. Yet determined resistance to desegregation was only overcome following the implementation by Congress of the 1964 Civil Rights Act which authorised the Justice Department and the Department of Health, Education and Welfare (HEW) to actively pursue desegregation through litigation, negotiation and termination of funds. This placed the weight of the federal government unequivocally on the side of the minority community. Over the next ten years decisions of the Supreme Court had the effect of enforcing the spirit of the 1964 Act. Thus within a decade the percentage of black pupils attending schools with whites had risen from 0.5 per cent (1961–2) to 86 per cent (1972–3).[9]

Indeed so successful was this process that attention turned from the often *de jure* segregation of the southern states to the apparently *de facto* segregation found elsewhere. Policy-makers have found this a more intractable problem as measures to 'bus' pupils between residential districts in order to ensure a racial mix in all schools has met resistance both locally and within the federal government. The Supreme Court has played a key role in the evolution of policy here. The principle that intentional segregation is illegal has not been challenged but the Court has been unenthusiastic in its endorsement of proposals to break down *de facto* segregation by area wide solutions that included 'busing' or the redrawing of district lines.[10]

Although in 1870 the fourteenth constitutional amendment guaranteed African-Americans the right to vote, most southern states quickly devised measures which prevented them exercising this right. The earliest successes of the civil rights movement were the Civil Rights Acts of 1957 and 1960 which demonstrated that the federal government was willing to help blacks secure the right to vote. Then, President Kennedy supported the constitutional amendment of 1964 which outlawed the use of a poll tax as a voting qualification. Important as these laws were, until 1965 the progress in voter registration was painfully slow. By the mid-1960s mass demonstrations were building up; they reached a violent crescendo in Selma in March 1965. A few days later President Johnson proposed a voting rights act which would remove obstacles to black political representation. This act, renewed and extended in 1970, 1975 and 1982, gave the federal government unparalleled powers to protect the voting rights of blacks, poor whites and other minority groups. Gaps still exist between black and white registration rates but they were dramatically reduced within five years of the original act. Registration and voting are of symbolic importance but they have also resulted in substantial increases in the number of African-Americans holding elected office. Moreover, the increased importance of the black vote has meant that black communities have been able to win concessions and appointments from white politicians and that racist campaign rhetoric has declined.[11]

The Civil Rights Act of 1964 played a part in strengthening the voting rights laws but also guaranteed blacks access to public accomodation, opened jobs and facilities to blacks and prohibited discrimination in federal aid programmes. This was supplemented by another Civil Rights Act of 1968 which aimed at ensuring fair housing practices by making discrimination illegal in the sale or rent of housing. The final law which established the current legal framework was the Equal Employment Opportunity Act of 1972 which broadened the coverage of the 1964 act and gave the Equal Employment Opportunities Commission the power to seek enforcement of its findings. Since the start of the 1970s attention has moved from Congress to the Supreme Court which has been responsible for setting the guidelines for affirmative action programmes; these will be discussed in the next section.

The logic behind *British* immigrant policy has been to complement that of the Immigration Acts. As Roy Hattersley put it, 'without integration limitation is inexcusable, without limitation integration is impossible'.[12] The main aspect of immigrant policy in the UK has been the introduction of anti-discrimination legislation in the form of the Race Relations Acts of 1965, 1968 and 1976. The first act set up conciliation machinery to deal with complaints about discrimination. It made discrimination in such public places as hotels, restaurants and on public transport unlawful on the grounds of 'race, colour, ethnic or national origin'. The 1968 act extended this to discrimination in employment, housing, the provision of goods and services to the public and the publication or display of discriminatory notices. The Race Relations Board was given more extensive powers to investigate complaints and a Community Relations Commission was formed to encourage harmonious race relations.

In 1976 a new act was introduced to combat indirect racial discrimination. This refers to treatment which may be described as equal in a formal sense but which is discriminatory in its effect on one racial group. For example, personnel recruitment which relies on word of mouth rather than public advertising may not be intended to disadvantage a particular sector of the community but if the company is a major employer and all its employees are white this recruitment practice may have the effect of preventing the employment of non-whites. This latest act was a much more determined and comprehensive effort to reduce and eliminate discrimination but weak government support since 1979 has limited its effectiveness.

In *France* a law was passed in July 1972 which prohibited both discrimination based on race or nationality and incitement to racial hatred. This was in response to the insecurities raised by earlier decrees placing strict controls on illegal immigration.[13] However, there was no provision for the reconciliation of complaints and no evidence that there had been any examination of the experience of Britain or the USA.

Until 1981 France had no overall immigrant policy; no specific plans or specialised institutions existed as it was feared that their creation would lead to segregation. The official view was that the formal guarantee of access to legal rights and social participation was enough to create equality. Still at the time of the 'immigration stop' of 1974 a series of twenty-five measures was introduced to encourage the integration of foreign workers into French society. Several aims can be perceived among these measures.[14] The primary objectives were to assimilate 'suitable' immigrants into French society and to maintain social peace. A distinction was made between 'good' immigrants – that is, white Portuguese who were to be encouraged to stay – and the 'bad' – that is, the young Africans who were perceived as causing trouble and who were to be encouraged to return home. So a degree of insecurity has been maintained among certain sections of the foreign worker community in order to ensure they remain mobile. Finally, there has been some acceptance of the need for special educational provision for the children of foreign workers. Previously the aim was to 'francify' them, to imbue them with the universal values of French civilisation. This often had the effect of cutting children off from their own language and culture. Now the policy was to encourage the development of their own culture and language in order to facilitate their eventual return to their countries of origin. Since 1981, the Socialist government had emphasised the right of foreign workers to live and work in France in security without loss of cultural identity.

Discussion of cultural pluralism in France has largely been couched in terms of allowing greater recognition of the separate language and culture of the Basques, Corsicans, Alsatians etc. rather than the needs of the new immigrant communities. At the start of the 1980s the Socialist Party subscribed to notions of cultural pluralism but later in the decade it shifted its emphasis towards an anti-racist policy which aimed to ensure the complete economic, political and cultural integration of the immigrants. The installation of a more or less Socialist government in 1988 and pressure on the right of centre parties to close ranks against the *Front National* probably means there will be no attempts to foster cultural pluralism in the near future.

Japan has not had any specific legislation which has made discrimination against Burakumin an offence. When challenged about this the government has simply pointed to the constitution, which in Article 15 declares: 'there shall be no discrimination in political, economic or social relations because of race, creed, sex, social status or family origin'. But such a law has been demanded. When the Special Measures Law (see p. 185 below) expired in 1987 the Liberation League made specific demands for a law which would make discrimination illegal. The ruling Liberal Democratic Party refused to consider these demands and the campaign for new legislation is not likely to be successful while the LDP remains in power.

Affirmative action

Whereas anti-discrimination legislation has the 'negative' aim of stopping minorities being discriminated against, affirmative action aims more 'positively' to improve their condition. Both in Japan and the USA minority policy has been composed of strong elements which amount to affirmative action.

In *Japan* some hoped that the democratic changes imposed by the US forces during the Occupation (1945–52) would create an environment in which discrimination against Burakumin would disappear. The massive destruction of life and property in the last year of the war meant that there was little difference in the nature of the poverty experienced by any sector of the community in the late 1940s. However, a series of events in the early 1950s demonstrated that discrimination remained a problem. The Buraku Liberation Movement emerged to publicise incidents of public and private discrimination and to insist that government take on responsibility for improving living conditions in Buraku communities. Isolated campaigns were successful in persuading local authorities to provide funds for improvement projects but it was only in 1960 that the central government agreed to establish a committee to investigate the situation. In 1965 it produced a report recommending a series of measures to improve housing and health facilities, to encourage attendance at schools and universities and to remove prejudice among the majority population. Four years later the Law on Special Measures for Dōwa Projects was passed and between 1969 and 1984 £7,000 million was spent building modern housing complexes, schools, hospitals and community centres. In addition grants were provided to enable Buraku children to attend schools and university.[15] There can be little doubt that the quality of the living environment in most Buraku communities has been transformed and that the level of school attendance at least up to high school level is now similar to that of the majority community. Nevertheless average incomes remain low – about one-half to two-thirds the national average – and, though improved, their communities remain distinct.

When the Special Measures Law was introduced it was intended to promote a series of measures over a ten-year period. As this period was about to expire the movement was able to win an extension of the programme at first until 1983 and then in a slightly reduced form until 1987.[16] It is now the government's position that all that it can do has been done and that it is powerless to do more to change attitudes.

In the *United States*, although enthusiasm for the thorough implementation of the desegregation of schools and the enforcement of voting rights acts had declined by the mid 1980s, the principles they enshrined were unchallenged. There remains fierce debate over the policy provisions which attempt to ensure fair employment practices. During World War II President Roosevelt introduced an executive order which forbad job discrimination among defence contractors. The order and the commission set up to enforce it expired once the war was over. In 1961 President Kennedy revived the idea of 'contract compliance programmes' in an executive order which forbad racial discrimination in all federally financed construction projects and this was extended by President Johnson to all private contractors and subcontractors doing work under, or related to, a federal contract. Those found guilty of discrimination could be punished by the loss of future or present contracts. The Office of

Federal Contract Compliance Programmes (OFCCP) was set up to enforce non-discrimination standards. This was of substantial importance since about one-third of the total workforce is directly or indirectly employed by the federal government.

Discrimination by private employers with twenty-five or more employees was prohibited by the 1964 Civil Rights Act and the Equal Employment Opportunity Commission (EEOC) was created to enforce the terms of the act. The powers of the commission were expanded in 1972 when its jurisdiction was extended to cover state and local government employees and private employers of more than fifteen employees. Further extension of its scope took place in 1978 when it became responsible for racial discrimination within the federal government.

However, the OFCCP and the EEOC insisted not only on non-discrimination but also on the implementation of programmes that would 'guarantee equal employment opportunities . . . including when there are deficiencies, the development of specific goals and timetables for the prompt achievement of full and equal employment rights'. By the 1970s these affirmative action programmes were requiring those with contracts to survey the number of minorities and women in each occupation group in their business and where their numbers were less than those in the community's labour force the company was obliged to establish numerical hiring goals and a compliance timetable. The EEOC also used affirmative action plans as part of its strategy from 1973. Under these plans an employer might set aside a certain number of job openings for qualified blacks. These were very controversial since white workers alleged they amounted to racial discrimination against them and thus were unconstitutional. The Supreme Court made judgements in 1978, 1979 and 1980 which, though not unequivocal, did leave government agencies with the power to negotiate and on occasion compel the implementation of affirmative action programmes. The use of quotas, timetables, goals or preferential treatment to overcome discrimination against minorities or women is strongly opposed by key members of the Republican party in Congress and neither President Reagan nor President Bush have been enthusiastic supporters. Progress towards equal employment and income equality for black Americans has been real but limited.[17]

Not all of the minority policies adopted in the United States or Japan have been affirmative action but the targeting of resources and the provision of preferential recruitment and training schemes have played a significant role. However, there seems to have emerged a consensus in Britain and France that overt affirmative action would not be politically acceptable. To the extent that similar measures have been introduced, they have not been overtly aimed at improving the educational or living standards of minorities. Usually they have been directed at areas such as the inner cities where greater concentrations of immigrants and their descendants are to be found. Two reasons might explain this difference. First, as immigrants their demands for active assistance from the state are not regarded as having high priority. Secondly, fringe parties in both countries have advocated anti-immigrant ideas which have been shared by many within the mainstream right-wing parties. There have been more votes in pandering to anti-immigrant ideas than in pressing for affirmative action – especially in France where few immigrants have the right to vote.

Policy community

Perhaps the most striking contrast between the four countries is the role played by the representatives of the minority groups themselves in the policy-making process. Whereas in Japan and to a lesser extent in the USA the organisations formed by the minorities themselves have taken the lead in campaigns for legislative change, in the UK and France measures have been devised and implemented mainly by the authorities with only peripheral involvement of the minorities themselves.

In *Japan* the Buraku Liberation League led the campaign during the 1950s and 1960s, demanding both the provision of preferential treatment and changes in the administrative arrangements that it regarded as responsible for many of its problems. Once the Special Measures were being implemented, the League played a key role in the administration of the projects. Often members of the League in effect decided who was qualified to receive the special school attendance grants or housing in the newly built apartment blocks.

Until the late 1960s the campaigns of the League had the support of all the opposition parties and the labour movement. This enabled the League's leaders to present their case with force. However, in the early 1970s a split developed within the league over the nature of discrimination and how to eliminate it.[18] Energy which might have been spent on campaigns for more special provision was diverted into internal argument.

In the *United States* the black minority, though large, was not well represented by a single organisation until the civil rights movement developed in the 1960s under the leadership of Martin Luther King with a singularity of purpose which stimulated creative policy-making under President Johnson's leadership. Once the process was underway there can be little doubt that the urban riots of the later 1960s encouraged further efforts to make sure that the policies devised were implemented in an effective manner. Political parties have not played an important role in the formulation of policy in the US. In general liberals within both parties have been more likely to favour affirmative action proposals but they have been implemented more enthusiastically by Democrat administrations, whether in the White House or City Hall.

The Supreme Court has played a crucial role. An examination of the chronology of the development of policy in any of the sectors of civil rights policy, be it voting rights, equal housing opportunities or fair employment policy, demonstrates that rulings of the Supreme Court have been at least as monumental as acts of Congress or executive orders. Not that this has always worked to the advantage of the minority groups. While the Brown *v.* the Board of Education decision in 1954 started the process of school desegregation, decisions in the late 1970s relating to the affirmative action programmes have hindered their development.

Immigrant groups in *France* and the *United Kingdom* have faced very different problems. In the UK most immigrants were eligible for citizenship and so voting rights were never a problem. When immigrants settled, their children were sent to the nearest schools and the segregation of schools has not been an issue except when some in the Islamic community have demanded segregated schooling. The diversity of the immigrant community has meant that it is not able to speak with a single voice, or even in harmony. Those with a Caribbean origin are divided by rivalry between islands. And, apart from the profound religious differences between groups originally from the Indian sub-continent, regional rivalries also prevent political unity. Representatives of these groups made little input into the process that led to the formulation of the race relations legislation.

The major problems which have been addressed are employment, housing and social discrimination. These have been the main targets of policy but in no area has there been much success. Since 1976 there have been no policy initiatives except in response to urban riots and these have usually taken the form of crisis management rather than considered proposals to deal with basic issues. Even relatively modest proposals for the implementation of contract compliance proposals based on the American model, or for the obligation of employers to monitor the ethnic origin of the workforce, have not been accepted. Until the 1970s the policy process was elite driven and deliberately intended to complement the immigration policy. Since 1979 the issue has been pushed off the agenda and the arrival in Parliament in 1987 of the first post-war black MPs has not changed this.

In the 1960s and 1970s there was an attempt to keep issues of race relations out of party politics and since 1979 the Conservative Party has not given these issues high priority. As members of the minorities are most likely to vote for the Labour Party and live in areas where there is little chance of Conservative success there is no electoral reason why they should. The Labour Party on the other hand has developed policies which might both improve living standards among the minorities and increase their role in the policy-making process.

French policy has been even less related to the wants or needs of the immigrants themselves. Very little minority policy has addressed such issues as equal employment opportunity, social discrimination or housing. As in the UK, the ability of the immigrants to influence policy-making has been hindered by their diverse origins. Though perceived by policy-makers as *Maghrebis* there is considerable difference in language and culture between, for example, Algerians and Malians. Moreover, a large proportion of these immigrants, not having citizenship, are unable to vote and are therefore unable to influence the political process directly. Thus they depend on the policy proposals of the political elite. In general when the Socialist Party has been in power, government has been more sensitive to the wishes of the immigrant minority but never to the extent of devising measures which direct significant resources to them or which provide a modicum of affirmative action. Across the French political spectrum there seems to be a consensus that policies which might protect and promote cultural identities would reduce the immigrants' incentive to strive for full national integration.

In each of our four examples the majority population seems to have acted as a 'brake' on the development of a minorities policy. The only exception to this might be in the United States in the mid-1960s when the case for voting rights and school desegregation was put so persuasively by King and his followers that it may have had the support of the majority in the US, if not in the South. Affirmative action proposals in each society have borne the brunt of most criticism as they have raised the prospect of 'reverse discrimination'. In the UK and less often in France this has led to policies which result in the provision of extra resources for minority groups being 'disguised' in the form of, for example, inner city improvement programmes.

Policy outcomes

There is a remarkable resemblance in the development of the minorities policy in the four states. The mid- to late 1960s saw a flurry of activity in terms of legislation and executive orders which were implemented with varying degrees of enthusiasm in the 1970s. But, on entering the 1980s, the issue had a much lower priority on the political agenda. One explanation of this might be that the global village created by modern media ensures issues which are fashionable in one political system attract attention elsewhere too. On the other hand, it might be that in the prosperous years after 1965 there were sufficient resources to permit governments to be generous to marginal groups. Before the oil shocks of the 1970s governments could spend time and money on minorities. Another explanation which cannot be immediately discounted is that the policies actually worked. The legislation and programmes introduced may have succeeded in reducing the problems encountered by minorities and thus the need for additional expenditure or more regulation.

In the *United States* since the mid-1960s the executive, judiciary and the legislature have been actively involved in the creation and implementation of minorities policy. This has led to radical and far-reaching changes. Protection of voting rights was assured by law in the 1960s and the legislation has been extended so that it will last at least until the mid-1990s. The desegregation of southern schools is now almost complete although the more knotty problem of segregated schooling in the north remains unresolved. Equal opportunity in employment has not yet resulted in any significant reduction in the gap between the average incomes of black and white families but the ongoing programmes of racial monitoring and affirmative action do seem to have had some impact on access by minorities to some hitherto closed occupational groupings. Nevertheless one cannot help but conclude that progress would have been faster if in the 1980s the White House had been occupied by a President who had taken a more active interest in this policy area than did Ronald Reagan.

A similar point applies to the *United Kingdom*. The 1976 Race Relations Act put into place a new administrative structure and provided a new sophistication which might have enabled the Commission for Racial Equality to make a real impact on race relations. However, starved of resources and standing at variance with the underlying non-interventionist philosophy of the Thatcher administration, it has been able to do little to improve the lives of the ethnic minorities. There have been changes in policy aimed at reducing discrimination, but these have been restricted to the problem of religious discrimination in Northern Ireland. There, sophisticated monitoring procedures have been introduced and implemented by the Fair Employment Commission and measures have been devised to try to eliminate discrimination. There is no question of such devices being introduced on the mainland unless the party in power changes.

Despite the variation in emphasis which has occurred in *France* depending on whether the right or the left was in charge, the ideology of French civilisation and culture has not been challenged. Indigenous minorities were regarded as little more than backward communities which would lose their idiosyncracies in the process of assimilation. It was accepted that the openness of French society would facilitate the process of full integration. The choice in France seems to be between this and a kind of economic 'insertion' into the economy of migrant workers under which they would be given training in order that they might work better while in France and acquire skills that would be useful when they returned home.[19] This was a policy pursued for a time in the 1970s under the bilateral agreements but it now appears to have been abandoned. Of the two, 'systematic cultural assimilation' seems to be preferable to 'insertion' but there seems to be no scope for ethnic pluralism which, however problematic, seems to be the option now favoured in the UK.

Japan's Special Measures Legislation was only intended to operate for ten years and it has now been decided that no new projects will be undertaken on behalf of the Burakumin. Certainly the special programmes have done a great deal to eliminate the outward manifestations of poverty and to improve standards of health and education. Employment patterns, though, remain untouched by the reforms and it is difficult to see how American style monitoring of employees would have any impact on this situation since the Burakumin Liberation League has sought to reduce rather than increase the availability of information which labels people as Burakumin. Nevertheless, given the ability of the Japanese government to exert firm leadership within the business community when the interests of the whole are threatened, it is difficult to believe that a determined Prime Minister with his Cabinet's support could do nothing if the political will was there. Moreover in the absence of any formal body which could periodically review the state of discrimination in Japan, it is hard not to be sceptical of the assurances of officials and politicians that nothing more needs to be done.

Prejudice remains, but even the Liberation League's leaders would accept that discrimination is not as virulent today as it was thirty years ago. Curiously the LDP and the JCP agree that there is no more the state should do. Further special treatment, they say, will only result in the problem persisting into the twenty-first century since treating the Burakumin as special encourages them to be regarded as different. If any further programmes are devised, they argue, they should be targeted not at Burakumin but at the urban or rural poor in general.

Japan has encountered the problem of illegal immigration somewhat later than the other states. The phenomenon only arose in the late 1980s and the government seems undecided about how to deal with it. This is in part due to a difference in attitude between ministries. While the Ministry of Labour would like a more relaxed policy, the Ministry of Justice (which controls visas) insists on maintaining strict control.

In each of the four states policy has mainly been aimed at integrating the minorities into the mainstream. However, there is a strategy which might be pursued in order to make minorities disappear – that of assimilation. Assimilation may take two forms. First, members of the minority may come increasingly to take on the characteristics of the majority until they no longer form a distinct minority – as Huguenot or Polish migrants have done in the UK. Secondly, the whole society may be regarded as an ever-changing 'melting pot' in which it is not the case of one group becoming like another but of all groups merging to form a single population – this is said (with only limited truth) to be the model presented by the USA.

However, there are a number of reasons why the scope that a government has to pursue an assimilationist policy is limited. First, there is the problem of 'visibility'. The more groups are distinguished by physical characteristics, particularly skin colour, the harder it is to achieve a manifest homogeneity; although the Burakumin provide striking confirmation that 'invisibility' is no guarantee of integration. Secondly, in a reasonably free society the extent to which members of different groups mix and merge is very much in their own hands and a government may be unable to exert much influence upon that process without resorting to unacceptably draconian measures. Thirdly, people may be reluctant to shed their group identities. The ideal of homogeneity has been increasingly under attack in recent decades; a society which is characterised by ethnic and cultural diversity has become for many people a condition to be fostered and cherished rather than an inconvenience to be eradicated. A policy of assimilation may therefore run into objections of principle as well as difficulties of practice.

The recent lack of interest in community relations issues does not appear to be the result of the overwhelming success of the policies in place. In each state the situation has improved over the past three decades and in ways that are partly attributable to the measures implemented. Policies have made a difference, yet there remains more to be done in each state: first in devising policies which will further minimise prejudice and discrimination and secondly in the elimination of the legacy of disadvantage. If ethnic communities are to be fairly treated, governments in each of these four countries will have to devote more time and resources to the problems encountered by the minorities and generated, consciously or not, by the majorities.

NOTES

1. B. D. Jacobs, *Racism in Britain* (London: Christopher Helm, 1988), p. 40.
2. W. Safran 'Minorities, Ethnics and Aliens: Pluralist Politics in the Fifth

Republic', in P. Godt, ed., *Policymaking in France* (London: Pinter, 1989), p. 185.

3. Ibid., p. 177.
4. I. J. Neary, *Political Protest and Social Control in Prewar Japan: The Origins of Buraku Liberation* (Manchester University Press, 1989).
5. J. McIlroy, 'The Politics of Racism', in B. Jones, ed., *Political Issues in Britain Today* (Manchester University Press, 1987), p. 215.
6. T. Hammar, *European Immigration Policy: A Comparative Study* (Cambridge University Press, 1985), p. 12.
7. G. P. Freeman, *Immigrant Labor and Racial Conflict in Industrial Societies: The British and French Experience, 1945–1975* (Princeton University Press, 1979), p. 73.
8. P. Fysh, 'Government Policy and the Challenge of the National Front', *AMSLF Review* (1987), p. 10.
9. R. Scher and J. Bulton, 'Voting Rights Act: Implementation and Impact', in C. S. Bullock and C. M. Lamb, eds., *Implementation of Civil Rights Policy* (California: Brooks/Cole Publishing, 1984), pp. 20–54.
10. H. Burns, 'The Activism Is Not Affirmative', in H. Schwartz, ed., *The Burger Years* (Harmondsworth: Penguin, 1988), pp. 95–108.
11. Scher and Bulton, 'Voting Rights Act', pp. 20–54.
12. J. Solomos, 'The Politics of Antidiscrimination Legislation: Planned Social Reform or Symbolic Politics', in J. Solomos and R. Jenkins, eds., *Racism and Equal Opportunity Policies in the 1980s* (Cambridge University Press, 1987), p. 37.
13. Freeman, *Immigrant Labour*, p. 92.
14. Hammar, *European Immigration Policy*, p. 146.
15. F. K. Upham, *Law and Social Change in Postwar Japan* (Cambridge, Mass.: University Press, 1987) p. 113.
16. This is discussed at greater length in F. K. Upham, 'Ten Years of Affirmative Action for Japanese Burakumin: A Preliminary Report on the Law on Special Action for Dōwa Projects', *Law In Japan: An Annual*, 13, 39 (1987).
17. H. R. Rodgers, 'Fair Employment Laws for Minorities: An Evaluation of Federal Implementation', in C. S. Bullock and C. M. Lamb, eds., *Implementation of Civil Rights Policy* (California: Brooks/Cole Publishing, 1984) pp. 93–117.
18. I. J. Neary, 'Socialist and Communist Party Attitudes towards Discrimination Against Japan's *Burakumin*', *Political Studies*, 34, 4 (1986), pp. 556–74.
19. Safran, 'Minorities, Ethnics and Aliens', p. 186.

FURTHER READING

Two volumes place the issue of British and French immigration in a comparative context: T. Hammar, *European Immigration Policy: A Comparative Study* (Cambridge University Press, 1985) and G. P. Freeman, *Immigrant Labor and Racial Conflict in Industrial Societies: The British and French Experience, 1945–1975* (Princeton University Press, 1979). As the issue of minorities has been less prominent on policy agendas so it has attracted less academic attention but a reliable source for recent developments in the UK is B. D. Jacobs, *Racism in*

Britain (London: Christopher Helm, 1988). For Japan chapter 3 of F. K. Upham, *Law and Social Change in Postwar Japan* (Cambridge, Mass.: Harvard University Press, 1987) provides a general description of the social context of the Burakumin problem and a detailed analysis of one instance of discrimination.

9   Law and order

Ella Ritchie

Introduction

The provision of law and order has always been considered a basic function of the state which is rarely, if ever, questioned, except by anarchists. Whilst all states accept the importance of law and order, different societies have different conceptions of what law and order means and entails.[1] For example, in France law and order encompasses both the narrow notion of individual security and a wider notion of *ordre publique* which means the security of the state, whereas in the United Kingdom law and order has traditionally referred to matters of individual security. In Japan it is difficult to identify a 'law and order' policy as such, since it does not generally feature on the governmental agenda; in the United States it is often difficult to separate the 'law and order issue' from the 'race issue'.

Given these differences across states, is it possible to arrive at a cross-national definition of law and order? For example, does the notion of *ordre publique*, which means the preservation of the existing political and social order in France, have an equivalent in the United States where the concept of the state has little meaning other than the machinery of state or federal government? In answering this it is helpful to disaggregate the concept of law and order.

Not all acts which are illegal arouse the same sort of public concern; it would be difficult to argue that in any of the four countries parking offences or art forgery could threaten the state or its inhabitants. We can distinguish three categories of offence which typically constitute matters of law and order:

1. assaults upon the person, such as murder, manslaughter, rape and the infliction of bodily injury;
2. attacks upon property, such as robbery, burglary, theft and vandalism;
3. collective acts of disorder such as riots, breaches of the peace and hooliganism.

What is it that makes some crimes a matter of law and order and others not? Why is the phrase law and order not usually applied to tax evasion, 'corporate crime', social security offences and the violation of health and safety regulations? The distinction may seem to be underwritten by little more than class or race prejudice. However, we can characterise law and order crimes generally both by who commits them and by what they entail. First, law and order offences tend to be those which visit immediate harm upon ordinary people. For example, assault, robbery and riot affect people directly. Thus it is not surprising that law and order is an area of policy in which public perceptions, often heavily shaped by the media, are especially significant in setting the agenda. In France, the UK and the USA, it is the fear of crime, as much as the reality of crime, which has shaped the law and order agenda.[2]

Secondly, for governments law and order offences may touch on the stability of the state, and potentially threaten the social fabric. The conflicts between students and the police in France in May 1968, and between striking miners and the police in the UK in 1984–5, are examples of this.

State involvement

In contrast to policy areas such as race relations or industrial policy, the state's involvement with law and order is not, in itself, a controversial matter. States have a near but not complete monopoly on the maintenance of law and order. Private security firms, vigilante groups, self-policing organisations (in some cases fostered and encouraged by the police) are increasingly common and in the United States privately run prisons are becoming more widespread. However, the part played by these private agencies in the maintenance of law and order remains very small and arguments over the proper balance between public and private provision have not figured significantly in debates about which policies should be pursued.

There are wide divergences between the four countries concerning how an ordered society is conceived and the ways in which governments believe that law and order should be preserved. A country's historical development affects the traditional scope of policing. The British state, for example, did not develop so extensively as the French state, nor did it acquire the same symbolic importance in the political system.[3] Consequently, policing in France has always had an explicitly political dimension, compared to the narrow conception in Britain. The British police force was built on the role of the local constable who saw his role as that of keeping the peace in the locality, whereas the historical role of the French police was not just to protect people and property but to safeguard the whole political system. In the United States a deep-rooted distrust of bureaucracy and a belief that democracy was best preserved through local elected politicians has led to a system of policing which is usually placed under direct political control. By contrast in Japan there is a belief that political interference in the police should be minimised. As Bayley notes,[4]

Americans distrust bureaucratic government and consider close supervision [of the police] by politicians indispensable to liberty. Japanese readily accept bureaucratic government and regard intrusions by politicians dangerous to liberty.

There are significant differences between the four countries in how governments maintain law and order. Broadly we can contrast countries such as France and the United States which emphasise law enforcement (often carried out in a highly coercive way) with those such as Japan and the United Kingdom which emphasise maintaining order with consent.[5]

There are two main dimensions which influence the organisation of a state's involvement in the field of law and order: civil/military and central/local. France is the most significant example of a state in which responsibility for law and order is shared between civilian and military organisations. The Ministry of Defence is responsible for about a third of the country's day-to-day policing. However, in the other countries policing remains largely a civilian matter with military troops being used only in matters of emergency, most notably the use of the National Guard to deal with riots in the USA.

More important differences arise from the balance between central and local involvement in maintaining law and order. In Britain and the United States the contemporary police forces have emerged from local forces, whereas in Japan and France policing has always been organised from the centre. In France the need for the state to defend itself against disruptive groups (such as Breton nationalists) has led to a hierarchical and centralised police force, which attaches a great deal of importance to its public order role. In the United States, by contrast, a federal structure of government, a strong dislike of centralised government and a political tradition which emphasises popular choice, has led to the most local and decentralised police force in the world, with approximately 40,000 police forces.

While the organisation and control of the police varies from country to country, all four countries have a special organisation for policing their national capitals. In these cases policing is under direct political control and often has more specialised resources at its disposal. Another similarity is the sharp distinction between urban and rural policing. Whereas there are wide differences in the nature of urban policing, rural policing tends to be organised in a similar way across the four countries, with an emphasis on community policing with few specialised resources.

Structure of policing

France

One of the most tangible manifestations of France's strong state is a highly visible and relatively coercive police force placed under the control of the government in Paris and its representatives, the Prefects, in the provinces. There was (and is) an expectation that much of the regulatory role of the state is carried out by the police.[6] Consequently, the average French person has much more contact with the police than the average Briton; for example the police issue visas, passports and driving licences. The police in France, like the police in Japan, expect to be involved in the daily life of the citizen.

There are two main policing forces in France; the *Police Nationale* (PN) under the Ministry of the Interior and the *Gendarmerie Nationale* (GN) under the Ministry of Defence.[7] The main difference is that the PN is a civilian force and is responsible for towns of over 10,000 residents while the *Gendarmerie* is a military force, resident in barracks and responsible for policing small towns and villages. In addition to these two forces there is a third, the municipal police, which is directly recruited by Mayors. In many local authorities this amounts to only one or two police, but in large conurbations it may consist of two or three hundred police. Municipal police have increased considerably during the 1980s and now amount to approximately 15,000 because local resources are being spent increasingly on law and order. Inevitably there is a considerable degree of conflict between the municipal forces and the PN.

The PN, reorganised in 1966 from the old *Sûreté Nationale*, is recruited nationally and polices the large conurbations. The two main branches of the PN are the uniformed urban police and the plain-clothes Criminal Investigation detectives. There are also divisions concerned with counter intelligence and political information. In addition the PN has a small division of security police, the infamous *Compagnies Républicaines de Securité* (CRS) which specialise in the maintenance of public order. The CRS are organised in a semi-militaristic fashion and are used to control strikes and demonstrations.

The GN is a branch of the Ministry of Defence but is legally obliged to respond to requests for assistance from civilian authorities. About 10 per cent of the *gendarmes* are auxiliaries – young men on national service who spend between 12 and 18 months in the force. The GN also has its own branch for dealing with public order, the *Gendarmerie Mobile* which can be deployed anywhere in France to maintain order. The *Gendarmerie* are a more professional force than the PN; they do not have the right to belong to unions and they tend to enter the political arena much less frequently than their civilian counterparts. Although the PN deal with the largest proportion of crime, in recent years the GN has extended its policing functions.[8] The individual *gendarme* or policeman is subject to strict hierarchical control reaching up to Paris. The local Mayor or Prefect can call on police support but it is central government which has the most control. Ministers of the Interior can, for example, deploy the CRS around the country to deal with actual or potential trouble-spots as they see fit. Police functions tend to be carried out in a highly regimented fashion with individual police officers exercising little discretion.

Various attempts have been made to reform the police during the Fifth Republic. The first, in 1966, went some way to reorganising the structure of the PN after several scandals involving the police.[9] The second was the ambitious Belorgey plan presented at the beginning of Mitterrand's first government, which attempted to change the emphasis in policing away from the public order function towards policing with consent and to bring the police under greater democratic control.[10] However, both the Gaullist and Socialist governments have discovered that it is extremely difficult to change the traditional structure of policing and to break down departmental loyalties which are fostered by a high level of specialisation. Under the Mitterrand Presidency there have also been attempts to improve the image of the police force and to make it more accessible to the public, but these efforts too have met with little success.

Japan

Until the end of the Second World War Japan had a highly centralised police force controlled and directed by the Ministry of Home Affairs. Pre-war police displayed authoritarian and militaristic tendencies and intervened extensively in the lives of individual citizens. Following the war and the introduction of liberal democracy, reforms were initiated, under the 1948 Police Act, which were designed to democratise and decentralise the police. These reforms were amended in the 1954 Police Act which established a police force which is in effect largely centralised and controlled by bureaucrats.[11] The police are headed by the National Police Agency (NPA), under the control of an appointed body, the Public Safety Commission (PSC). Political neutrality is ensured by stipulating that the composition of the six-member PSC is mixed, with no more than three members belonging to the same political party. This system is replicated at the Prefectural level. The role of the PSCs is to formulate the basic policy for the operation of the police forces but its constitution stipulates that it is not to intervene in the day-to-day running of the National Police Agency. The PSCs are, however, responsible for appointing the Secretaries General of the police forces. In practice this system gives an enormous amount of power to the bureaucrats.

There are 1,200 police stations in Japan, servicing the larger towns and conurbations, 6,100 police boxes (*koban*) and 9,000 residential police stations (*chuzaisho*). The two latter are the most significant feature of the Japanese system; they are a means of exercising social control by integrating the police into the local community. Police are highly regarded in Japan and the population accepts that the police will monitor people's lives closely.[12] Indeed many citizens organise themselves into volunteer crime prevention associations to assist the police in keeping a watchful eye on the population. The pattern of small town policing where each police officer has responsibility for about one hundred families is followed even in Tokyo where the neighbourhood policeman *omawari-san* – Mr Walkabout – will typically visit each household and the workplace of each of his 'residents' once or twice a year. Consequently even urban dwellers regard the patrolman as a part of their family's community.

Each police force has its own Public Security Division, the most important arm of which is the riot squad. These riot squads contrast very markedly with the typical community policeman; they are highly specialised, extremely well equipped and often brutal in their treatment of demonstrators. The PSD are typically divided into sections dealing with student movements and extreme radicals.

The United Kingdom[13]

The contemporary structure of policing in the United Kingdom is based on a tradition that the forces of law and order should serve the local area rather than the state. Consequently there is no national police force. Policing is decentralised into forces which are part funded by local authorities and to some extent controlled by them.[14] However, while there are variations between forces, all operate within a common framework which is determined and monitored by central government. Thus policing in the UK is decentralised but not as diverse as it is in the USA and it shares a professionalism and uniform set of standards with its counterparts in France and Japan. Policing arrangements have been characterised as 'more like a federation of states united by a common culture and a federal government than they are analogous to a collection of independent states with autonomous goals and independent cultural characteristics'.[15]

Since 1964 the police in England and Wales have been organised into forty-three police forces, each under the direction of a Chief Constable. Each force has its own specialised branches, such as the Criminal Investigation Division and the Drugs Unit which themselves are devolved to divisions within the force. Apart from the Metropolitan Police, which is directly responsible to the Home Secretary, all forces are to some extent accountable to local police authorities, which are composed of two-thirds elected councillors and one-third appointed magistrates. In principle police authorities control the police budget and are responsible for appointing new Chief Constables and their Deputies. In practice the Home Office can and does intervene in both these areas. In addition, the Inspectorate of Police, which is directly responsible to the Home Office, monitors police forces to ensure that they act in accordance with Home Office circulars. Police authorities have no control over the operational aspects of the police and while they do try to influence police policy through control of the budget, in practice it is the Chief Constables who determine both the operational strategy and way resources are used in their force.

In the last twenty-five years policing has become more professional, specialised and centralised.[16] The 1964 Police Act greatly reduced the number of forces as well as curtailing local control over the police and increasing the power of the Home Office. The new police authorities were on the whole more willing to defer to the professionalism of the police.[17] Latterly increasingly sophisticated equipment and weaponry has led to the development of specialised units within the police. In the 1960s a police officer could try to tackle a disturbance with a dustbin lid and a truncheon; in the 1980s special units with sophisticated riot gear were called on to deal with riot situations. By the 1980s all police forces had Police Support Units trained in crowd and riot control. However this specialisation needs to be kept in perspective. In the late 1980s only about 1.5 per cent of the British police were trained to deal with riots compared to 21 per cent of the French police force.

Increasing centralisation has taken place through the amalgamation of forces and the increasing control of budgets by central government. The controversial National Reporting Centre, established after the 1972 miners strike, made it possible for the Home Office to co-ordinate 'mutual aid' or the facility of one police force to give help to a neighbouring force in time of crisis. The National Reporting Centre was used extensively by the Conservative government to move police forces around the country during the 1984–5 miners strike.

Although most changes in the police have been in the direction of specialisation and the increasing use of technology, there have been countervailing trends. It became apparent in the mid-1970s that relations between the police and racial minorities were at a low ebb. At the same time there was a recognition that increasing specialisation and the use of 'fire-brigade' tactics for routine policing often led to a breakdown in police–community relations and escalated violence. The idea of community policing seemed to provide a panacea for these problems.[18] As a result some forces reintroduced permanent beat officers and tried to strengthen links with the community. The influential Scarman Report which followed the Brixton riots in 1984[19] took some of these ideas further by advocating the establishment of Police Liaison Committees and by stressing the importance of widening recruitment to the police to try and reflect the composition of the communities which were being policed.

The United States

The American belief in the democratic value of localism is reflected in highly decentralised and varied policing arrangements. The structure, organisation and recruitment of police forces varies not only from state to state but also within the states themselves. There are five levels of policing[20]: (1) the federal level, consisting of federal agencies such as the Federal Bureau of Investigation and the Federal Drug Enforcement Agency; (2) the state forces which principally concentrate on criminal investigation work and traffic; (3) some 3,000 county forces supervised by sheriffs; (4) the cities and townships which account for a further 20,000 police forces; and (5) a further 15,000 forces in villages and boroughs. In total there are 40,000 police forces in the United States – an astonishing 80 per cent of which employ fewer than 25 officers.

Each police force is bounded by a geographical area but in practice jurisdictions overlap and many crimes are investigated by several police forces. For example, an organised drug racket across two states might involve the FBI, the Federal Drug Enforcement Agency and state and local forces. Inevitably this overlap in jurisdictions and the lack of standardisation across police forces leads to conflict and competition between the various police forces. As Brewer et al. note,[21]

It can hardly be emphasised enough that such overlapping jurisdictions can lead to rivalries between forces, duplication of effort and ultimately a less efficient prosecution of the criminal.

The police do not exhibit the same professionalism as in the UK nor do they have the same high status as police in Japan. Police are recruited locally and there is often difficulty in filling places. Once in place officers receive little training and career progression can be influenced as much by political factors as by the experience of the police officer.

The two most striking features of the American system are the high level of local political influence on the police and the variety of police organisations. The most common arrangement is for the head of the police department, the police chief, to be appointed either by the directly elected Mayor or by the city manager (who in turn will have been appointed by the mayor or city board). However, there are still a number of directly elected police chiefs, largely in rural areas, and most sheriffs are elected. What this means in practice is that police forces are likely to enter directly into the political arena to compete for resources and will be more responsive to the needs of local politicians and of the local electorate than in any of the other three countries. Local funding of police and the politicisation of the police will mean that the quality and nature of policing may reflect and play upon dominant local interests.

During the 1960s police forces developed specialised units, such as the Special Weapon and Tactic Units (SWATs), to deal with the problems of riots and public disorder. These specialised units reduced the role which the National Guard had previously played in supporting police forces in dealing with public disorder. Paradoxically, at the same time in some urban areas there was a move away from the traditional crime-fighting role of the police towards the service role, with an increasing emphasis on community policing.

Policy community

The law and order policy community is dominated by governmental actors and by the corporate professionals, the police. In general the consumers of the policy – the citizens – are not organised and do not influence policy outcomes except in a general way through the ballot box. In Britain and France law and order features quite prominently on party agendas and in the United States the nature of policing is often determined by electoral preferences. In contrast to other policy areas such as social minorities, there are no distinct groups representing the 'users' or the 'beneficiaries' of the policy. In a sense we all benefit from law and order policy but we only recognise the benefits of the policy to maintain law and order when outcomes such as safe streets or peaceful demonstrations are threatened. Citizens tend to notice the inadequacies of the policy rather than its benefits. There are some groups, such as civil rights groups and anti-racist organisations, which seek to alter the agenda of law and order policy. However, these groups do not usually play a significant role in determining policy as they are often regarded as outsiders by the policy community.

Legislatures, the judiciary and public opinion only influence the policy agenda intermittently. For example, Parliaments in the UK and France have changed the legislative framework of policing in the last twenty years and Commissions of Enquiry, which followed the outbreaks of civil unrest in the United States in the 1960s and in the UK in the late 1970s and 1980s, gave some groups the opportunity to influence the future shaping of policing. In the United States the Supreme Court, grand juries, magistrates and ombudsmen as well as civil courts can all influence policy. However, the role of these bodies is often responsive rather than initiatory.

In all four countries the police play a key role in the policy community because their consent is essential to effective implementation. The police do, and must, exercise a great deal of discretion in executing their duties.[22] In everyday policing most police officers can decide what law to enforce and against whom to enforce it. Even in public order situations the activities of the police on the ground can be vital in containing or escalating disorder.

In both the UK and the USA police chiefs are able to wield considerable power over politicians and control bodies. In the USA police chiefs are in an almost unassailable position in their ability to determine the priorities of their departments. They are openly engaged in the political arena and canvass lobbies and the public for support.[23] In the UK the individual mark of chief constables on local policing can also be seen. For example, James Anderton, Chief Constable of Greater Manchester, directed police resources into rooting out drug abuse, pornography and other symptoms of 'moral decay'. Even in more centralised systems it may be difficult for ministers to control the professionals. In France a succession of Ministers of the Interior failed to reorganise the Paris Police, largely because of the power of the Prefect of Police for Paris.

Police unions or their professional representatives normally have a close institutional relationship with politicians in the policy community. In the UK the Association of Chief Police Officers (ACPO) and the Police Federation are consulted about policing policy and new legislation. While these groups may not always agree with government policy they are nevertheless seen as vital partners in the policy-making process. Ideological and professional divisions within French police unions means that it is possible for the government to play off one group against another.[24] Nevertheless the unions, such as the *Fédération autonome des syndicats de police*, are very powerful and any major reform has to be negotiated with all the groups. One of the reasons for the failure of the Belorgey reform proposals was the united hostility of all major police unions to large-scale reform and to closer monitoring of the police by the public.

Policy agenda

The late twentieth century has seen increasing social tensions in all four countries, many of which have manifested themselves in social disorder and conflicts between the police and the population. The increasing politicisation of student groups, the growth of protest groups and a new activist style of politics beginning in the 1960s raised new law and order issues. While the intervention of the police in industrial relations and civic unrest is not new, the 1970s and 1980s have placed such interventions in a very public light. Increasing public awareness of police tactics and police misuse of power, and a growing recognition of the importance of safeguarding individual liberties and minority rights, have made policing an increasingly controversial issue.

During the last thirty years there has been a steadily rising crime rate in France, the UK and the USA. In Japan the crime rate fell until 1970 and there has been a very slight rise since then. However, wide national differences still remain: Japan is a relatively orderly country with low crime rates in most categories (see table 9.1). A similar pattern can be seen in the area of public order. The United States experienced ghetto riots in many major cities in the 1960s, a pattern repeated on a much smaller scale in the UK in the 1980s. There were major clashes between the police and students in France and in the United States in the 1960s and between police and strikers in France in the 1960s and in the UK in the 1970s and 1980s. While there have been no inner city problems in Japan there have been a few, very violent, clashes between the police and left-wing organisations and between the police and protest groups. The confrontation between the police and protestors at Tokyo's Narita airport began in the late 1960s, reached a violent peak in the 1970s and continued unresolved into the 1990s.

There are significant variations in how prominently law and order features on a country's political agenda. In France, the UK and the USA law and order is an important and defined policy area while in Japan it is not. Although the crime rate is increasing in Japan and there have been outbreaks of social unrest, these are rarely defined either by the government or by the media as problems of 'law and order'. For example the occasional panics over violence in schools, teenage prostitution and motorcycle gangs are defined as problems of youth rather than of law and order. Thus the Radical Students Movement in the 1960s was presented by the government as an issue about the reform of the universities and was placed firmly on the educational agenda. This contrasts dramatically with the 'events' of May 1968 in France when a student revolt was immediately politicised by the government and presented as a potential collapse of

Table 9.1. *International comparison of number of offences known to the police, crime rate, and clearance rate (1984)*

Country	Homicide			Robbery			Rape			Larceny		
	Number of cases known to the police	Crime rate[a]	Clearance rate (%)	Number of cases known to the police	Crime rate[a]	Clearance rate (%)	Number of cases known to the police	Crime rate[a]	Clearance rate (%)	Number of cases known to the police	Crime rate[a]	Clearance rate (%)
France (Population 54,832,000)	2,712	4.9	83.7	57,907	105.6	21.6	2,859	5.2	80.8	2,196,587	4,006.0	15.3
Japan (Population 120,235,000)	1,762	1.5	97.2	2,188	1.8	78.8	1,926	1.6	89.6	1,365,705	1,135.9	58.7
England and Wales (Population 49,763,600)	1,613	3.2	76.4	24,890	50.0	22.4	4,325	8.7	85.1	2,660,401	5,346.1	31.3
United States (Population 236,158,000)	18,692	7.9	74.1	485,008	205.4	25.8	84,233	35.7	53.6	10,608,473	4,492.1	17.9

Note: [a] Per 100,000 population
Source: Adapted from a table in *White Paper on Police* (National Police Agency, Government of Japan, 1986).

public order. Paradoxically, there is a high level of organised crime in Japan organised around the *yakusta* or gangs. The Japanese police have a symbiotic relationship with the *yakusta* and, in order to keep non-syndicate crime under control, they often turn a blind eye to their activities.[25]

In France and the UK law and order has an important place on the national political agendas. Local issues such as rural policing and police corruption quickly find their way into the national arena. In France the law and order debate centred around the coercive use of police power in strikes and demonstrations in the 1960s. In the 1970s the agenda moved on to the question of the treatment of foreigners and immigrants and in the 1980s centred on the inability of police forces to deal with the growing problem of inner city crime. In the UK the problem of lawlessness and the increasingly authoritarian nature of the British police have become part of the mainstream political agenda under the Thatcher administrations. In addition to the regular clashes between police and supporters at football matches, numerous *causes célèbres* such as police handling of industrial disputes at Saltley and Grunwick, of inner city disturbances in Brixton and Toxteth and the treatment of hippy convoys have helped to keep these issues high on the agenda.

In the United States problems of law and order generally fall under the auspices of state governments. At state level since the 1960s there has been considerable concern over the breakdown of law and order in the major cities and over police handling of minority groups. In some cases the issue has become 'federalised'. Sometimes the President is forced to act on an issue because of the scale of the problem. For example, the impact of the race riots in the 1960s was such that President Johnson set up the Law Enforcement Assistance Agency which was designed to channel funds to state governments to support effective programmes of crime control. On other occasions the President chooses to take up the issue because of overlapping policy concerns. For example in September 1989 President Bush defined the 'crack' drug problem as a matter of national public order, which needed more resources from the federal government. While crack, a cocaine derivative, certainly was an increasing problem, the social panic it engendered allowed the President to present his new administration as 'tough'. The President also used the issue of crack as a means of furthering his foreign policy objectives: namely, strengthening American influence over countries in Central America.

Media coverage of both crime and policing have, quite independently of personal experience, heightened the public's awareness of crime. Worries about crime are often felt out of proportion to an individual's likelihood of being a victim, and fear of crime has itself become part of the law and order agenda.[26] These fears, often whipped up by the media, can be exploited by politicians who capitalise on public anxieties. For example, part of the National Front's success in France in municipal, European and legislative elections between 1983 and 1986 was due to the way in which Jean Marie Le Pen, the National Front leader, played on people's general feeling of insecurity and linked these anxieties to the issue of immigration. Heightened public awareness of insecurity also meant that the Socialist government abandoned its earlier proposals for a radical reform of the police in favour of policies which responded to the public's desire to see a more effective and assertive police force. In Britain the Conservative manifesto for the 1979 election effectively interwove the problem of industrial unrest with that of rising crime rates so as to present the Conservatives as the party most committed to law and order. In the United States many Mayors fight local elections on the law and order ticket and the issue has been on the national agenda for Presidential elections ever since Barry Goldwater used it in his bid for the Presidency in 1964.

While the law and order agenda may vary according to 'objective' circumstances, such as student protests or a wave of strikes, it may also vary because of political strategy by a government or because the police themselves place issues on the agenda in order to strengthen their bargaining position with government. For example, certain constabularies in the UK used the issue of rural disorder in the late 1980s to argue for increased resources.[27]

Two main issues underlie the law and order agenda. These are first, the effectiveness of the policies and secondly, how the policies are implemented. Clearly the effectiveness of any policy is an important issue, and given the way in which law and order problems are presented to and perceived by the public, there tends to be a preference for policies which yield quick and conspicuous results.

The second issue underlying the agenda is how policies are implemented and at what cost. This issue raises the question of the relationship between order and liberty which is fundamental to liberal democracy. On the one hand people want effective laws and policing in order to secure a peaceful society; on the other hand they may find the price which they have to pay to achieve these results too high. Curfews, such as those imposed in some large American cities in the late 1980s, may be successful in reducing street crime but they may also be regarded as an unacceptable infringement of citizens' liberties. Stop and Search policies have been advocated vigorously by the police in France, and in the UK for some categories of offence (such as drink driving), but politicians regard them as unacceptable. Telephone tapping may bring results in trapping individuals involved in organised crime but may be regarded as an unacceptable violation of privacy by the average citizen. Recent changes in the nature of policing in France, the United Kingdom and the United States have served to heighten this debate. The increasing use of computer technology for collecting information about the population has been of immense concern to civil rights groups and the paramilitary capability of most police forces raises worrying questions about the use of coercion.

The debate about the balance between individual liberties and the power of the state has tended to focus on two related issues: first, the use and abuse of police powers and secondly, the question of the control and accountability of the police. Criticisms about the abuse of police power centre not only on the tactics employed in policing disorderly situations but also on how everyday policing is conducted. Incidents of police brutality, entrapment and evidence fixing are an increasing concern in all four countries. Even Japan has not been immune from such scandals.[28]

More substantially, there has been a debate in the UK, the USA and to a more limited extent in France about the control and accountability of the police. Although the concepts of control and accountability are often linked they do have different meanings. Control is the capacity to shape policy while accountability is the responsibility for their action of those who take decisions. As we have seen, methods of controlling the police vary in the four countries, ranging from directly elected police chiefs, to control by local authorities, the judiciary, central government or any mixture of these. However, operational activities of the police cannot in fact be adequately controlled by politicians or bureaucrats. Although there has been some debate about improving the ways in which the police are controlled, most of the debate has been about making the police more accountable. The police are, to some degree, financially and politically accountable to the bodies which control them but police operations on the ground have raised important issues about the abuse of police power.[29]

Citizens can take out a criminal or civil prosecution against the police but this route is invariably slow and expensive. In France, the UK and the USA citizens can complain formally about police abuse of power; in the event of a complaint the police investigate themselves. In France the *Inspection Générale de la Police Nationale* investigates serious complaints against the police. In the United Kingdom complaints go before a Police Complaints Authority, which since 1976 has included a small independent element. In the United States practices vary across police forces but most police departments have a specialised internal investigatory unit, the Internal Affairs Division, to investigate complaints by the public or judiciary. These systems of self-regulation are generally ineffective and do not adequately protect the individual against possible misuse of police power. However, reformers have met with great difficulty in effecting any change which will reduce the role of the professional in checking on standards. In Japan the high degree of internal discipline within the police means that cases involving police misuse of power are rare. Even so there is no real check on the police. Citizens can take complaints to the Human Rights Bureau in the Ministry of Justice but this body only has the power to make recommendations. The Public Safety Commissioners can ask the police to investigate complaints but in reality they do so infrequently.

Policy outcomes

Law and order is not an area which is likely to bring many electoral benefits to governments. Publics tend to notice when law and order policy is unsuccessful rather than when it is successful. In this sense law and order is as much an issue for oppositions as for governments. Public disorder and criminality are unpredictable and difficult to contain. Governments may spend much time and effort in changing the legislative framework, or in putting more resources into policing, but achieve few results. Ultimately the policy outcome may depend more on the activities of the police or on wider social trends than on any particular design of the government.

At first sight, tackling the social conditions that cause crime would seem to be the best solution for law and order problems. The relationship between deprivation and disorder has been emphasised in Commissions of Enquiry following the race riots in the United States and in the influential Scarman Report in the United Kingdom. Why then does this option not figure more prominently in law and order policy? Basically it is because democratic governments want quick and conspicuous results more than long-term solutions. Governments are therefore inclined to turn for results to policing and punishment rather than to policies whose impact is more imponderable and long term and which may anyway require significant redistribution of resources.

However, contemporary governments have not ignored this wider aspect of policy altogether. In the 1970s and 1980s there were many experimental schemes in the USA and France for dealing with problems of law and order. In the USA innovative schemes in Massachusetts have aimed to reduce unemployment in inner city areas by targeting and socialising alienated groups with a view to reducing the crime rate. In France the Socialist government of François Mitterrand introduced widespread reforms in the area of law and order. New Inner city policies were partly based on the premise that social deprivation, family instability, school failure, lack of job prospects and a negative self-image all contributed to a drift by young people towards anti-social and destructive behaviour. There was a deliberate policy of penetrating immigrant and other socially isolated communities through a well-structured system of resources and support. In 1981 the government set up a National Crime Prevention Council and all major urban centres were encouraged to set up their own local councils to bring together local councillors, civil servants, voluntary workers, judges and prosecutors. These schemes have run with considerable success in many of France's major urban conurbations, such as Lille and Marseilles. However, it has been difficult for the government to extend the schemes more generally over France. The Socialists themselves have acknowledged that the widespread adoption of a more innovative approach to inner city problems needed a change of public attitude.

Another way to tackle crime is to introduce preventative measures to contain crime. One such approach has been to encourage citizens to police themselves. Neighbourhood Watch schemes[30] were first introduced on an experimental basis in the United States in the late 1960s; they were often coupled with schemes designed to reduce the fear of crime in the inner cities. These schemes were also adopted by the Conservative government in the UK in the 1980s. For the Conservatives the schemes served two purposes. On the one hand they formed part of the campaign to reduce crime and, on the other, they formed part of the Conservatives' policy of fostering a sense of civic responsibility or 'new citizenship' in the community. One of the drawbacks of such schemes, which has been identified in the United States, is that Neighbourhood Watch may tend to encourage vigilantism and/or racism in communities and so may actually exacerbate problems of alienation and possibly increase levels of crime.

In Japan the nature of policing emphasises prevention. The high degree of social control exercised by the Japanese police has gone some way to ensuring that 'organised' crime (with the important exception of the *yakuza*) does not arise. Close monitoring of the population by the police, combined with the enthusiasm of the public for keeping the police informed of anything suspicious, certainly helps to prevent crime. However, it seems that the Japanese case is not for export, as experience in the UK and the USA suggests that a high police presence and close interference in people's lives may serve to exacerbate tensions.

In the UK preventative policing has often taken the form of community policing. Community policing, which is based on a romantic interpretation of the role of the nineteenth-century English bobby,[31] stresses the maintenance of the Queen's Peace rather than the enforcement of law, policing by consent rather than by coercion, less technology and reactive policing and more permanent beat officers. This pattern of policing was adopted by several police forces in the UK in the early 1980s. While the presence of more police on the streets certainly helps to reduce people's fear of crime, there is little evidence to show that it improves police–community relations in inner cities or that it reduces the likelihood of public disorder. Studies in the United States show that the success of community policing depends on an existing level of trust between the police and the community.[32] Community policing in Birmingham (Handsworth) in Britain appeared to be successful during the early 1980s, but it did not prevent serious disturbances breaking out in 1985. Yet there is also considerable evidence to show that polarised relations between the police and ethnic communities formed part the background to many race riots in the United States and to inner city disorders in Britain. Measures designed to improve understanding between the police and communities which they serve, such as improved training and the recruitment to the police from minority groups, must go some way, over time, to improving the situation.

The main thrust of government policy for dealing with law and order is to deal with crime itself. This has the potential of bringing down the crime figures more rapidly and of showing the public that 'something is being done'. Dealing with crime has taken two main forms – legislation and more effective policing. In the last thirty years all four countries have passed a considerable body of legislation dealing with matters of public order. In general this legislation has been designed to clarify and strengthen police powers, or to limit the freedom of strikers and demonstrators.

At the same time all four countries have increased spending on the police and have channelled resources into both technology and personnel. There has been increasing use of computer technology and of specialised weapons and equipment particularly in the area of riot control. In the late 1960s there was a massive injection of both federal and state capital into policing in the USA under the Law Enforcement Assistance Agency and this pattern was repeated in the UK in the 1980s under the Thatcher administrations and in France under the 1986 police modernisation programme. Increased resources were channelled into computer technology and more specialised weapons and equipment as well as into the workforce.

To the frustration of governments, however, increased spending on the police may not actually lead to a decrease in the crime rate. Experience in both the United States and France has shown that reducing or increasing the level of policing appears to have little effect on the actual level of crime. Use of technology, specialised weapons and riot techniques may encourage overzealous policing and consequently further distance the public from the police or heighten tension between communities and the police. Governments have become increasingly aware of this syndrome and consequently policy in France, the UK and the USA has tended to simultaneously use 'fire-brigade' policing and community policing, which emphasises policing with consent.

There is strong evidence to suggest that good community policing is best ensured when the police come from the locality in which they are working and are to some extent representative of it. Research into the causes of the ghetto riots in Detroit and Chicago in the 1960s showed that white policing of black areas contributed to the escalation of the troubles. Strenuous efforts were subsequently made to recruit police from minority groups and a policy of positive discrimination resulted in the number of blacks in American police forces rising from 7.5 per cent in 1972 to 13.1 per cent in 1983. The authoritarian, bureaucratic and repressive nature of the Parisian police force can, to some extent, be accounted for by its recruitment patterns. Young recruits are reluctantly sent from the provinces to Paris where they serve in specialised units. They have little or no identification with the areas they police and they tend to retreat into rigid organisational values rather than building up good relations with the community.[33]

Crime figures may seem to provide hard data on policy effectiveness, data which is unbiassed by individual experience or by media sensationalism. However, differences in the way that police forces collect and categorise these data, and shifts in the balance between reported and unreported crime, make evaluations based upon these figures extremely hazardous. Moreover, crime rates can be affected by factors which are quite outside a government's control. For example, because crime is more prevalent amongst young adults, it is likely that the decline in the 18–25 year cohort in Western societies will at least slow down the increase in the crime rate. Law and order policy can, itself, affect crime rates 'perversely': more vigorous and effective policing, and a greater willingness of the public to co-operate with the police and to report crimes, may result in an increase, rather than a fall, in recorded crime. Thus a symptom of success can easily be misread as indicative of failure.

A successful policy on law and order is one that contains crime and defuses potentially disruptive situations with a minimum of conflict and a maximum of consensus. The success of law and order policy is not simply determined by the policy output of government; it is also shaped by authority patterns in the state and by the relationship between the police and the public. Superficially, the fact that less crime is committed in Japan than in the US and more crime is cleared up in Japan might suggest that law and order policy and policing is much more effective in Japan than in the US. However, in reality, the explanations for this apparent success are complex. Japan is a country with a high degree of social conformity and no tradition of individual rights. Japanese society is subjected to a high level of policing to which the individual citizen assents because of the high level of trust placed in the police. Police are given considerable help and information by the public. Once suspects are caught they are put under heavy pressure to confess. By contrast the USA is a pluralistic and individualistic society and has a judicial system which places a strong emphasis on individual rights. Gun ownership is extremely high. The police in the US are not held in very high esteem by the ordinary population and there is less unsolicited co-operation between communities and the police. While some of the inefficiencies of the American system of policing, such as the overlap and competition between forces and the low level of professional training, might go some way to explaining the high crime rate and low clearance rate, much of the explanation for the difference lies in broader social and cultural factors.

Thus, it seems unlikely that the Japanese system of policing, described by Bayley as 'heaven for a cop', could be exported wholesale to other countries. Integration into the community is vital if the Japanese police is to perform the wide range of social roles ascribed to it. This degree of integration is unlikely in any of the other three countries studied here. Given the importance of cultural variables in determining the effectiveness of law and order policy how much can countries learn from each other?

There are some similarities in the social problems facing advanced liberal democracies and there is some evidence that countries are looking to each other in order to learn how to control social discontent and foster harmony. Specific policies have been copied from one country to another; initiatives such as private prisons, electronic tagging of offenders and community policing projects have been imported from the United States into the UK. Some elements of Japanese policing such as the *koban* have made an appearance in large American cities and the French police have begun to look to the Anglo-Saxon model of policing as they try to switch the focus from public order policing to community policing. Nevertheless, the distinctive pattern of law and order policy in each of the four countries is shaped more by the authority patterns in each state than it is by any specific policies. A 'successful' law and order policy may have little to do with government policy and would be unlikely to have the same effects in a different state.

NOTES

1. For a useful discussion of the concept of law and order see P. Norton, ed., *Law and Order in British Politics* (Aldershot: Gower, 1984), introduction, pp. 1–16.
2. See for example S. A. Scheingold, *The Politics of Law and Order: Street Crime*

and Public Policy (London: Longman, 1984) pp. 38–43; and *Taking Account of Crime: Key Findings From The 1984 British Crime Survey* (Home Office Research Study No. 85) ch. 5, pp. 33–42.

3. See J. E. S. Hayward, *Governing France: The One and Indivisible French Republic* (London: Weidenfeld and Nicolson, 1983), pp. 149–55 for a discussion of the relationship between the police and the state.

4. D. H. Bayley, *Forces of Order: Police Behaviour in Japan and the United States* (Berkeley and Los Angeles: University of California Press, 1976), p. 193.

5. This distinction is made by I. K. MacKenzie and G. P. Gallagher, *Behind the Uniform: Policing in Britain and America* (Hemel Hempstead: Harvester Wheatsheaf, 1989), pp. 138–42.

6. See article 92 of the Code Municipale.

7. J. Roach, 'The French Police', in J. Roach and J. Thomaneck, eds., *Police and Public Order in Europe* (London: Croom Helm, 1985), pp. 113–22.

8. In 1988 the National Police was responsible for dealing with 66.7 per cent of recorded crime. *Aspects de la criminalité et de la délinquance constatée en France en 1988* (Paris: Documentation francaise, 1989).

9. See P. Stead, *The Police of France* (London: Macmillan, 1983), pp. 97–103.

10. For a discussion of reforms of the police under Mitterrand see R. Levy and F. Ocqueteau, 'Police Performance and Fear of Crime: The Experience of the Left in France Between 1981 and 1986', *International Journal of Sociology of Law*, 15, 3 (1987), pp. 259–80.

11. For a formal description of the structure of the Japanese police see *The Police of Japan* (Tokyo: National Police Agency, 1987) and for an interpretation of their role see K. van Wolferen, *The Enigma of Japanese Power* (London: Macmillan, 1989), ch. 7, pp. 181–201.

12. Bayley, *Forces of Order*, pp. 84–102; see also L. Craig Parker, *The Japanese Police System Today: An American Perspective* (Tokyo and New York: Kodansha International, 1984), pp. 181–90.

13. The structure of policing here refers to England and Wales.

14. For a brief summary of the structure of policing in the UK see J. Brewer et al., *The Police, Public Order and the State* (London: Macmillan, 1988), pp. 14–21.

15. E. M. McLeay, 'Defining Policing Policies and The Political Agenda', *Political Studies*, 38 (1990), p. 629.

16. See J. Benyon and C. Bourn, eds., *The Police: Powers, Procedures and Proprieties*, (Oxford: Pergamon, 1986), pp. 18–37.

17. The police authorities which were the most assertive were in the Labour-run Metropolitan Counties created in 1972. These were abolished on 1 January 1986.

18. For a view of community policing by a former Chief Constable see J. Alderson, *Policing Freedom* (Plymouth: MacDonald and Evans, 1979).

19. The Brixton Disorders 10–12 April 1981, *Report of an Enquiry by the Rt. Hon. Lord Scarman*, Cmnd 8427 (London: HMSO, 1981).

20. This section is adapted from Brewer et al., *The Police, Public Order and the State*, pp. 109–17. See also I. K. McKenzie and G. P. Gallager, *Behind the Uniform*, pp. 27–9.

21. Brewer et al., *The Police, Public Order and The State*, p. 111.

22. There is an enormous literature on the role of the police as implementers of

policy. See for example M. K. Brown, *Working the Street: Police Discretion and the Dilemma of Reform* (New York: Russell Sage Foundation, 1987) esp. pp. 3–9; and R. Morgan and D. J. Smith, eds., *Coming to Terms With Policing* (London: Routledge, 1989) ch. 1, 'Policing Priorities on the Ground', pp. 1–30.

23. See L. W. Potts, *Responsible Police Administration* (University of Alabama Press, 1983), pp. 60–6.
24. There are a large number of unions representing the French police. About 15 per cent of police officers belong to the mainstream trade unions, the CFDT, the CGT or the FO. The others belong to special police unions. The largest of these is the *Fédération autonome des syndicats de police (FASP)* which is close to the Socialist party. Others are the *Union des syndicats catégoriels de police* (USCP) which is centre right and the small but extremely active extreme right *Fédération professionelle et indépendente de la police* (FPIP). The inspectors and commissioners belong to their own professional organisations.
25. See W. A. Ames, *Police and Community in Japan* (Berkeley and Los Angeles: University of California Press, 1981), pp. 105–27.
26. See Scheingold, *The Politics of Law and Order*, pp. 37–43 for a very clear analysis of the way in which fear of crime is politicised.
27. McLeay, 'Defining Policing Policies', pp. 630–2.
28. Van Wolferen, *The Enigma of Japanese Power*, p. 200.
29. On procedures for investigating complaints: for France see J-M. Ancian, *La Police des polices* (Paris: Balard, 1988) esp. conclusion, pp. 237–48; on Japan see Ames, *Police and Community in Japan*, conclusion, pp. 215–28; on the UK see Benyon and Bourn, *The Police*, pp. 286–93; on the USA see L. Potts, *Responsible Police Administration*, pp. 64–73.
30. For an evaluation of Neighbourhood Watch schemes see Morgan and Smith, *Coming to Terms with Policing*, pp. 138–52.
31. See Norton, *Law and Order in British Politics*, pp. 84–96.
32. See for example D. Rosenbaum, *Community Crime Prevention: Does It Work?* (Beverly Hills: Sage, 1986).
33. D. Monjardet, 'Questionner les similitudes', *Sociologie de travail*, 2 (1989), p. 199.

FURTHER READING

There are no comparative studies of law and order or policing which cover the four countries examined here. However, J. Brewer et al., *The Police, Public Order and the State* (London: Macmillan, 1988) covers Great Britain and the United States and gives a useful conclusion on the problems of comparing law and order policy. I. K. MacKenzie and G. P. Gallagher, *Behind The Uniform* (Hemel Hempstead: Harvester Wheatsheaf, 1989) compares policing in Britain and the United States. The classic study by D. H. Bayley, *Forces of Order* (Berkeley and Los Angeles: University of California Press, 1976) assesses the Japanese system of policing from an American perspective. Bayley's glowing descriptions of the Japanese police should be read with K. van Wolferen's more critical analysis, *The Enigma of Japanese Power* (London: Macmillan, 1989) chapter 7, pp. 181–201. Another very useful work on Japanese policing is W. A. Ames, *Police and Community in Japan*

(Berkeley and Los Angeles: University of California Press, 1981). There is very little written in English on the French police; the best overview is J. Roach, 'The French Police', in J. Roach and J. Thomaneck, eds., *Police and Public Order in Europe* (London: Croom Helm, 1985) pp. 107–39; the chapter by A. Guyomarch, 'Adversary Politics, Civil Liberties and Law and Order', in P. Hall, J. Hayward and H. Machin, eds., *Developments in French Politics* (London: Macmillan, 1990) gives a clear background to the policy issues. There are numerous studies of British policing and of law and order; J. Benyon and C. Bourn, eds., *The Police: Powers, Procedures and Proprieties* (Oxford: Pergamon Press, 1986) gives an excellent study of recent changes in policing and R. Reiner, *The Politics of the Police* (Brighton: Wheatsheaf, 1985) looks at the role of the police in the state. Literature on the American police tends to focus on criminal justice, or sociological studies of policing. However, J. Q. Wilson, *Varieties of Police Behaviour* (New York Atheneum, 1978) gives a good flavour of the different styles of American policing and S. A. Scheingold's excellent study, *The Politics of Law and Order* (London: Longman, 1984) gives a policy perspective.

Part 3

Perspectives

10 Implementation

Michael Clarke

Patterns and perspectives

Students of policy analysis quickly become aware of the importance of implementation as they try to explain why policies are as they are, and why they have the effects that they do. Once policy analysts come to consider questions of 'effectiveness', for example, it becomes obvious that policies tend to suffer from 'slippage'. This happens when what is done in a government's name is neither what was fully intended nor expected.[1]

But though evidence of 'slippage' is never difficult to collect, it is also clear that many other patterns of implementation can also be discerned. Some slippage may constitute unanticipated success in other areas as policies have unintended but beneficial spin-offs. Police drug swoops, for instance, often fail in their primary objective of catching major drug dealers, but frequently net a large number of other types of offender. Or, as seen in chapter 5, the United States has invested very large amounts of money in the defence sector, where the slippage between the intention to produce given types of weapons and the actual output of them has frequently been spectacular, even farcical.[2] But US military spending has nevertheless provided an important subsidy to its high-technology industries, whatever the costly failures of individual programmes.

Nor is 'slippage' the only discernible pattern of implementation. Some policies are inherently easier to implement than others: some policies are self-implementing, where a government only has to announce its policy for it to be enacted. An example of a self-implementing decision would be where a government chooses to recognise, and so legitimise, something – a new foreign government, for example, or a pay deal between a public sector employer and its workers. Other policies are intended to fail in the implementation stage, where it suits policy-makers to be seen to enact a policy without having to live with the consequences; and some policies involve so much technical complexity in their normal operation that critical choices are effectively taken by the implementers who cope with its routine complexity.[3] It is difficult, in other words, to draw a clear distinction between policy-makers and implementers. Everyone involved in a policy is to some extent a policy-maker and discrete decisions are very hard to find. A government 'decision' breaks down into a set of smaller sequential decisions, each one of which has to be implemented in some way to give effect to other contingent decisions. Similarly, we should appreciate that the output of a policy – what the governmental machinery does – is not the same as the impact of it – the effect on society. Policy outputs, therefore, may be successful and consistent but fail to have the desired impact on society; perhaps because they were based on a false premise as to cause and effect. Governments, for example, may efficiently manipulate their interest and exchange rates but find that such policy outputs fail to have beneficial impacts on their economy because the intellectual understanding of the relationship between economic cause and effect has become seriously deficient in the contemporary world economy.

At the risk of over-simplification, it is possible to give some coherence to such observations by drawing a useful distinction between 'top-down' and 'bottom-up' perspectives on implementation. The top-down approach is the most common perspective to adopt, though in fact it emerges more as an ideal type than a pervasive reality. It assumes that we can usefully view the policy process as a series of chains of command where political leaders articulate a clear policy preference which is then carried out at increasing levels of specificity as it goes through the administrative machinery that serves the government. It is 'a running argument, a chain of linked problems and tentative solutions . . . a chain within which issues are increasingly solidified'.[4] In this perspective the leadership sends preferences and authority down the line, which are translated by officials into definitions, procedures and precedents; while officials at lower levels perform a monitoring and filtering process to make sense of all the information coming up the line as the policy impact is felt.[5]

The top-down approach rests on certain assumptions. Chief among them is that leaders are able to take clear decisions which are capable of being further specified at lower levels. Another is that the decisions in question embody an accurate intellectual expression of the relationship between cause (the output) and effect (the impact). Another is that there is efficient communication between leaders and officials; that there is no inherent reluctance within the bureaucracy to execute the decisions; that the leadership is able to monitor and control the bureaucracy. A further assumption is that the bureaucracy has adequate links with any non-governmental agencies (such as sub-contractors or private institutions and firms) which will have to become implementers and that there is no overwhelming opposition to the policy from those agencies. Finally, not the least important assumption is that within this policy network *appro-*

priate actions are taken, at the *right time*, in the *correct order*, without significant dilution of *coherence and authority*.[6] Not surprisingly, these conditions are difficult to meet, or may only be met after several attempts over a good period of time. Pressman and Wildavsky have referred to this as 'the complexity of joint action': the trade-off between the tendency for political commitment and policy coherence to diminish, over the time it takes to achieve the prerequisites for effective top-down implementation.[7]

The alternative to top-down perspectives sees the implementation process as more likely to work from the bottom up. This perspective sees the 'flow of policy' as taking precedence over leaders' attempts to impose single, meaningful decisions upon it. The assumptions of this perspective are that political discretion is highly constrained by the past experience and conventional wisdom as to what is possible; that the conditions in which implementation has to take place are constantly changing, so that decision-makers must adapt their preferences to what is implementable rather than to what is desired. It also assumes that leaders are more concerned with policy-steering than policy-making. From a bottom-up perspective the key to understanding policy is to appreciate the coalitions which build up between different implementation agencies – sections of a government, quasi-governmental organisations, outside interests, and so on. Leaders translate their preferences into policy, therefore, not by making discrete decisions but by becoming involved in the coalitions of implementing agencies – from presidential offices to private firms – in an attempt to inject their political authority into the policy machinery so as to alter some of its characteristic procedures.[8] Effective leaders are those who can influence implementation coalitions, or even form their own, *and maintain them* for long enough to achieve their objectives. In bottom-up perspectives the bureaucracy is politically significant at all levels, and though formal authority resides more at the top of the bureaucracy, it does not necessarily follow that the top will be the most powerful part of it.[9]

The earlier chapters provide good examples of both top-down and bottom-up processes. Some policy sectors give great credence to one as opposed to the other. Most show examples of both. Indeed, almost any detailed case-study within a single policy area will reveal elements of both perspectives. Most government activity embodies at least some attributes of leaders' choices, which change over time in both direction and intensity, and galvanise the policy process. Between times government activity is powerfully moulded by the prevailing coalitions among implementing agencies and by the standard operating procedures embodied within them. The trick for the policy analyst is not to choose between perspectives as a way of explaining a particular sector or governmental process, but rather to spot when each type of perspective is most helpful and to develop a sense of the nature of the relationship – the constant tension – between 'chains of command' and 'implementing coalitions'.

The fact that implementation can be seen in such different ways reveals how intimately it is connected to the most basic assumptions we make about the whole business of policy-making: whether we regard elected politicians as having real power; how they are influenced; how they may be opposed; how power is wielded within a political system, and so on. Implementation studies provide one way of asking how government works: 'the micro-structure of political life'.[10] More specifically, certain themes are common to any pattern of policy implementation. An outline of the most relevant of them allows the analyst to draw some comparisons both between countries and sectors.

Expectations and intentions of policy-makers

All implementation studies are based on some assessment of what the analyst assumes policy-makers have in mind as their policies are enacted. Clearly, whether leaders are injecting a distinctive personal initiative into the process, or merely presiding over the steady momentum of the bureaucracy, the expectations that leaders have of policy provide important yardsticks of evaluation and will determine how the system 'learns' from its own performance.

Leaders' intentions and expectations work in complex ways. The most obvious feature is that they change over time as political and bureaucratic circumstances alter. The 'privatisation policy' of the Thatcher Governments in Britain, for example, assumed different rationales as the confidence of the government grew in winning a second, then a third, term in office. In essence, the main intentions of privatisation in the period prior to 1983 were to put some of the ailing industries that the state had taken under its wing back into the marketplace, and to use the cash thereby raised to help reduce public sector borrowing. As such, the policy was unexceptional and might indeed have been adopted by many a government faced with the same circumstances. During the Conservatives' second term, however, privatisation was extended to some of the public utilities such as telecommunications and gas, and the realistic intentions behind it began to alter as the government saw in it a way to introduce greater efficiency into the workings of the industries concerned through the promotion of at least limited competition in areas that had previously been regarded as natural monopolies. In the late 1980s, however, as the Conservative government entered its third term, the intentions behind the privatisation policy reached their widest and most ambitious extent:

privatisation was no longer an aspect merely of industrial policy but had become one of the chief means by which a social revolution could be promoted in Britain. Privatisation would create a 'share-owning democracy' in which nearly all production would be accountable through the mechanisms of the marketplace. Privatisation would promote the 'enterprise culture' which in some of its loftiest formulations would even bury socialism, not just in Britain but throughout the developed world.[11]

Privatisation policies offer a particular example of a more general phenomenon. Throughout the world governments have tended to define some of their most central policy objectives in terms of the market. There are longstanding differences in the way particular Western governments have viewed market forces, but in the 1990s the market has become ubiquitous as trends towards integrating international production and the deregulation and extension of service sectors have produced an apparently irresistible international dynamic. 'The market', as Hula points out, is often assumed to embody certain attributes that make it appropriate as a policy instrument: it is a distributive mechanism; where it does not exist, it can be created; it is responsive to incentives; it tends towards efficiency; it is thought by many to be politically neutral insofar as it is not motivated by moral or ideological judgements. Indeed governments are sometimes thought to face tasks so similar to those faced by the market that a functional equivalence can be assumed between them.[12] In several sectors dealt with in this study, and to differing degrees in all of the countries examined, market mechanisms are increasingly being used (a) as a means to achieve other objectives, and (b) as a policy objective in their own right.

The health policy agenda in all four countries has tended to shift from the 'provision' of health care to the 'containment' of health care costs. In this case the political objective is a reasonably clear top-down preference – to save public money – and in some countries market mechanisms have been introduced into health provision in an attempt (generally unsuccessful) to achieve it. Such mechanisms have become particularly attractive to governments, however, since health care is an area where governments have found it notoriously difficult to impose top-down policy-making in matters of detail and have found themselves unable to stop the growth of health spending. The detailed allocation of health resources, for example, between preventive medicine and transplant surgery is very much in the hands of the medical profession who are in a position to make expert judgements about the efficacy of one type of expenditure over another, so government policy-makers cannot penetrate very deeply into the health policy community and cannot act as an effective arbiter between financial provision and demand for services.[13] But the adoption of a more market-orientated approach offers governments the prospect of creating a frame-

work within which demands and resources might be balanced by influencing the actions of medical professionals through a requirement that they
make choices according to the disciplines of the market.[14] This was the
philosophy behind the proposals of Mrs Thatcher's Conservative government to introduce an 'internal market' to Britain's National Health
Service. It was also the thinking lying behind the United States government's encouragement of Health Maintenance Organisations and other
systems of competitive primary care (see chapter 7).

In the case of industrial policy, market conditions are regarded by
Western governments as simply unavoidable. The policy of building up
and backing 'national champion' companies has been effectively dis-
credited, though it still holds some residual credibility in French policy-
making circles.[15] In general, however, governments have assumed that
market conditions are paramount in the promotion of national industry.
Highly interventionist economies are no longer regarded as viable and the
purpose of governments' industrial policies has become to help their
industries adapt themselves and prepare for the rigours of the world
market. Of course, such 'adaptation' has certainly involved measures of
protection and various devices of overt and covert subsidy. But, rightly or
wrongly, governments have generally come to agree over the last decade
that the general purpose of industrial policy is not to direct the national
economy or provide socially desirable jobs, but to help predominantly
international companies operate in the marketplace in such a way as to
benefit *national* economies. Thus although Britain's industrial policy is
predominantly defensive while Japan's is more innovative and assertive,
both countries nevertheless define their policies in market terms.

Governments' approaches to industrial policy over recent years have
been to try to facilitate ways in which their industries can become sensitive
to the market and hence work essentially from the bottom up. One thing
all governments have learned from their experiences of industrial policy in
the 1970s was that, 'There is no one best way, no single approach works in
all circumstances.'[16] Market-oriented industrial strategies offer the prospect of a more variable approach. The indications are that this is likely to
happen anyway. Mergers and acquisitions, and more recently the promotion of joint ventures between major international companies, are already
driving national industrial policies along – and perhaps much else besides.
As *Business Week* pointed out in 1987, 'Corporate chieftains have eclipsed
governments in the quest for an integrated Europe.'[17] In all major
industries, firms are merging or co-operating across national boundaries
in order to meet market competition in the 1990s. European electronics
companies have merged and co-operate between themselves: even US
aerospace and Japanese automobile companies – market leaders in their

industries – have established foreign partners for their new product development. Now the service industries have begun to follow suit. As the traditional professions become deregulated so lawyers, accountants, architects, advertising agencies and financial firms are on the verge of becoming genuinely internationalised in a series of 'supermarket companies' which will offer a wide range of services to the multinationals that need them. Where national governments operate industrial policies which would contradict these trends – by opposing deregulation in certain sectors, for example – they risk being marginalised and damaging their industrial base. They have little choice, and in the 1990s little inclination, to do anything other than define their policy agendas in terms of the market.[18]

The hold that 'the market' presently has on the paradigm within which policy-makers operate is only one example of the importance of perceptions in the way policies are defined and what is expected of them. More overtly social policies, such as those relating to law and order or the treatment of minorities, tend to be characterised by very perceptual, rather than empirical, goals. That is to say that policy-makers will articulate a range of objectives in respect to public order and the treatment of minorities, and some of them may indeed constitute sincere long-term objectives, but for many policies in these sectors the realistic intention and the element that requires some particular implementation, is that which contributes to *perceptions* of an orderly and assimilated society. Thus, in both these sectors, it is appropriate that governments should enact legislation to give effect to their stated policies. This is something that is normally within their control and can be implemented in a traditional top-down manner.

As policy-makers are very well aware, however, the existence of law is no guarantee of a change in social behaviour. Indeed, rigorous top-down implementation of anti-discrimination legislation, for example, can provoke even more discrimination and set back the longer-term objective. For this reason, many such policies are intended not to be implemented strictly, but rather to indicate a symbolic commitment to some particular attitude which is thereby furthered for being officially sanctioned, and perhaps tested in the courts. Many policies which on paper imply specific implementation requirements, may in reality simply be expected by their creators to make a statement, the success of which is to be judged by its contribution to a social consensus. To take another example: in the 1970s both the United States and British governments entered into major public debates over educational reform which, at first glance, appear to be directly comparable. Why then did the American 'School Improvement Program' have a favourable impact on the US educational agenda, whereas the British 'Great Debate' simply reinforced an acrimonious stalemate over the future of education between the government and educational interest groups? The comparison is instructive, for while the US program quite explicitly represented 'a bottom-up approach to policy-making' that was intended to provide guidelines by which 'school communities' could define their own requirements – it was intended to *generate* a flow of policy upwards[19] – the British Great Debate was established to *legitimise* a choice that had already been made – 'to gain support for central government intervention in securing an educational system more relevant to the world of work'.[20]

Implementation perspectives, therefore, have to begin by considering how policy-makers – operating from the top down or from the bottom up – define their own objectives and what criteria of success they adopt. What constitutes a 'policy', therefore, still more what constitutes a 'decision' within it, will be in the eye of the beholder. Furthermore, policies and decisions come in all shapes and sizes: some are designed to produce goods and services directly; some to create the conditions in which others can do so; some to facilitate procedures; some to delay or manipulate procedures; some to strike a posture, some to do nothing whatever, and so on. The key question is not merely: 'what do policy-makers want?' when they articulate policies and take decisions; but 'what do they want to implement?', which is not at all the same thing.

Environment of implementation

Another major theme in policy implementation is the analysis of those environmental conditions that determine the ways in which implementation will tend to operate in any given case. Some professional groups, such as the police or the armed forces, are more conducive to smooth top-down implementation, while others, such as medical or educational professionals, make it virtually impossible. Some sectors, such as industrial policy, naturally require more indirect forms of policy implementation, and so on. Three issues are particularly relevant when trying to compare the conditions under which policies are implemented. These concern the arenas of implementation, the agencies of implementation and the question of opposition to the policy persisting into the implementation stage.

Arenas of implementation

The first is the degree to which the national or the sectoral arena is the more appropriate frame of reference within which implementation takes place. This distinction can take two forms. One is that there is a difference between a national and a transnational arena of implementation. Policy towards culture and the arts, for example, is implemented in a national context, whereas agricultural policy for European Community countries, and to a lesser extent for other OECD members such as Japan and the United States, is implemented in a transnational – sectoral – context since agriculture is now a profoundly international issue.[21] Industrial policy also offers a clear example of a sector which, as we have seen, transcends national boundaries. Governments' policies may be targeted on the national economy, particularly where they are concerned with the older industries that have demanded, and received, a high degree of protection from their governments. Newer industries, however, cannot in any case be easily protected at a national level – though there are degrees of 'regional protectionism', especially in Europe – so that the evolution of new industries promotes the growth of more internationalised industrial policies. A transition is therefore taking place in industrial policies whereby the older industries are fighting protectionist rearguard actions while the newer industries are tending to drive policy along. To have the desired effects, a modern government's industrial policy must address actors and issues within the whole industrial sector, which has significant international dimensions. Since the last decade has witnessed a boom in foreign acquisitions and most major industrial companies in Europe now engage in joint international ventures, governments have to implement their industrial policies if not as a European policy, at least in a manner that is compatible with market trends in Europe. Implementation in such a wide sectoral context is bound to be more indirect and involve the use of intermediary agents and mechanisms – hence the greater reliance on market forces.

At the other extreme, policies on ethnic minorities constitute a relatively narrow policy sector and are implemented in a national context. Though ethnic minorities certainly cross national boundaries in many parts of the world and have to be regarded in general as an international phenomenon, the treatment of minorities in the United States, Britain, France and Japan is primarily an issue of domestic politics. Moreover, the implementation of minority policies is paradoxical. For governments generally realise that policy *impact* requires changes in social behaviour, which is almost impossible for a government to engineer. So governments settle for rather limited policy *outputs* in respect to minorities – legislation, statements of principle, selective subsidies, etc. – which can be implemented directly by the agents of national government and tend not to require the co-operation of a wide range of intermediaries.

The other dimension of this distinction between nation and sector is between those policies which are by their nature implemented mainly by the machinery of national government, as opposed to where the weight of implementation falls on sectoral actors who are not part of the national government. The United States, for example, is less affected by the outside world than any other developed state and implements most policies only in its own national context. But such is the size, diversity and federal nature (not to mention the ideology) of the country that very few policy areas are directly implemented by national government. Defence and foreign policy, the US post office, medicare funding, social welfare policy and some aspects of energy and transport policies are implemented directly in a vertical fashion from the centre of national government, and can be understood as a reflection of nationally determined priorities. Almost all other policies in the United States, however, have to be implemented horizontally and are less the outcome of national mechanisms of implementation than of those mechanisms characteristic of diverse policy sectors: state and local government, the policies of private charities, local industries, etc. Industrial policy in the United States, for example, is a clear case of a major policy that is driven more by sectoral or regional conditions than by preferences in Washington. What matters most are the structures of particular industries and the desires of local and state governments to subsidise production in their localities.

Agencies of implementation

The second issue affecting the environment of implementation concerns the number and type of agencies involved in a policy's implementation. Some policies will require the co-operation of a large number of government agencies; many will also require the co-operation of an even larger number of non-governmental agencies; and an increasing number of policies require the co-operation of foreign non-governmental agencies. Clearly, as the number of implementing agencies increases, procedures become extraordinarily complex. The intrinsic power of such agencies within the policy network is also a major factor determining the circumstances in which a policy will be implemented.[22] In the case of health policy, for example, members of the medical profession constitute important policy implementers. Indeed, in some accounts so too do doctors' receptionists and secretaries, since they have the power to affect the public's access to health provision.[23] The medical profession is not easily controlled by government and occupies a powerful position by virtue of past tradition, present expertise and regulation of future entry into it. Law and order policies, on the other hand, offer a good example of a policy area where the major implementing agencies are generally centralised, are controlled by the state – even if they are sometimes administered at local level – and are accustomed to obeying orders from above. Indeed, in France, the military is still an official enforcer of civil law. Thus, while in the case of law and order governments must obtain the support and co-operation of the public, which can be achieved in a very direct way through publicity and national debate, in the case of health policy a government must gain the co-operation of the medical profession in any practical action, through which (and *only* through which) it will gain the confidence of the public.

Governments are generally faced with an increasing number of diverse agencies through which they must implement their policies. The forces of transnationalism create infinitely more foreign agencies in sectors such as agricultural policy, defence, trade policy, industrial or monetary policies, even for the United States and Japan. And greater reliance on market forces, encouraging increased privatisation all over the world, has the effect of bringing new, private actors into several policy sectors that were previously more centralised. Thus, contemporary health policies have begun to involve insurance companies in their implementation, education policies require more co-operation from private companies and financial institutions, even law and order now involves an increasing number of private contractors. As the Western state 'retreated' during the 1980s it relinquished responsibility for certain functions and left behind a more complex and less predictable arena of actors within which policy imple-mentation would in future have to take place.

In this situation, all top-down policies have a tendency to take on bottom-up characteristics, since the relevant implementing agencies have to be aggregated into workable coalitions. Where the agencies remain within the government's direct remit, 'coalitions' are necessary not so much to get everyone to agree but to maintain an acceptable level of efficiency in a more diverse policy environment. Where agencies are outside the government's immediate influence, 'coalitions' are crucial to maintaining a modicum of agreement since agencies invariably find their own circumstances changing. The implementation of policies on ethnic minorities provides a neat example of the different sorts of coalitions that policy-makers have to maintain. It is relatively easy to maintain coalitions of those agencies dealing with legislative action in respect to ethnic minorities: these are generally within the government's direct influence and are more likely to be populated by a social elite which will tend to agree with official government positions. Such agencies include the legislature which will enact the law, the judiciary which will interpret it, government officials and members of quangos, task forces, and charitable watchdogs which will attempt to monitor it. The same might well be true of coalitions to promote greater racial equality within the education sector, though here the number of relevant agencies will be far greater. Beyond that, however, ethnic minority policies are expected to have some impact on the housing and industrial sectors, which are more diverse, are more likely to be in private hands and to reflect a wider spectrum of opinion. Holding together coalitions in these sectors long enough for the policy to have some impact is an altogether different and more demanding task.

The third major issue in the environment of implementation is the degree of political or ideological opposition to a policy. Until now we have only dealt with implementation problems in a management sense, where problems arise from complexity and opposition takes the form of diminishing commitment or incomprehension. But one of the most important factors in the policy environment is where overt political opposition is expressed through the implementation process: what Hood refers to as 'quasi-administrative' limits on government's ability to administer.[24] The necessary coalitions of implementing agencies normally involve actors who are quite properly 'party political'. Governments have to work through local authorities, or, in a federal system, through state governments which may be controlled by a party opposed to the national governing party; they have to deal with sectoral authorities, for example in agriculture or education, which may be similarly party political; and they have to deal with professional groups, such as doctors, teachers or lawyers, which may choose to oppose a government's policy by *becoming* party political, at least for the time during which the policy is controversial.

In this respect, national structures and styles of government have a major bearing on the degree to which overt political opposition arises within the implementation process. Some policy sectors, of course, are more inherently ideological than others. Industrial policy tends to be an arena of partisan conflict, certainly in Britain and the United States. The same is true in a different way in regard to policies for ethnic minorities. If minorities policies are not always debated in party political terms, they nevertheless cast a long shadow over the party arena, where it is frequently acknowledged that such issues can be manipulated to great effect. Nevertheless, national political traditions and the structures through which they are expressed are probably the most important determinants of the degree of overt political opposition that is involved in policy implementation. British and French political traditions tend more towards party politicisation than do those in the United States and Japan. But there is no shortage of vigorous dissent over the implementation of policies in the United States and Japan. The United States, for instance, experienced prolonged street violence during the Vietnam War. Likewise, Japan witnessed vociferous demonstrations over the Security Treaty in 1960, and an orchestrated legal and illegal protest since 1965 over the building of Narita International Airport outside Tokyo. But in Britain and France, with their more adversarial political traditions, even vigorous dissent is institutionalised to a greater extent within the political system. This can have the effect of giving effective veto powers to certain groups over the successful implementation of policy and can inhibit policy innovation on the part of governments. The political power of French wine-growers during the 1970s, for example, placed an effective veto over the French government's ability to implement its European Community obligations in respect to the wine regime, just as the party political structure of Ulster Unionism in Britain has repeatedly exercised a dramatic veto over several governmental policies, most notably the attempted imposition of power-sharing arrangements for the province in 1975. The party politics of local government in Britain provide another case of an institutionalised political tension that has proved during the last decade how easily it can create trench warfare between central and local government in the implementation of a range of important policies.

Where radical policy is enacted in such contexts, it may well spark intense political conflict. During the 1980s the 'New Right' governments of Margaret Thatcher in Britain and Ronald Reagan in the United States enacted a series of radical, market-orientated, conservative policies. In both cases, the general direction of policy excited fierce intellectual discussion within their societies. The general nature of the arguments over 1980s conservatism were remarkably similar in both countries. Yet in Britain, opposition to the thrust of policy and to the implementation of it took very public, party political forms, which became increasingly bitter in the 1980s. The Reagan administration certainly 'took on' certain groups in the pursuit of its policies, such as the air traffic controllers who entered into a prolonged strike in 1981, but in general the Reagan administration encountered the most effective political opposition to its policies at the Congressional and federal stages, rather than in the process of detailed implementation.

Instruments of implementation

The final major theme concerns the instruments that policy-makers can employ to execute their policies. Policies can be enacted through direct policing, through coercion, blackmail, inducements, through pressures to conform, or through the reinforcement of values and appeals to reason. In practice, a mixture of all of these techniques is applied most of the time in attempts to implement policies.[25] At one end of the spectrum compliance is physically enforced, as in the case where demonstrators are prevented by police from occupying a certain area. Physical policing of this sort can only be carried out in very limited circumstances and is always financially (and politically) expensive. Even the police states of Eastern Europe could not physically police their major cities in November 1989 when the citizenry demonstrated en masse.

At the other extreme, policy-makers hope to appeal to values and logic so as to create a self-policing regime which draws sustenance from some common ethos, as can exist for periods when societies face grave external threats to their existence. As a rule, leaders will always frame their policy announcements in terms of the political values peculiar to that society which might encourage compliance. At lower levels, managers and officials will frame their appeals to subordinates in terms of the professional ethos of their own bureaucracy. The most impressive sources of those values to which politicians and managers can appeal are usually implicit and it is difficult to establish how deeply rooted they may be. There is evidence from chapters 2 and 8 that values encouraging social and political conformity are both strong and deeply rooted in Japan. In Britain, however, such values may be relatively pervasive but less deeply rooted. Britain has been characterised as a society in which the settled establishment of interest groups has produced a common pattern of 'consultation-leading-to-self-regulation', where policing of policy can become implicit. The converse of this, as we have noted, is that radical departures from the pattern can produce an implementers' nightmare in Britain as tended to happen in the 1980s. Policy-makers would like to implement their policies only by appeals to values, though in reality large parts of the less attractive end of the spectrum will be overtly or covertly employed.

Coercion forms a large implicit part of the implementation of many policies. Coercion is distinguished from physical policing in that it relies on an implied tangible threat. Law and order policies, for example, can only work where there is a large measure of self-policing: they rely on the fact that most citizens uphold the law most of the time and are generally prepared to inform on those who do not. Areas where these conditions do not apply rapidly become 'no-go' areas to any police force. The vast majority of police work relies on public consent. Yet behind the continual appeals to values inherent in law and order policies, there is always the coercive threat of tangible punishment to encourage good behaviour at the margin.

Blackmail is a more popular policy instrument than is normally assumed. For blackmail implies some tradeoff between different interests.

Policy-makers engage in overt blackmail when they pursue 'affirmative action' programmes, wherein they withhold public contracts from companies that have not been sufficiently affirmative in eradicating discrimination within their organisation. They blackmail public sector trade unions with the threat that disruption will turn the public against them. And they engage in covert blackmail when they create package deals that will encourage compliance by holding at risk some of their subjects' other interests. As major customers for so many important industries, both central and local government in modern states have great opportunities to use blackmail as a policy instrument, not just in industrial policy, but in health policy, education, defence, agriculture – any policy sector, in fact, in which government spending looms large.

The manipulation of incentives is probably the clearest instrument of implementation. Organisations or individuals are paid for their work, either in money or in kind. Social status, promotion and honour may be part of the inducement since it is logical that policy-makers should reward other bureaucratic agencies in some proportion to their commitment to shared goals. Tax relief or the provision of financial grants is a favoured way of manipulating such rewards: it can be enacted and monitored centrally and has immediate impact. Tax concessions have been used in United States health policies, for example, in order to help promote hospital building programmes, and are used by all four countries analysed here as an instrument of industrial policy. The disadvantage of tax relief as reward is that it is difficult to use it in a discriminating way. It is a potent but blunt instrument, and in certain sectors, such as industry and agriculture, is now subject to international regulation (through the European Community, for example) on the grounds that it may constitute hidden subsidy and unfair competition. Other sorts of payments are easy to imagine, however, as where market forces are introduced into health policy and doctors are offered financial inducements to practice in the regions that need a higher proportion of doctors. As noted in chapter 6, however, this has not generally been a successful technique, since there are limits to what financial inducements can achieve, if unaccompanied by other appeals to conformity.

Another technique of implementation is rule-making. Rules, of course, come in many shapes and sizes. Some – surprisingly few – are enshrined in law, interpreted by the judiciary. Many more are formal administrative rules, wherein implementing agencies may well be given the task of interpretation (usually backed up by an appeals procedure). Some rules are merely for 'guidance' wherein advice is offered to implementing agencies, but backed by the prestige of government.[26] In federal systems rule-making takes a more legalistic form, since the authority structures between national and state government are normally set out in formal constitutional terms. Relations between central and local government in unitary political systems are traditionally based upon more informal versions of rule-making, where central government is able to indicate its interpretations and preferences and have local authorities take notice of them in their more particular circumstances. The Japanese experience in industrial policy offers a good example of the most informal type of political rule-making. For here the government has taken advantage of what in chapter 5 is called the 'market-conforming' nature of Japanese industrial culture and has offered extensive 'administrative guidance' to Japanese industry, mainly through MITI. Such guidance is not legally binding but nevertheless commands a strong acceptance within Japanese industrial circles – though, even this is backed up by a range of inducements and covert blackmail techniques. In all cases where the making and interpretation of non-legal rules is an important aspect of implementation, power will tend to devolve to those who have to apply the rules to specific cases, and they will interpret the rules according to their own political values. This sort of rule-making, in other words, will tend to support bottom-up perspectives of implementation.

The final type of instrument is appeals to values and reason.[27] Cynics will argue that such techniques can never be effective on their own, but that rather misses the point. For, in reality, single policies are never implemented on their own. As we have seen, what constitutes 'policy' is more in the eye of the beholder. In the confused reality of policy-making, endless subordinate decisions are being taken and enacted all the time, many of which will not be intended to do more than strike a posture or reinforce a point. So appeals to values and reason will always be a part of any definable policy, and in the case of self-implementing policies – the enormous output of government that is declaratory – such appeals may make up a predominant part of policy implementation.

Conclusion

This chapter has outlined the importance of implementation as a perspective on policy-making. It is clearly only one of many perspectives, but no example of policy-making is properly explicable without it. Most analysts bring an intuitive top-down image to their study of policy-making, partly because policy analysis has traditionally proceeded from rationalistic assumptions: the expectation that policy is made by political leaders and carried out by government officials. This, however, represents an idealised picture of the policy process in most developed countries. Though elements of a rationalistic explanation apply to all policy areas, the study of implementation tends to challenge such implicit assumptions and suggests instead that policies can be better understood if the top-down approach is augmented by the bottom-up approach. Whichever mix of these assumptions is adopted, three general themes have been identified which are the key concerns of all implementation studies: how policy-makers define their objectives; how the environment varies within which policy-makers have to try to achieve their objectives; and the instruments and techniques which are available and appropriate to given policies in particular circumstances.

This raises a deeper question about comparative policy implementation. Are patterns of implementation more similar within countries with their national traditions and structures of power, or within policy sectors with their common concerns and international links? Where should policy analysts focus their attention? This is not an easy question since every case of policy implementation is different and generalisations are notoriously difficult to make. Nevertheless, these and other studies suggest that implementation is more similar within major policy sectors where the gross similarities dominate the politics of implementation, rather than within national contexts, where different political traditions are more likely to affect only the style and nuance of policy implementation.

A comparison between inner city policy and foreign policy puts this question in a concrete form. Leaders' attempts in the United States to regenerate inner city areas have tended to take the form of using intermediaries within a horizontal power structure. Governments establish an agency – a task force or a special executive, for example – that ranges right across the policy area in question. Political leaders find it almost impossible to become involved in the detail of policy at more than one or two removes, and certainly find it difficult to maintain an active personal interest for any length of time given the other calls on their attention. So they frequently try to maintain their control by the use of such special intermediaries who transcend the normal political hierarchy.

On the other hand, implementation studies of foreign policy reveal key policy-makers becoming deeply involved in a vertical power structure in which they promote their policies directly in a series of complex bilateral and multilateral relationships with implementing agencies. French foreign policy-making, for example, is particularly noted for the way in which the Presidential Office deals separately with other interested ministries and encourages vertical structures of implementation. Are such differences due to the fact that some national government styles, such as the French, will favour more vertical structures of authority, while others, such as that of the United States, characteristically work in a more disaggregated and horizontal way? Alternatively, should we account for such differences by the fact that foreign policy, for example, is amenable to centralised (vertical) policy-making, whilst inner cities policy, by its very nature, has to operate in a decentralised and more horizontal way?

Both positions are sustainable, but in general the common factors within policy sectors may prove more influential than national styles. The major policy sectors of the OECD countries have become significantly transnational in recent years as they have reacted to the high levels of interdependence characteristic of the Western world. This has become an established fact for industry, agriculture, competition rules and defence policies. It is also beginning to happen in social security provision, immigrant policies and law and order and employment policies. All of these policy sectors offer evidence of the pervasive nature of international influences on modern government. It would be wrong, nevertheless, to assume that national frameworks are unimportant in the study of policy implementation. For the implementation perspective, in presenting the 'micro-structure' of political life, is concerned precisely with the importance of small variations in the structures of power and political nuances as ways of accounting for different policy outputs. But the conviction grows that where national differences in policy implementation are evident, they are driven more by domestic needs to present governmental action in a particular way rather than by the imperatives of the policy sector itself.

NOTES

1. One of the earliest expressions of slippage was in Graham T. Allison, *Essence of Decision* (Boston: Little Brown, 1971).
2. See, Asa S. Clark et al., eds., *The Defense Reform Debate* (Baltimore: Johns Hopkins, 1984): Edward N. Luttwak, *The Pentagon and the Art of War* (New York: Simon and Shuster, 1985).
3. Michael Clarke and Steve Smith, 'Perspectives on the Foreign Policy System: Implementation Approaches', in Michael Clarke and Brian White, eds., *Understanding Foreign Policy* (Aldershot, Edward Elgar, 1989), pp. 165–72.
4. David Lewis, 'Improving Implementation', in David Lewis and Helen Wallace, eds., *Policies into Practice: National and International Case Studies in Implementation* (London, Heinemann, 1984), p. 204. Lewis is also paraphrasing here from Michael J. Hill, *The Sociology of Public Administration* (London: Weidenfeld and Nicolson, 1972).
5. Andrew Dunsire, *Implementation in a Bureaucracy* (Oxford: Martin Robertson, 1978), pp. 222–3. See also Andrew Dunsire, *Control in a Bureaucracy* (Oxford: Martin Robertson, 1978).
6. Michael Clarke and Steve Smith, 'Conclusion', in Steve Smith and Michael Clarke, eds., *Foreign Policy Implementation* (London: George Allen and Unwin, 1985), pp. 171–3.
7. J. L. Pressman and A. B. Wildavsky, *Implementation* (Berkeley: University of California Press, 1973), p. 92.

8. Dunsire, *Implementation in a Bureaucracy*, pp. 124–31. See also Michael Inbar, *Routine Decision-Making: The Future of Bureaucracy* (London: Sage, 1979).
9. See Morton Halperin, *Bureaucratic Politics and Foreign Policy* (Washington, D.C.: The Brookings Institution, 1974).
10. W. I. Jenkins, *Policy Analysis* (Oxford: Martin Robertson, 1978), p. 203.
11. See Patrick Dunleavy, and R. A. W. Rhodes, 'Government Beyond Whitehall', in Henry Drucker et al., eds., *Developments in British Politics 2* (London: Macmillan, 1986), pp. 135–40: Michael Moran, *Politics and Society in Britain* (London: Macmillan, 1985), pp. 191–8.
12. Richard C. Hula, 'Using Markets to Implement Public Policy', in Richard C. Hula, ed., *Market-Based Public Policy* (London: Macmillan, 1988), pp. 9–16.
13. Martin Burch and Bruce Wood, *Public Policy in Britain* (Oxford: Basil Blackwell, 1986), pp. 116–17.
14. Bette S. Hill et al., 'Practical Issues in Developing Competitive Contracting for Home Care Services', in Hula, *Market-Based Public Policy*, pp. 84–95.
15. Albert Bressand, 'Beyond Interdependence: 1992 as a Global Challenge', *International Affairs*, 66, 1 (1990), pp. 49–50.
16. J. L. Metcalf, 'Industrial Strategy 1975–79', in Lewis and Wallace, *Policies into Practice*, p. 118.
17. *Business Week*, 31 August 1987.
18. Ron Smith, 'The Political Economy of Britain's External Relations', in Lawrence Freedman and Michael Clarke, eds., *Britain in the World* (Cambridge University Press, 1991).
19. Gaynor Cohen, 'Education: Back to Basics in the USA and Britain', in Lewis and Wallace, *Policies into Practice*, p. 79.
20. Ibid., p. 88.
21. For a cross-national study of arts and cultural policies see Caroline Bray, 'Cultural and Information Policy in Bilateral Relations', in Roger Morgan and Caroline Bray, eds., *Partners and Rivals in Western Europe: Britain, France and Germany* (Aldershot: Gower, 1986), pp. 78–101. On agriculture see Graham Avery, 'Europe's Agricultural Policy: Progress and Reform', *International Affairs*, 60, 4 (1984), pp. 643–56.
22. See Carol H. Weiss and A. H. Barton, eds., *Making Bureaucracies Work* (London: Sage, 1980), S. Dawson, 'Organizational Analysis and the Study of Policy Formulation and Implementation', *Public Administration Bulletin*, 31 (1979), pp. 52–68.
23. Burch and Wood, *Public Policy in Britain*, p. 224.
24. Christopher Hood, *The Limits of Administration* (London: John Wiley, 1976), p. 7.
25. *Ibid.*, pp. 118–33: Dunsire, *Control in a Bureaucracy*.
26. Burch and Wood, *Public Policy in Britain*, pp. 176–8.
27. On the importance of values see John L. Anderson, *Public Policy-Making*, 2nd ed. (New York: Holt, Reinhart and Winston, 1979).

FURTHER READING

The most impressive study of implementation probably remains the two volumes by Andrew Dunsire, *Implementation in a Bureaucracy* (Oxford: Martin Robertson, 1978) and *Control in a Bureaucracy* (Oxford: Martin Robertson, 1978), both of which provide an intellectual history of all the issues in policy implementation. Excellent works that established the groundwork of contemporary implementation studies are by Christopher Hood, *The Limits of Administration* (London: John Wiley, 1976); Christopher Hood and Andrew Dunsire, *Bureaumetrics* (Aldershot: Gower, 1981); and J. L. Pressman and A. B. Wildavsky, *Implementation* (Berkeley: University of California Press, 1973). Good collections of implementation case studies can be found in David Lewis and Helen Wallace, eds., *Policies into Practice* (London: Heinemann, 1984); Steve Smith and Michael Clarke, eds., *Foreign Policy Implementation* (London: George Allen and Unwin, 1985); and Talib Younis, ed., *Implementation in Public Policy* (Aldershot: Dartmouth, 1990).

11 Evaluation

Peter Jones

Policies are concerned to make things happen or to make them not happen. They are about promoting, maintaining or preventing states of affairs. It is natural therefore to ask of a policy whether it is, or has been, successful in achieving its aim, whether that aim is the right one, and whether the means adopted for its pursuit are acceptable. That is the ordinary stuff of political argument. Indeed, if policies were never evaluated, the whole enterprise of policy-making and implementation would be curiously nonsensical. How can we think of ourselves as adopting or pursuing a policy without having some idea of what our aim is, why we are pursuing it and why we are pursuing it in that particular way? In other words, the 'evaluation' of policy, in however exact or crude a form, is an indispensable part of the policy process.

The term 'evaluation' is often used to denote a retrospective activity: we do something and, once we have done it, we 'evaluate' how well we have done. Evaluation is often conducted in this retrospective way but it should not be thought of as something which should occur only at the end of the policy process. Evaluation is involved, implicitly if not explicitly, at the very beginning of the process, when one policy is pursued rather than another. It is also an activity which can, and in various ways often does, go on during the life of a policy. A distinction is sometimes made between 'summative' evaluation which appraises a policy only after it has been implemented, and 'formative' evaluation which is conducted during the implementation of a policy and the findings of which can be used to modify the policy itself.[1] Clearly evaluation has more point if it can be used not merely to satisfy our curiosity but also to guide present or future policy-making.

It is frequently remarked that the policy process is not a 'rational' one and, indeed, very often it is not. All sorts of factors influence the evolution, design and adjustment of policies which make those processes something other than sober and detached considerations of all of the values and information relevant to policy decisions. But even if the policy process itself is not rational, that is no reason why the policies which emanate from it should not be subjected to rational assessment. This chapter will examine what is involved in making that assessment.

What then do we mean by the evaluation of public policy? To evaluate means simply 'to determine the value of'. However, 'determining the value' of a policy is something that can be construed more or less broadly. At its broadest it would involve appraising a policy by reference to all those criteria, including matters of basic value, which we believe should figure in policy judgements. More narrowly, a policy may be evaluated only in its own terms. That is, we may concern ourselves only with whether a policy succeeds in achieving its own aims. Most of what are described as 'evaluation studies' are evaluative in this more limited sense. The goal or goals of a policy are taken as given; the evaluator is concerned only to assess the policy's success in achieving those goals. In other words, this narrower approach is concerned to judge a policy only by standards 'internal' to the policy itself, while the more comprehensive approach would also invoke criteria 'external' to the policy. In the second part of this chapter I shall examine what these 'external' criteria might be. However, I shall begin by considering some of the issues involved in assessing a policy's effectiveness in securing its own aims.

Evaluating the success of a policy

In principle, assessing the success of a policy might seem an uncomplicated business. We need not grapple with difficult questions of value since the values by which the policy's success is to be judged are embodied in the policy itself. All we need do is go out into the world and discover whether the policy actually achieves what it is intended to achieve. In reality, assessing a policy's success is rarely as straightforward as that.

Identifying goals

Frequently, it is far from easy to identify the goals to which a policy is committed. There are a variety of reasons why this is so.

Goals often remain unstated. A government may embark upon a course of action without articulating a detailed account of what it hopes to achieve through that action. Thus the evaluator may be left to infer the point of a policy from the nature of the policy itself or from the unofficial remarks of government ministers and officials.

Even where goals are stated, they are often formulated in such general terms that it is hard to know what would count as success and what as failure. Suppose for example that a series of changes in the organisation of health care were prefaced by a statement that these measures were designed to improve the quality of care delivered to patients. There are so many different components of health care, and so many different dimensions of 'improvement', that it would be difficult to know quite how the success of the measures should be tested. From a politician's point of view, vagueness of this sort may be an asset rather than a liability. If a purpose is formulated generally, it may win the approval of all; a more precise and measurable formulation may attract unwelcome controversy. Nor need politicians be overly keen to expose themselves to appraisals of the success or failure of their policies.

In addition, a policy may have not one goal but many. For example, a government's targeting of funds on inner cities may be intended to enhance their physical environment, improve the economic lot of certain deprived groups, prevent social disorder, and so on. Thus, there may be several standards by which the effectiveness of that policy should be tested and which of these goals, if any, should be regarded as primary may be quite unclear. Moreover, if a policy has multiple goals, those may not be wholly compatible. For example, that distribution of resources within inner cities which does most to alleviate economic hardship may not coincide with that which does most to reduce the risk of social disorder. Elderly members of the population, for example, are likely to do better if the first is the primary goal; teenagers and young adults will do better if it is the second.

The goals of a policy may also shift over time. This may be because those goals simply 'drift' during the life of the policy or because they are consciously revised in the light of experience and changing circumstances. There is nothing intrinsically exceptionable in that – although goals that are consciously redefined are likely to be more defensible than those whose effective content is changed by influences such as institutional inertia or organisational interests. But changes in the content of goals may leave evaluators unsure of which goals they should adopt as the basis for their evaluation.

And, of course, there may be a difference between the announced or ostensible purpose of a policy and its real purpose. For example, a government anxious to reduce public expenditure may introduce changes in medical services on the ostensible grounds that these will result in improved health care when what it is really aiming for is financial savings. Suppose that the policy fails to achieve its ostensible purpose but succeeds in achieving its real purpose. In that case, what appears to be a policy failure might, at another level, be considered a policy success.

Whose goal?

Things are further complicated by the fact that policies may have other than purely 'public' purposes. Government ministers may present their policies as directed towards public aims, but privately they may also be concerned that those policies should advance their own careers and enhance the chances of their party's being re-elected to office. Things are at their happiest when public, partisan and private purposes coincide and sometimes they do. The best strategy for politicians keen to advance their careers may lie simply in their sponsoring successful public policies and that might also prove the most effective strategy for a governing party seeking re-election. After all, liberal democracy is supposed to function via these sorts of political incentives. Unfortunately, this happy coincidence of purposes is not inevitable. For example, in a particular policy area at a particular time, the public interest may be best served by the maintenance of the status quo; yet the politician's career may be better promoted by a policy which is innovative, disruptive, and 'high profile'. Similarly, governing parties often aim to curry favour with voters by producing consumer booms in the period running up to an election, even though that sort of economic manipulation may ultimately be harmful to a society's economic development. Clearly if we are evaluating policy as 'public' policy, public purposes must be our ultimate concern, however sincerely or insincerely they are intended by their sponsors.

Despite the obstacles and difficulties that the would-be evaluator may encounter in identifying a policy's goals, that identification is an essential preliminary to evaluating a policy's success. Without establishing a policy's goal, we can still establish what have been the *effects* of government action or inaction. That activity is sometimes described as 'goal-free' evaluation but it really amounts to *establishing*, rather than *evaluating*, what has happened.[2] We may also form our own judgements about the 'goodness' or 'badness' of those effects. But we cannot assess whether those effects amount to a *policy success* or a *policy failure* if we remain ignorant of whether they are the outcomes that the government was aiming to bring about.

Assessing the impact of policy

The most obvious test of a policy's success is whether it has had the impact it was intended to have. Again, this can be more or less difficult to ascertain. For example, if a government decides that scientists should be legally free to experiment on embryos, or that the legal voting age should be reduced, it has only to make the necessary changes in the law and the desired state of affairs will have been produced. But suppose a government wants to reduce the incidence of crime or to eradicate racial discrimination. Those outcomes are much less directly under its control and consequently there is much greater scope for a gap to develop between what a policy is designed to achieve and what it actually achieves.

Thus, we shall need data which indicates a policy's impact. That data may be readily available, but often it is not. If it is not readily available, it may be costly to collect. It may also be difficult to collect for a quite different reason: it may be that the effects aimed at in a policy are not easy to detect or measure. For example, reliable data on changes in people's attitudes towards other racial groups will usually be more difficult to obtain than data on unemployment levels amongst different racial groups. If and when that data has been gathered, its interpretation may not be straightforward. Crime statistics, for example, might have the appearance of hard data but, as we saw in chapter 9, recorded crime is not the same as reported crime and reported crime is not the same as actual crime.

The other main issue that arises in assessing the impact of policy is that of distinguishing the policy's effects from other variables that impinge upon its area of concern. How, for example, do we isolate the effects of a specific industrial policy when so many other national and international influences, including other policies, affect a society's economy? How do we discover the impact of a new mode of policing when so many other factors might simultaneously affect the level and pattern of crime in a society? If things improve after a policy has been implemented, can we be sure that all or any of that improvement was the effect of the policy? If things get worse, has the policy failed, or might things have been still worse without it?

Here I can give only the briefest description of a number of techniques which can be used to assess a policy's impact.[3]

1. *Experiments*: In fully experimental tests of policies, individuals, localities, or whatever are the relevant units, are assigned randomly to two groups – a control group and a treatment (or experimental) group. The policy is delivered only to the treatment group. Randomising should ensure that there are no initial differences between the two groups. Thus the impact of the policy can be gauged from differences between the groups that appear after its implementation. For example, attempts have been made to establish the effect of various sorts of financial aid upon the conduct of people released from prison by conducting experiments of this sort.[4] Although this is usually reckoned to be the most reliable of methods, it is impracticable for very many public policies. It may also be morally objectionable and politically difficult deliberately to deliver the expected benefits of a policy to some and not to others.

2. *Quasi-experiments*: These are more commonly used to assess the impact of policies. Like experiments, they compare a group that has received the policy with one that has not, but they are *quasi*-experimental in that membership of the two groups is not determined randomly. Quasi-experimental methods aim to compare two groups which, in the absence of randomising and apart from their receipt or non-receipt of the policy, are as alike as possible. For example, water may be fluoridated in one locality, but not in another highly similar locality; the dental health of the populations of the two localities can then be compared to establish the effect of fluoridation. The effects of different modes of policing or of different forms of health care provision may be tested in the same way. Alternatively, statistical techniques may be used to construct the relevant comparison. Clearly the success of quasi-experimental methods depends very much upon how fully they manage to control for significant variables other than the impact of the policy itself.

3. *Before-and-after studies*: If a policy is delivered to an entire society, comparisons of the type required by experiments and quasi-experiments will be impossible – unless, that is, we use another society as the comparator. Cross-national comparisons of policy impacts may yield insights but, given the large differences between societies, these are likely to be suggestive rather than reliable. In these circumstances, the most satisfactory test available to the evaluator may be a comparison of circumstances before and after the policy. Crime levels, for example, may be compared before and after the introduction of community policing or of neighbourhood watch schemes. Industrial development in economically depressed areas may be compared before and after the introduction of regional aid. The main hazard of this method is that it does not eliminate influences other than the policy that may affect the 'after' situation, although more sophisticated versions of this technique can attempt to detect and adjust for these.

4. *After-only studies*: If the evaluator was unable to collect data in advance of a policy's being implemented, his sole option may be an 'after-only' study. That is, he may be reduced to comparing circumstances after the policy has been implemented with whatever can be gleaned about the pre-policy condition from people's recollections and from whatever useable data survives from the past. Clearly, this is the least reliable of the four methods.

One distinction that analysts are keen to make in measuring the impact of policies is that between *outputs* and *outcomes*. A policy's outputs are the goods and services it produces, whereas a policy's outcomes are the states of affairs produced by those outputs. For example, doctors and hospitals should be regarded as some of the outputs of health policy, just as police officers and prisons constitute part of the output of law and order policy. Intended outcomes are the states of affairs that those outputs are intended to yield – a healthy nation and the containment of crime; actual outcomes are the outcomes that they actually yield. A distinction between outputs and outcomes cannot always be maintained; for example, if a government assumes responsibility for delivering uncontaminated water to each household and does so via publicly owned water companies, the outcome would seem identical with its output. But, more often than not, the distinction is both meaningful and significant. There is also scope for a distinction between *resources* and *outputs* since the budget allocated to a policy is distinct from the specific goods and services into which those resources are translated.[5] The significance of these distinctions for evaluation is that, ultimately, it is outcomes, rather than resources or outputs, that should supply the test of policy. Because resources and outputs (how much money, how many police officers, how many hospital beds, etc.) are often more easily quantified and calculated than outcomes, there is a temptation – often yielded to in political argument – to allow resources and outputs to become the measures of public policy. But, clearly, a health policy which demands increased public expenditure but which does not deliver better health care, or a policy which increases the number of police but which fails to produce any improvement in law and order, cannot be reckoned an effective or successful policy.

Side-effects

Policies often have side-effects; that is, they sometimes produce consequences other than those that their sponsors intend. These ought not to be ignored. The side-effects of a policy will often become apparent to policy-makers only after the policy has been put into operation. In that case they can figure only in a retrospective evaluation of the policy. But unintended effects need not always be unanticipated effects. They may be unintended only in that they are the known, but unwished-for, effects of policy and, in that case, some account can be taken of them in initial decisions about policy. Nor need side-effects always be 'bad'. For example, government efforts in Britain to reduce the spread of AIDS by persuading people to change their sexual behaviour, have also resulted in a reduction in the incidence of venereal disease. In the United States, speed restrictions, intended to reduce the consumption of fuel by motor vehicles, had the welcome side-effect of reducing traffic accidents. However, side-effects may also be unwelcome. Protectionist measures designed to prevent domestic industries from being undermined by foreign competition may simultaneously encourage those industries to become less efficient and therefore even less able to compete in international markets. One school of thought believes that welfare measures help to create a culture of 'dependency' amongst the recipients of welfare so that welfare policies themselves help to perpetuate the problems that they are, in part, designed to solve.[6] A policy's side-effects might be so adverse that they outweigh any and all of its intended benefits.

Clearly it would be odd to evaluate a policy while totally ignoring these side-effects, but taking them into account further complicates the evaluation. We have then to concern ourselves with how the positive value of a policy's intended effects should weigh against the negative value of its adverse side-effects. In other words, it becomes difficult to keep the evaluation 'value-free' since, while a policy's goal provides a yardstick for measuring the policy's effectiveness in securing that goal, it is unlikely to provide us with criteria for appraising the merits or demerits of the policy's side-effects. How, for example, are we to weigh the success of a policy in providing low-cost energy through the use of fossil fuels, against the unintended (and previously unanticipated) side-effect of its producing acid rain? How should we evaluate an economic policy which succeeds in its aim of creating greater mobility of labour but which unintentionally, but perhaps predictably, contributes towards the break-up of more families? If evaluators are determined not to allow their own values to intrude into the evaluation, they may attempt to use the policy-maker's own judgement of what is acceptable and unacceptable by way of side-effects and take that as their yardstick. However, there is reason to doubt whether, in practice, they will be able to identify 'the policy-maker' for that purpose or the significance that that policy-maker would have given to various sorts of side-effect.

The comparative nature of policy judgements

One further complication is that appraisals of policy are, or at least ought to be, comparative in nature. While it may be interesting and informative to discover how close a policy comes to fulfilling some ideal of efficacy, that of itself does not establish whether it is, or is not, the 'best' policy. If a policy falls short of attaining its goal, it may still be adjudged the best policy in that all of the available alternatives would fall even further short of the target. Similarly, a policy which comes close to fulfilling its aim might still have been outperformed by one of its rivals. In other words, the practically significant standard by which policies are to be judged is not some absolute ideal of attainment but rather the standard set by its rivals. How do we establish what *that* standard is? That again may not be easy. Rival policies may be untried policies so that we have little to go on but presumption and imagination. Even when rival policies have been tried, they may have been used in significantly different circumstances so that it is difficult to come up with conclusive verdicts on the relative merits of rival policies. For example, Western analysts sometimes look with envy at the organisation and methods of the Japanese police, but that organisation and those methods might operate much less successfully if they were transported to the very different social and cultural circumstances of Britain or the United States. Even in the same society, different times and different geographical areas, can present significantly different contexts for policy.

Another kind of comparative judgement is also very important. All policies (or almost all) make a call upon resources. As far as resources are concerned, therefore, policies compete not only with rival policies in the same policy area but also with policies in other areas devoted to quite different goals. Here we begin to stray beyond the issue of policy success and to enter the realm of policy goals and the relative values that should be given to them. But at least part of this calculation may turn upon the relative success of different policies in attaining their different goals. Two policies may have goals of different importance but, if the policy devoted to the less important goal is likely to enjoy a greater degree of success, it may be reckoned the better investment.

Implementation

Finally, some account must be taken of implementation in evaluating policy. Assuming that we can make a working distinction between the general design of a policy and the specific measures by which it is implemented, we then have two possible sources of policy failure. A policy may fail because it is poorly designed for its purpose. But it may also fail because it has been implemented incompetently. If the fault lies in its implementation, it would be quite misleading to declare the policy itself a failure. On the other hand, if failures occur at the implementation stage not because of incompetence or sabotage but because the policy is inherently difficult to implement, that is a factor which ought to figure in the evaluation of the policy itself.

Values in public policy

From technical judgement to value judgement

Up to now we have looked at how we might go about evaluating a public policy in terms of its own aims. But a comprehensive evaluation must go beyond that to consider whether the aims to which a policy is committed are the right ones. Generally these more fundamental questions about the 'rightness' of a policy are abjured by those who describe themselves as 'policy evaluators' or 'programme evaluators' – and with good reason. Once we pass from (internal) questions concerning a policy's efficacy to (external) questions concerning the values upon which it is based, evaluation ceases to be a matter of technical expertise and becomes an exercise in value-judgement. In other words, we move from the realm of technical judgement to the arena of political argument. Yet it would be absurd to ignore this area of policy evaluation just because it assumes a contentious character. In the remainder of this chapter, I shall map out the various dimensions of value-appraisal that relate to public policy and indicate how this aspect of policy evaluation can also be approached in a systematic way.

One preliminary point before I pass on to that. Public policy is inevitably the subject of political dispute, but not all of that political argument stems from conflicts of value. A large portion of it stems from the sorts of issues that I have already examined. Consider questions such as 'will these financial measures curb inflation?', 'will those economic policies promote industrial growth?', 'will that penal policy reduce crime?'. Questions like these are at the centre of political debate in most liberal democracies yet none is, in itself, a 'value-question'. Each is about whether a particular policy will, as a matter of fact, bring about some desired aim. Of course, these questions are typically difficult to answer conclusively – that is why they are so disputed – but that does not turn them into questions of value; it means only that they are empirical questions that are difficult to answer. These questions may also become entangled with other questions which *are* questions of value (e.g. 'are these financial measures fair?', 'is this penal policy humane?'). But we should not be tricked by this. If questions about the probable consequences of a policy become entangled with questions about the values embodied in that policy, we should disentangle the questions rather than treat them as though they were a single question with a single answer.

Let us now turn to those policy questions that are rightly perceived as issues of value. The history of humanity presents us with a vast array of different ideas about what should ultimately guide public policy. Since in this book we are concerned with public policy in liberal democracies, the analysis that follows will be confined to the sorts of values that are likely to arise in the context of those societies, although that still encompasses an enormous diversity of ideas.

Goals and wants

Policies, I have said, aim at goals. How then do we determine which goals should be pursued? One simple answer is that the goals of public policy should be set by the 'wants' of the public in whose name it is conducted. A 'liberal' society is one whose citizens are given scope to determine for themselves what sort of lives they lead rather than having a comprehensive conception of the good life imposed upon them. A 'democratic' society is one whose policy is, in some sense, ultimately determined by the *demos* (the people) who form the citizenry of that society. It would therefore seem consonant with both the liberal and the democratic claims of these societies that the goals of public policy should be set by the wants of the public at whom it is directed.

The political philosophy which is most associated with this approach to public policy is utilitarianism. Utilitarians hold that policy-makers should aim to maximise the 'utility' of a society. 'Utility' may be characterised variously as 'happiness' or 'welfare' or 'preference-satisfaction', but the idea fundamental to utilitarianism is that 'good' consists in maximizing human well-being and that ultimately we achieve that by satisfying people's wants. However, the claim that, other things being equal, it is better that people's wants should be satisfied rather than frustrated, is by no means unique to utilitarians. It would be unusual to find anyone nowadays who would quarrel with that claim. What is unique to utilitarianism is the belief that *all* values can be reduced to the single ultimate value of utility and that, as we shall see, is much less widely accepted.

On this view then we have a simple test by which all public policy is to be evaluated: how fully does it satisfy the wants of the relevant population? The application of that test requires a number of calculations to be made. It may be that a population is unanimous in some of its wants. Every community, and every member of a community, is likely to want an unpolluted environment, the absence of disease, and security from violence. However, we cannot go very far before we run into the need for 'trade-offs'. Personal security, health care and education may all be desirable but they all make demands upon public resources; more of one means less of the others and, to that extent, these goods are in competition with one another. Individual citizens are likely to have different views on what is the 'optimum' combination of these competing goods. People's wants may also conflict in more obvious ways. For example, some people might be quite happy to see natural environments disrupted or destroyed if that is what is required to construct an efficient transport system; others might not. Somehow, therefore, we have to decide whose wants public policy is to satisfy and whose it is to frustrate. The mere facts about people's wants cannot tell us how *that* issue should be resolved. However, another issue is logically prior to that one: are 'wants' the only morally relevant data on which public policy should be based? There are a number of reasons why we might think not.

Alternatives to wants

First, the wants of a population may be extremely difficult to discover in any very refined way, particularly if we remember that what policy-makers would really need if they were to be faithful to this standard would be information about people's *relative* preferences between a vast range of goods. Indeed, on many matters of public policy most people may have no wants to elicit because they have never confronted those matters and formed wants in relation to them. How many people, for example, could articulate their wants in respect of the aerospace industry or the finer points of monetary policy? Policy-makers may often therefore be forced to presume what people's wants would be or should be.

Secondly, people's wants may be based upon incorrect or inadequate information. Should policy-makers have to defer to ignorance and error? Is it not better that they should 'adjust' for public misperceptions? The possibility that people's wants are misinformed is one reason why we can sometimes make a distinction between what people want and what is really in their interest. We are justifiably suspicious of characterisations of people's interests which depart too radically from what those same people actually want. Nevertheless, if public policy should ultimately aim to promote human well-being, that would imply a departure from people's (apparent) wants in these sorts of cases.

Thirdly, some wants may be adjudged evil and improperly satisfied. Consider people who have racist wants and who want to see the members of a racial minority done down. Should those wants count equally alongside other wants in determining public policy? One could answer yes and then hope that the wants of the would-be persecutors would be outweighed by the contrary wants of those whom they wish to persecute. However, that is a risky tactic. Should public policy be equally responsive to all wants no matter how morally grotesque their content?[7]

Fourthly, we can look at the same issue the other way round. Are there certain wants to which public policy should give special status? People are sometimes given to asserting claims of 'need' rather than of 'want'. State provision of welfare goods, such as social security and health care, is often justified as meeting the basic needs of citizens. The concept of need is a complicated and vulnerable one but its use signals the belief that certain goods are crucial to human well-being and that the provision of those goods is therefore of greater moral urgency than the satisfaction of 'mere' wants.[8] Of course a need could be understood as nothing more than a 'strong want' but the language of need appeals to what can be objectively identified as essential to a person's well-being rather than to what, subjectively, people intensely desire. It therefore seeks to prioritise claims to public resources by reference to something other than people's wants and their intensity.

Another way in which wants are discriminated amongst is by the assertion of 'rights'. 'Rights' are sometimes characterised as 'trumps'.[9] If my rights come into conflict with your preferences, the significance of their being my *rights* is that they 'trump' or 'override' your preferences. For example, there are good reasons for holding that my wishes as to how I should live my life should have a different status from your wishes as to how I should live my life. Thus we might hold that people have a right to live their lives as they choose no matter how many other people would prefer them to live in some other way. What rights people have, if any, is much disputed, but, as with needs, the language of rights signals the belief that public policy should not be wholly determined by a calculus of want-satisfaction.

This leads us on to a fifth and more severe way in which it may be claimed that public policy should be guided by something other than public wants. What may be reckoned right or good for people may be quite different from what they themselves want. We have already touched upon one way in which this may be so. People's wants may be based upon incorrect information or mistaken judgements. However, more radically, people's wants may conflict with a model of what human beings would ideally be like and how ideally they should live. Governments may for example subsidise 'high culture' but give no similar support to 'low-brow' entertainment on the grounds that one is intrinsically superior to the other. Similarly, governments may discriminate against wants that, for some reason, they believe to be unfortunate – they may, for example, prohibit non-medical drugs, ban pornography and impose penal taxes upon the consumption of alcohol and tobacco. Beyond that, it might be deemed a proper task of public policy to shape the very wants that people have. Health education campaigns, for example, seek to induce people to revise their life-styles. Policy on the education of children has to address the issue of what kind of people it should be aiming to produce. More radically still, the wants of mature adults may be regarded as no more than the flotsam of an imperfect world and therefore legitimate targets for transformation. 'Consumerism', for example, is sometimes viewed in this light, particularly in relation to growing concerns about its environmental consequences. In liberal democratic societies there will be limits to how far a government can or should go in seeking to impose a conception of the good life upon its citizens. Nevertheless, we should recognise that public policy can be driven by beliefs about what is for people's good, or about how they ought to conduct their lives, which owe little or nothing to what they themselves actually want.

None of this is intended to argue that we should forsake wants as properly giving direction to public policy. It is meant to indicate only that there are other candidates – needs, rights, beliefs, ideals – which compete for that guiding role, and that public policies often lean heavily upon those other concepts.

Maximising and distributing

Another important dimension of public policy is that it is policy for a *public*. How much does that matter? What difference does it make that public policy is concerned with the wants or interests or good of a *society* rather than a private individual?

There are traditions of political thinking which would stress the integrity, the commonality, of a society so that society itself can be conceived as a collectivity with a single identity analogous to that of an individual. That society is then conceived as possessing a single good which is equally the good of all of its citizens. That way of thinking can be more or less grandiose but commonplace instances of it occur every time someone appeals to 'the national interest' or 'the public interest' or 'the common good'. Of the policy sectors dealt with in this book, law and order can be most readily viewed in this way. In large measure, law and order is a good which, if it is made available to any member of society, is made available to all. It is a good which we share – even criminals do not wish to be victims – and a good which we enjoy publicly rather than privately. Defence is another familiar example of a good of this sort. In some respects the same is true of health and industrial policy – there are many ways in which a society benefits collectively from having a healthy population or a buoyant economy.[10]

But to suppose that all of public policy might be viewed in that way would be unduly optimistic. People's wants or needs or goods often compete or conflict so that no 'common good' is available to guide public policy. Let us revert to the simple case where people have different and competing wants. How should a policy-maker respond to that? One possibility is the *maximising* approach. If we are concerned to satisfy wants but we cannot satisfy all wants, then we are to aim for as much satisfaction as possible. There is a simple logic in that view. If want-satisfaction is good, then surely it is better to have more rather than less of it; so, if we cannot achieve total satisfaction, we should go for maximum satisfaction. Maximising may often entail satisfying the majority but it is not to be simply identified with majoritarianism. Account should be taken of the strength or 'intensity' of people's wants as well as of their number and that may sometimes result in satisfying a minority. Moreover, where compromise is an option, the optimal solution may lie in satisfying everyone somewhat rather than in satisfying some completely and others not at all.

Although the maximising approach is most easily illustrated with reference to wants, it need not be confined to them. The maximising approach is equally available if we adopt needs or interests or some ideal-based standard as our criterion or, indeed, some 'mix' of these. Things can get very complicated if policy-makers are expected to take account of qualitatively different considerations (such as wants, needs and rights) in calculating the social optimum. Even so, it may still be held that the maximising approach is the right one and that policy-makers have simply to grapple with these difficulties as best they can.

However, maximising is only one way of responding to the diverse demands that public policy has to confront. Another type of response is distributive in character. If we use the familiar image of the cake, the maximiser is interested in the size of the cake (in its being as large a cake as possible), whereas the distributor is concerned with how the cake is divided up (in its being divided fairly or justly). The contrast and tension between these two concerns is a favourite theme of political theorists. There may indeed be occasions when maximising would seem to demand something other than a 'fair distribution' so that we have to decide to which we are more committed. But it would be silly to pretend that these must be mutually exclusive concerns. If something is of value, we usually worry both about its being promoted and about its being distributed fairly. For example, we would be dissatisfied both with a poor level of health-care that was fairly distributed and with a good level of health-care that was unfairly distributed. In other words, we want a large cake, fairly sliced.

Some sectors of public policy are primarily distributive in character. Policies concerned with racial equality, for example, aim to ensure that the distribution of opportunities in a society is not skewed by racial prejudice. In other policy areas, distribution may be a more incidental consideration. Law and order policy, for example, is typically concerned with containment of crime in society at large. Even so, the resources devoted to the maintenance of law and order can still be distributed across a society in a more or less equal way.

The area of policy in which distributive issues bulk largest are those which bear most directly upon people's income and wealth, such as economic, taxation and welfare policies. Here there are a great variety of competing notions of what constitutes a fair or just distribution.[11] Need, desert, merit, contribution to the public good, respect for established property rights, all enter the lists as possible principles of social justice. There are also those who would claim that the very notion of social justice is a 'mirage' and that, by and large, a society should simply accept whatever distribution emanates from the free market.[12] Various combinations of these principles are also possible. For example, 'basic need' might be taken to justify securing a minimum of economic well-being to everybody, typically in the form of a 'welfare state', but beyond that minimum more or less modified market outcomes might be thought acceptable.

It is also in this area that a tension between maximising and distributive principles is most likely to be felt. If more rapid economic growth requires greater incentives which in turn require greater economic inequality, and if social justice requires intervention in the market to reduce inequality, we face a classic conflict between maximising aggregate economic output and distributing income and wealth justly. John Rawls's celebrated 'difference principle' is one way of dealing with that conflict: distribute equally unless distributing unequally will work to the advantage of everybody, particularly the worst-off section of society (for example, through creating incentives which, in turn, lead to the creation of greater wealth in which everybody will share).[13] Not surprisingly, Rawls's principle has not met with unanimous approval. Some believe it allows too much inequality, others believe that it is unduly restrictive. Still others, particularly utilitarians, hold that Rawls is wrong to subordinate maximising to distributive considerations.

In other areas of policy what is fair or just might seem less open to dispute, particularly where 'equality' seems the obvious requirement. Surely, all citizens should be equal before the law, all should be equally protected by the police, all should have equal access to publicly provided health care, and all should be able to benefit equally from public education. However, beneath the simplicity of these egalitarian principles there may still lurk difficult distributive decisions. All may have an equal claim to health care and to personal security, but just what that requires may not be obvious when it comes to allocating resources to the treatment of different sorts of illness or to the prevention of crimes to which some are more at risk than others.[14] All children may have an equal claim against the state to education, but how far does that require an unequal distribution of educational resources to take account of the different social and economic backgrounds of children, and what does it imply for the resourcing of tertiary education which not everyone will receive?

State involvement

One other factor which is highly relevant to distributive matters is the division between publicly and privately provided goods. Should every-thing be potentially the concern of *public* policy? Are there matters which are not properly the business of the state at all? We have seen that the extent and the acceptability of state involvement varies from sector to sector and, to a lesser degree, from country to country. That the state should maintain law and order is uncontroversial. But there is much less consensus on what the role of the state should be in relation to health care, industrial affairs or social minorities. Why these differences of view? Arguments about the propriety of state involvement can turn upon straightforward considerations of efficiency. Does a national health service like the British deliver health care more efficiently than one like the American which is more squarely based upon private provision? Does state intervention in industry ultimately promote or retard a society's economic development? In other words, the issue of state involvement may be approached in a purely pragmatic spirit – whether and how the state should intervene, it may be argued, should depend entirely upon what works best.

However, this issue may also turn on differences of a more principled kind. One useful general contrast is between teleocratic and nomocratic conceptions of the state.[15] The term *teleocratic* derives from the Greek word *telos* meaning 'end' or 'purpose'. On the teleocratic view, the state is regarded as vehicle for the pursuit of some collective end or *telos* – which end can be as various as maximum happiness or the godly society. The term *nomocratic* derives from the Greek word *nomos* meaning 'law' or 'rule'. On the nomocratic view the state has a more limited and secondary role. Its purpose is not to pursue any first-order end of life but merely to establish rules and conditions within which its citizens can pursue their own ends. It is best to think of these as 'ideal types' since few actual states will have been pure examples of either. Even so, the distinction does point to a significant difference in the way that the state's purpose may be understood.

The 'liberal' in 'liberal democracy' points to a nomocratic bias in how the role of the state is conceived. For example, in liberal societies it would be unacceptable for the state to adopt and to impose upon its citizens a particular vision of the godly society or, more generally, to give its citizens no freedom to determine the course of their own lives. Clearly, the nomocratic view gives the state a more limited authority than teleocratic views. However, it would be a mistake to see the contrast between teleocracy and nomocracy as simply equivalent to that between more and less state intervention. Nomocrats might also give an extensive role to the state. Social democrats and non-Marxist socialists, for example, seek more state intervention than is acceptable to their more *laissez-faire* opponents, but that is not usually because they aspire to impose a particular form of life upon a population. They too would subscribe to a broadly nomocratic vision of the state. It is just that, being less impressed with the sanctity of private property than their opponents, or less persuaded of the justness of market outcomes, they see a greater need for the state to intervene if life chances are to be distributed amongst the members of a society in a just or fair way. In large measure, therefore, ideological disputes in Western societies about how extensive the state's role should be are better understood as contests between rival versions of the nomocratic view than as conflicts between nomocratic and teleocratic conceptions.

Means

So much then for the various ways in which the ends or goals of public policy may be conceived. But important value-questions also arise in relation to means. The pursuit of a good end does not justify the use of any means and evaluations of the rights and wrongs of public policy have therefore to attend to strategies as well as to goals. We may want a reduction in crime but are we willing to see that achieved by licencing widespread intrusions into privacy, such as telephone-tapping, or by setting aside the normal rules of evidence and increasing the risk of innocent defendants being found guilty? We may want greater racial equality, but to what extent should we be able to speed up that process by engaging in 'reverse discrimination'?

Perhaps the boldest form of constraint upon the pursuit of public goals is the assertion of rights. We have already seen how rights may be thought of as 'trumps'; they have also been characterised as 'side-constraints' in that they set limits to what governments may do in pursuit of their goals.[16] The US Bill of Rights functions in just this way. It makes a number of areas of life 'immune' from the powers of Congress or any other public body so that a government is constitutionally constrained to pursue its aims in ways which respect those rights. However, not everyone would agree that there should be such absolute constraints upon what governments may do. Public policy is often a matter of choosing not between good and evil but between competing goods or between competing evils. Just as we have to accept trade-offs between competing ends, so, it might be argued, we cannot avoid trade-offs between desirable ends and undesirable means. In truth, the range of moral possibilities available to us in dealing with conflicts between ends and means is as great as that presented by competing ends.

Processes

A final dimension of policy evaluation relates to the processes by which policy is evolved. How we regard a decision often depends not merely upon its content but also upon the processes by which it has been reached. We regard some ways of making decisions as more legitimate than others. For example, people will often find a policy they dislike more acceptable if they are satisfied that all of the 'legitimate interests' were consulted and taken into account during its formulation.

There are commentators who would play down this distinction.[17] Decision-making processes, they would say, are themselves to be evaluated purely in terms of their results: a good decision procedure is one that produces good decisions. Thus, in the end, everything must still turn on the goodness or badness of the content of policies. It would, indeed, be odd to think of structuring and evaluating policy-making processes while paying no regard to the quality of policy that issued from them. But this uncomplicated view is too uncomplicated. We do think of processes being more or less legitimate in and of themselves. How else, for example, can we explain the aura that surrounds 'democracy' in the modern world? One obvious reason why this matters is that people have different ideas about what constitutes 'goodness' or 'badness' in a policy; thus, it is no good telling them to adopt the 'best' policy. If people hold conflicting views about the merits of different policies, they have to have some way of determining authoritatively which policy is to be adopted. People can then agree that the policy which emerges from that process is the policy which is 'rightfully' adopted and implemented, even though some of them continue to believe (perhaps correctly) that, as far as its content is concerned, it is the 'wrong' policy.

Conclusion

This sketch of the kind of value judgements that public policy requires of us is intended to be broad rather than deep. Obviously it leaves a great deal unsaid. In particular, I have said little or nothing about 'ideologies' such as socialism, liberalism and conservatism. Disputes over public policy are frequently presented as clashes between those ideologies, especially in the politics of European states such as Britain and France. My own neglect of ideologies in this chapter is not entirely accidental. If political argument is represented as no more than a battle between a number of 'isms', each of which is a self-contained and coherent set of ideas which shares nothing in common with other 'isms', it is misrepresented. Values and ideals are not that simple or tidy. Anyone who is seriously interested in the value dimension of public policy is well advised to push past ideological slogans to an examination of the claims that hide behind them. Of course, that need not make the resolution of value disputes any easier. It may reveal that the battle lines are less clearly drawn than party politicians would have us believe; but it may also expose significant differences amongst those who are supposed to subscribe to the same ideology.

If we cannot expect everyone to agree in their evaluation of the goals of public policy, we may still hope for clear and agreed verdicts when we investigate whether policies succeed in achieving their goals. Yet the difficulties that I outlined in the first part of this chapter may cast doubt upon the feasibility of even that more limited form of evaluation. Technical evaluations of public policy have been conducted much more extensively, and in much more sophisticated forms, in the USA than elsewhere. Yet it is common to find American policy analysts commenting disparagingly upon the achievements of policy evaluation and upon its very limited impact on the formulation of public policy. Three concluding remarks are therefore in order. First, not every appraisal of a policy will be dogged by all of the difficulties that I have catalogued. Secondly, evaluators may have given greater attention to those policies that are more difficult to evaluate just because their skills are most needed where the success or failure of a policy is least readily apparent. Thirdly, we should remember Aristotle's dictum that we should seek only 'as much exactness as the subject matter admits of, for precision is not to be sought alike in all discussions'. Policy-makers may often have to settle for crude, impressionistic and tentative evaluations, but simply shrugging their shoulders and abstaining from any kind of evaluative judgement ought not to be an option.

NOTES

1. This distinction comes from Michael Scriven, 'The Methodology of Evaluation', in Ralph W. Tyler, Robert M. Gagne and Michael Scriven, eds., *Perspectives of Curriculum Evaluation*, AERA Monograph Series on Curriculum Evaluation, No. 1 (Chicago: Rand McNally, 1967), pp. 39–83.

2. For a discussion of 'goal-free' evaluation, see Michael Quinn Patton, *Utilization-Focused Evaluation* (Beverly Hills, Calif.: Sage, 1978), pp. 109–13.

3. For brief accounts of these methods, see Martin Bulmer et al., *Social Science and Social Policy* (London: Allen and Unwin, 1986), ch. 8; and Carol H. Weiss, *Evaluation Research* (Englewood Cliffs, N.J.: Prentice-Hall, 1972), ch. 4. For more detailed accounts, see Peter H. Rossi and Howard E. Freeman, *Evaluation: A Systematic Approach*, 4th ed. (Newbury Park, Calif.: Sage, 1989), chs. 5–7; and T. D. Cook and D. T. Campbell, *Quasi-Experimentation: Design and Analysis Issues for Field Settings* (Skokie, Ill.: Rand McNally, 1979).

4. Rossi and Freeman, *Evaluation: A Systematic Approach*, pp. 291–4, 301–4.

5. Brian W. Hogwood, *From Crisis to Complacency? Shaping Public Policy in Britain* (Oxford University Press, 1987), p. 227.

6. Charles Murray, *Losing Ground* (New York: Basic Books, 1984).

7. Different proposals for dealing with this issue can be found in Ronald Dworkin, *Taking Rights Seriously* (London: Duckworth, 1977), pp. 234–8, and Robert Goodin, 'Laundering Preferences', in Jon Elster and Aanund Hylland, eds., *Foundations of Social Choice* (Cambridge University Press, 1986), pp. 75–101.

8. On the concept of need, see Brian Barry, *Political Argument* (London: Routledge and Kegan Paul, 1965), pp. 47–9; David Miller, *Social Justice* (Oxford: Clarendon Press, 1976), pp. 122–50; Raymond Plant, 'Needs and Welfare', in Noel Timms, ed., *Social Welfare: Why and How?* (London: Routledge and Kegan Paul, 1980), pp. 103–23.

9. This way of understanding rights derives from Dworkin, *Taking Rights Seriously*. For other analyses of the nature and significance of rights, see Jeremy Waldron, ed., *Theories of Rights* (Oxford University Press, 1984).

10. Economists have given the term 'public good' a more precise meaning than it has in ordinary language. In this more precise sense, a commodity or service is a public good if (a) consumption of it by one person does not reduce its availability to other persons ('non-rival consumption'), and if (b) it cannot be made available to one person without its being made available to all ('non-excludability'). The standard example of a public good is a lighthouse. Judged by these more exacting criteria, examples of the sort that I have given in this paragraph are likely to rank as 'impure' public goods.

11. For accounts of competing theories of justice, see David Miller, *Social Justice*, and Tom Campbell, *Justice* (London: Macmillan, 1988).

12. F. A. Hayek, *Law, Legislation and Liberty*, vol. II, *The Mirage of Social Justice* (London: Routledge and Kegan Paul, 1976).

13. John Rawls, *A Theory of Justice* (Oxford University Press, 1971). There is a vast critical literature on Rawls; for a representative sample, see Norman Daniels, ed., *Reading Rawls* (Oxford: Blackwell, 1975).

14. On distributive issues in relation to health care, see Norman Daniels, *Just Health Care* (Cambridge University Press, 1985).

15. This distinction, and the terms 'teleocratic' and 'nomocratic', come from the lectures of Michael Oakeshott. For his development of that distinction, see his *On Human Conduct* (Oxford: Clarendon Press, 1975), parts II and III.

16. Robert Nozick, *Anarchy, State and Utopia* (Oxford: Blackwell, 1974), pp. 28–35.

17. See, for example, William Nelson, *On Justifying Democracy* (London: Routledge and Kegan Paul, 1980).

FURTHER READING

A useful introduction to the technical activity of evaluation is Carol H. Weiss, *Evaluation Research* (Englewood Cliffs, N.J.: Prentice-Hall, 1972). Peter H. Rossi and Howard E. Freeman, *Evaluation: a Systematic Approach*, 4th ed., (Newbury Park, Calif.: Sage, 1989), provide a fuller but still general treatment of the subject. Michael Quinn Patton, *Utilization-Focused Evaluation* (Beverly Hills, Calif.: Sage, 1978), outlines an approach to the evaluator's task which is worldly wise without being world weary. Briefer overviews of policy evaluation can be found in Melvin J. Dubnick and Barbara A. Bardes, *Thinking about Public Policy* (New York: John Wiley, 1983), and Brian W. Hogwood and Lewis A. Gunn, *Policy Analysis for the Real World* (Oxford University Press, 1984). Four books which relate contemporary political theory closely to public policy are Robert E. Goodin, *Political Theory and Public Policy* (University of Chicago Press, 1982), Albert Weale, *Political Theory and Social Policy* (London: Macmillan, 1983), Brian Barry, *Political Argument* (London: Routledge and Kegan Paul, 1965), and Michael Laver, *Social Choice and Public Policy* (Oxford: Blackwell, 1986).

12 Comparison

Martin Harrop

This concluding chapter examines the four countries, and then the four sectors, together. We retain the same headings used in the earlier chapters.

One theme of this chapter is the extent to which policies are now shaped in an interdependent world. The traditional assumption behind cross-national comparisons was that countries could be regarded as independent of each other, thus providing a large sample of countries from which to develop and test general theories. Of course that assumption has always been a simplification but it has now become positively misleading. Elements of an international dimension can now be seen in the context, agenda and processes of policy-making in most of the sectors we have examined.

The international environment forms much of the *context* of national policy-making. Policy-makers in each country share a policy context formed by the international economic cycle of prosperity, recession, depression and recovery. As Grant notes in a discussion of industrial policy, 'no matter how the economy is to be guided, the process must relate more to international competitive conditions than to internal political preferences'.[1] This was a lesson learned painfully by President Mitterrand of France when at the start of his administration he unwisely launched expansionist policies when other countries were exercising restraint. International organisations such as the EC also form an increasingly important part of the context of national policy-making. Indeed, they help to harmonise policies across countries.

The policy *agenda* is also becoming international. Similar problems (such as an increase in crime) show up in different societies at a similar time and some solutions (such as community policing) are considered, though by no means consistently implemented, throughout the liberal democratic world.[2] The mass media and international conferences ease this process of policy diffusion. Policy-makers in one country seek to emulate the successes of colleagues overseas. Broader shifts in priorities also echo round the liberal democratic world. For example, Cerny argues that the 1980s witnessed a shift from the welfare state to the competition state as industrial policy became a higher priority for governments, particularly but not only in France and Britain.³ The 'competition state' is concerned with the selective use of state resources to stimulate private firms to achieve international competitiveness. This move towards the competition state reflected growing economic interdependence and a shift in the climate of elite opinion throughout the liberal democratic world.

Some policy-making *processes* also develop in similar ways across countries. For example, in industrial policy, admittedly one of the most international of sectors, Grant has identified a shift away from the 'corporate state'.⁴ Except for some of the smaller consensus democracies, high-level negotiations between government and peak associations representing business and unions have become little more than talking shops. Instead we have what Grant calls 'the company state', a concept similar to Cerny's idea of the competition state.

This does not mean the nation-state can be dismissed. Nations differ in the severity with which problems arise and in the range of solutions which it is feasible for them to consider. Fundamentally it is still national policy-makers who seek solutions, even if the problems are shared, and it is still national policy-makers who are accountable to national electorates. Common problems do not mean common solutions; interdependence does not mean convergence.

Comparing countries

National situations

The issue of economic growth is common to the national agenda in all four countries. In terms of economic performance over most of the post-war period, the countries have divided into two pairs – the growth economies of France and Japan and, relatively speaking, the declining economies of the United Kingdom and, more recently, the United States.

For thirty years or so after the war, France and Japan played the easy game of catch-up. Initially helped by American aid, France changed from a predominantly agricultural society into a modern, industrial economy. Japan's growth was even more spectacular as the country became a major actor on the world economic stage. As in most industrialising countries, the state played a significant role though in both cases there was a natural dynamic to the process, assisted by the general expansion of the world economy. In France, state intervention took the form of indicative planning and direct involvement in the economy. In Japan, the state showed rather more ingenuity, nudging industrial development in the desired direction through specific policies (for example, tax breaks for investment in preferred sectors) and through acceptance by industry of a general leadership role for the state. The hidden hand of Japan's government was as effective as the French state's more direct role but it did not threaten the Japanese tradition of 'cheap government'.

In Britain and the United States, coping with relative decline has moved up the elite agenda. In Britain, and so far to a lesser extent in the United States, the management of decline – adjusting popular demands to the contemporary capacity of the state to supply – became a major political task. The British decline came earlier in the post-war period with the retreat from empire and the vulnerability of its economy to post-war international competition. The United States still maintains super-power status and a domestic economy large enough to give some insulation from the world economy (see p. 10). But in the 1980s even America had to attempt to deal with declining international confidence caused by massive trade and budget deficits. While France and Japan had benefited from creating new industries, Britain and the United States faced the harder task of modernising or dismantling old ones. In responding to these problems, the United States benefited from the leading position it (unlike Britain) had maintained in many high-tech industries.

As all four countries became industrial economies competing in a world economy, so there was some convergence in their national situations. Declining agricultural sectors, over-capacity in heavy industry and strong competition in manufacturing and assembly from newly industrialised countries were shared problems. Even Japan's growth economy had to confront a decline in its steel, aluminium and shipbuilding industries. This convergence was accelerated by the recession of the early 1980s. All four countries must also now come to terms with cross-border institutions, particularly the European Community and transnational corporations.

Of course, economic concerns involve distribution as well as production. In Britain and France, the slicing of the pie between classes, and increasingly between regions, has been a key source of political conflict, detracting from efforts to increase the size of the pie itself. This sensitivity towards distributive issues is not so highly tuned in Japan or the United States. All four countries have also had to confront the political strains caused by demographic change: rural depopulation in France, population ageing in Japan and the growth and/or changing composition of ethnic minorities in France, the UK and the USA.

Constitutions

In fashioning their societies to succeed internationally, what hand have elites been dealt by their constitutions? Constitutions contribute more to ineffective than to effective government. For example, the American constitution embodies the dispersal of power between the federal government and the states, on the one hand, and between executive, legislature and judiciary, on the other. These features reflect a general cultural preference for limits on government power. In consequence policy can fail at numerous points, not least in implementation, and major policy innovation is difficult. This characteristic was not so apparent in the era of American hegemony but has become more apparent as the state seeks solutions to relative decline. America must rely on its President to pull piecemeal policies together. Constitution notwithstanding, the President has the potential to 'go public' – that is, to mobilise public opinion behind a programme of change. But this almost always means policy-making by crisis. To handle any problem, the President must first turn it into a crisis – if it is not one already.

Although France also has a directly elected President, the political reality there is different. Constitution-makers invariably seek to overcome the defects of the previous constitution. In designing the Fifth Republic, they sought to strengthen the executive so as to overcome the instability of the Fourth Republic. Combined with France's unitary system and a prestigious bureaucracy, this yielded a much stronger executive than in the United States. But it would be wrong to overplay the significance of purely constitutional contrasts. During the Fifth Republic the role of the state has shifted towards regulation rather than planning, even though the constitution has stayed the same.

A comparison of Britain and Japan confirms the limit of purely constitutional explanations of policy-making. The post-war Japanese constitution was modelled on the British cabinet system. But despite these constitutional similarities, the contrasts in policy-making are sharp. Britain has an adversarial style; the Japanese preference is to avoid explicit confrontation. The role of the state in British society is clearly circumscribed; in Japan the border between state and society is less clearly drawn. These are important differences and, whatever the explanation for them, constitutional similarities cannot be among them.

Actors

Executive and bureaucracy If the executive (i.e. political appointments) stands at the bridge of the modern state, the bureaucracy (i.e. civil service appointments) forms the engine room. The nature of, and the relationship between, these institutions strongly influences what (and how) policies are made. Inevitably considerable weight in policy-making lies with the bureaucracy – and the question then is whether this is used to play department politics (as in the United States and, to a lesser extent, Britain) or also to pursue some broader notion of the national interest (as traditionally in France and Japan).

The United States has the most fragmented executive and bureaucracy. Departments and bureaux can frustrate presidential objectives by forming alliances with client groups and Congress, which influences their budget. For routine policy-making this process of alliance-building works reasonably well. Bureaux are the basic operating units and they need to come up with new programmes to justify their continued existence. These ideas then need to be sold to other players, a process which reduces the chance of indefensible schemes reaching the statute book. However, this system produces only marginal adjustments. Major innovations need intervention by the President, interventions which can become snarled up in the slow track of routine policy-making.

In Britain, by contrast, policy-making is more contained. The governing party controls both Parliament and the budget. This makes policy initiatives feasible, if not easy. The bureaucracy inevitably initiates much routine policy but lacks its own vision – reflected in the bureaucratic preference for strong rather than weak ministers. Thus although the number of political appointments is much lower in Britain than the United States, political control of the bureaucracy is less of a problem.

France and Japan, on the other hand, have traditionally powerful bureaucracies which have gained further kudos from presiding over post-war economic growth. In both countries, civil servants frequently contribute to the public debate over policy. This would be unthinkable in Britain, where civil servants still like to hide behind the stifling convention that ministers are responsible to Parliament for all the actions of all their civil servants. In France, movement between the administrative, political and business elites further strengthens the bureaucratic input into the elite agenda, particularly as there is more movement out of the bureaucracy than into it. (In Japan, however, civil servants stay in the one department until late in their careers, when they may move out to work for a relevant interest group or firm.) The influence of the Japanese civil service is further increased by the unusually rapid turnover of ministers there.

As France and Japan have modernised, so the capacity of the bureaucracy to lead rather than follow other groups in society has tended to decline. Certainly in Japan economic modernisation means it is harder for MITI to steer industrial development now than it was, say, thirty years ago. The economy has become less manoeuvrable. In France the strategic role of the bureaucracy in the economy has also declined though the bureaucratic elite remains highly influential.

Within the political system as a whole, the bureaucracy no longer seems to be gaining ground. Its grip on specialist, technical matters remains strong but there has recently been clearer political direction of the bureaucracy in Britain and Japan. In Britain, Mrs Thatcher offered a clear vision and selected senior civil servants who helped her to achieve it. In Japan the ruling party has colonised the bureaucracy, a characteristic phenomenon of dominant party systems. Indeed it is more accurate to say the LDP is merging with, rather than controlling, the bureaucracy. 'Serving the national interest' is coming to mean 'serving the LDP'. However this leads to inertia and means innovation is difficult except in a crisis. Thus Japan (a dominant party) and the United States (weak parties) both end up with a policy style which militates against major change.

Parties Parties can give direction to the policy process. In office, they form the political executive and direct the policy process. In opposition, parties are left free to think up new ideas. True, these must pass an electoral hurdle before the party returns to power but as many elections are referendums on government performance this gives oppositions some freedom in policy formation. Is it therefore to the party, and paradoxically to the major opposition parties, that we should look for the main agency of policy innovation in the modern state?

A strong two-party system as in Britain does allow for policy innovation. Once elected, a governing party has a clear run until the next election. But its long-term impact also depends on the autonomy of the state (what does it matter which party governs if none can do so?) and on the willingness of opposition parties to accept the reforms when they come to office. Without this acceptance, the British system degenerates into adversarial, see-saw politics. Thus the significance of party to policy-making in Britain rests on the relationship between governing and opposition parties.

In Japan, by contrast, there is not a dominant party system but a dominant party. The LDP is now intertwined with the bureaucracy; its aroma is the smoke-filled room rather than the breath of fresh air blown into Whitehall by a new governing party in Britain. What gives the British system its momentum is the existence of ideological factions within parties; these seek to capture the party and, through it, the state. The LDP is even more factionalised than Britain's parties but the factions are personal and contribute little to the policy process. Policy development depends more on a process of consensus-building among policy tribes. The LDP looms over this process but does not participate as a single actor within it.

Parties are much weaker in the United States and France. In the USA a pragmatic non-partisan style gives a certain flexibility to make policies which might actually work. There is less adversarial posturing than in Britain. But the risk is drift – failure to make policy at all. While American parties have become organisationally weaker, French parties have become more disciplined since the 1950s. In France, as in Britain, party factions – political clubs in France – have been important in opposition in redefining the political direction of parties. In that sense they have helped to initiate policy. In addition, under cohabitation, French parties have placed some restrictions on executive freedom. However the French political system is still executive dominated rather than party dominated.

Pressure groups The freedom to organise, and lobby government, is a hallmark of liberal democracy. For the early pluralists, the role of the state was to act as an umpire between competing interests.[5] Yet in reality an effective state must favour certain interests over others; indeed coherent leadership is based on long-term alliances between the state and particular social forces. This tension between pluralistic and effective government is resolved differently in each of the four countries.

The United States comes closest to the pluralist model. Pressure groups of all kinds exploit the divisions between the executive, the bureaucracy and the legislature. Well-organised groups confront a disorganised state. As long as the American economy remained internationally competitive, this was a recipe for successful political management. The big firms made decent profits, their employees were well paid and, in consequence, politicians stood a good chance of re-election. Only a disorganised underclass was left out. But this is not a system which adapts easily to shocks, as the slowness of response to the budget and trade deficits in the 1980s showed.

Japan is furthest from the pluralist model. Big business in Japan is equally if not more dominant than in the USA but the relationship with the state is closer to an explicit coalition. Transnational companies are more independent of government in the 1990s than were national companies in the 1960s but, even so, intimate links remain between the peak business organisations and the bureaucracy. These are oiled by exchanges of personnel between the two sectors. As a Japanese Ambassador to Britain once commented, the old boy network works better in Japan than in Britain. The Japanese political map is also more clearly signposted; firms and groups know exactly which department is responsible for a particular area. In Britain and even more in the United States, the division of responsibilities between government departments is more variable and confusing.

If the United States combines strong groups with a weak state, Fifth Republic France is traditionally viewed as a strong state with weak groups. Many interests in France, including the unions, are themselves divided ideologically into competing groups. French peak organisations have not achieved the coverage of Japan's Keidanren. In fact France's policy environment is not unfavourable for those firms which are politically well connected and favoured by the government's industrial strategy. For large firms, a centralised state has the advantage that there is just one number to ring. (In France, as indeed in all the countries in this study, small and medium-sized enterprises are much less influential than big firms.) In adapting the French economy to international demands, the difficulty is not so much the relationship between the business and political elites as the aspirations of the political elites themselves – particularly the failure of Mitterrand's 'go-it-alone' socialism and the survival of other nationalist traditions.

Britain has a long tradition of consultation by the bureaucracy with producer groups. Where the American government issues regulations, Britain's makes gentlemen's agreements. At the same time, there is much less interchange of personnel between the elites than in the other countries and little sense of a shared strategic purpose. In fact neither business nor labour organisations have sufficient members (nor sufficient control over those they do have) to implement any common strategy. However, the relative strength of the labour movement did make modernisation more difficult to achieve until the 1980s. For a long time Britain illustrated Olson's thesis that a long-established pluralist system is likely to produce a weak state in which powerful interest groups veto change.[6]

While big business has disproportionate leverage over government in all four countries, by no means is it the only influential sector. The farming lobby has had well-established relationships with agricultural ministries and, in Japan, with the LDP. Other high-status professional groups – for example, lawyers and doctors – also have considerable clout. In general, however, the grip of these groups on the policy process has declined, reflecting some crowding of the policy environment as new non-producer groups (such as consumer and environmental groups) gain recognition. In Britain, and to some extent also in France, government has sought deregulation of professional monopolies in an effort to stimulate competition and produce visible benefits for voters.

Arenas

The arenas in which policies are made vary from country to country. The only common themes are that in each country the full Cabinet is no more than a ratifier of policies made elsewhere – and that 'elsewhere' usually includes the bureaucracy. In Japan policy tends to bubble up from fairly low within the ministries, though the top echelon of civil servants has become more important as issues increasingly cut across departmental boundaries. In the United States, policy initiatives often spring from bureaux, in the absence of expertise and a broader programme at higher levels.

The United States is exceptional in that Congress (and its committees) and the courts are also important policy-making arenas. This wide range of arenas works against cohesive policy-making. The 'broad brush' approach which is needed to have any chance of getting legislation through Congress leaves plenty of scope for interpretation of detail by the courts and the bureaucracy. In the other countries the courts have much less say and the significance of the assembly is not so much as a policy-making arena but as a body whose reaction policy-makers must anticipate.

Leaving aside the United States, it is easy to exaggerate the impact of arenas on the content or style of policy. After all the selection of arena may itself be a political decision as with ministers who sideline an issue into an official enquiry, or pressure groups which 'go public' because of failed negotiations with the civil service. This point is clearest in Japan. There policy-making involves discussions between bureaucrats, LDP representatives, Dietmen and pressure groups. The precise arena may change – the Diet one day, the ministry the next – but the faces stay the same.

Equally the arena often reflects more than it determines the salience of an issue. All the countries show evidence of a 'dual track' along which policies can move: the fast track for crisis situations or highly political policies, where Presidents or Prime Ministers are involved and policy innovation is feasible; and the slow track for routine matters, where options are fewer, top leadership is not involved and the bureaucracy, and indeed pressure groups, are more important.

In the 1980s sub-national government became a more important political arena. France and Japan made efforts to encourage innovation at local level though both remain centralised states. In the federal United States, the fifty states have always had considerable vitality but their role has been growing in health care, transport, economic development and the environment. The centralising trends in Britain are exceptional in a comparative context but even these have stimulated a stronger central–local axis to political debate.

One trend in all four countries is the increasing stress placed by sub-national governments on attracting investment. The United States has not one industrial policy but fifty; in Britain local and regional bodies have competed hard for foreign investment; in France local authorities have set up offices in Brussels to liaise directly with the EC; and in Japan localities have launched their own technology parks. This concern with economic development, if only in terms of local areas fishing against each other in a limited pool of outside investors, runs against an interpretation of local government as concerned only with social and welfare tasks.

Instruments

The instruments of government should never be neglected. The effectiveness of government depends in part on the range and effectiveness of the instruments which give effect to policy.

Laws are an essential instrument but statistically far from the most important. In most countries the making of laws is a slow and cumbersome process; indeed the United States has difficulty in making them at all, except perhaps in election years. But laws, once passed, are enforceable. They also provide a context within which subsequent policies must be made. In Japan, basic laws are an additional instrument. These are important in demonstrating the importance attached to an issue and in paving the way for more specific legislation. They are roughly equivalent to the Queen's Speech in Britain.

In all four countries, secondary or delegated legislation is now quantitatively the main instrument of policy-making. Even the United States, where Congress and the courts have traditionally been suspicious of delegated authority, now governs primarily through administrative regulation. Delegated legislation means that executive agencies are given by statute the authority to make rules which have the force of law. Orders, regulations and statutory instruments are the means by which departments flesh out the skeletal outlines of the primary legislation. While laws are made in the legislature, regulations are made in the bureaucracy, usually after close consultation with affected interests. Indeed such consultation is legally required in Britain and the United States. Legislative scrutiny of delegated legislation is often cursory or non-existent.

Indeed in France administrative influence on policy-making goes beyond delegated authority. Certain fields of policy are covered wholly by decrees instead of laws. In addition the President can issue decrees in advance of legislation. This enhances the power of the executive. And in all four countries new agencies can be created or existing practices can be changed, even though such developments do not require legislative approval. For example, the executive order by the American government in 1948 to racially integrate the Armed Services proved to be highly significant.

In two countries – France and Japan – indicative plans are an additional instrument of policy. But as the economy becomes more complex, specialised and international, these plans have become looser and less influential. They were more influential in creating a modern economy than they are in refining it. Indeed in France recent trends towards decentralisation and deregulation run against the planning ethos. What distinguishes France and Japan is not so much the formal plan as the willingness of the state to use more subtle instruments of economic policy such as procurement procedures and funding of research and development.

The allocation of government funds to departments is a prime instrument for expressing priorities. In fact, most funds are committed to existing programmes and any change is at the margin. Even so, the politics of allocation is highly revealing of the overall policy process in a country. The United States, for example, has difficulty in making budgets at all and Congress is heavily involved in the process. Elsewhere, procedures are more effective and more executive-dominated, involving negotiations between spending ministries and the finance ministry, with appeals going to higher political authority. The Japanese budgetary process is particularly significant in that it demonstrates how much interpenetration there now is between the bureaucracy and the LDP and how, despite this, public spending is still kept on an extremely tight rein.

Comparing sectors

State involvement

In the sectors we have examined, the involvement of the state in the policy process varies more by sector than by country. State involvement is greatest in law and order and immigration control, more recent and indirect in industrial and health policy, and least developed in minorities policy. These contrasts between sectors are clear and consistent. The only major exception is the health sector, where state provision does vary enormously between nations.

Why does the involvement of the state differ so much from one sector to another? One reason is that some sectors are more integral to the existence and functioning of the state. Law and order is a traditional, core responsibility of the state. If a state fails here, it ceases to exist. With the emergence of the modern state system, states have also claimed the right to control immigration and the residential status of immigrants. It is difficult to imagine any state contracting out the core of these functions to private agencies.

By contrast, the involvement of the state in industry and medical care represents a more recent extension to the state's activities. In all four countries, the role of the state expanded in the thirty or so years after 1945, initially as governments led post-war reconstruction.[7] The growth of the public sector was greater in France, and particularly in Britain, than in Japan and the United States. Basic industries were taken into public ownership in Britain and France. Public spending on medical care increased in all four countries though only Britain introduced full public provision through the National Health Service.

Public policies towards ethnic minorities came later, and remained weaker, than state regulation of the economy and medical care. Between 1963 and 1974 all four countries introduced legislation to improve the position of minorities. The 1960s witnessed the high tide of liberal optimism about the capacity of the state to 'improve' behaviour. American initiatives proved influential, providing an example of the diffusion of public policy across liberal democracies. The efforts of liberal elites did have some impact on the position of blacks in the United States and the Buraku in Japan. But governing parties saw no electoral pay-off from legislating to help minorities, anti-discrimination laws were difficult to enforce, and parties of the right did not share these liberal concerns. Compared to the other sectors, the state's role remained feeble, consisting in large measure of lukewarm attempts to promote good practice.

Policy communities

A 'policy community' is simply a group of actors with a shared interest in, and focus on, a particular policy area.[8] There is no doubt that such communities can be identified in most of our sectors. In health, for example, the health and finance ministries, doctors' associations, insurance organisations and medical administrators form the core of the community. These actors focus on such shared problems as controlling costs, responding to the AIDS problem, and confronting an ageing population. Industrial policy is the only sector in which a single policy community is difficult to identify. This is because industrial policy is a broad category containing a variety of distinct policy 'villages' within its territory. In other sectors a single community is easier to spot.

In the ecological sense, a 'community' refers to a group adapting to a shared environment. This ecological metaphor helps to understand policy communities. Like any other inhabitants of a common territory, the members of a policy community are usually in contact, often in agreement and sometimes in conflict.[9] The most important shared concern is the desire to prevent outsiders from muscling in and upsetting established relationships. For example, the home affairs ministry and prison managements will resist admitting newly formed prisoners' associations to the policy process. Some broadening of policy communities has in fact occurred in this and other sectors but it is still far from easy for newcomers to find a niche once a set of relationships has been established. At the same time as wanting to keep outsiders firmly on the outside, the inhabitants of a policy community also share a desire to extract maximum resources from external bodies, notably the Finance Ministry.

These two objectives – keeping things cozy within the community and maximising resources received from outside bodies – often conflict. This is because extra funding will normally have strings attached. For example, the Health Ministry may only be able to secure more funds from the Treasury if it promises to monitor the effectiveness of the extra expenditure, monitoring which doctors' associations are sure to resist. Faced with such a conflict, policy communities, and especially interest groups, will usually seek to maximise autonomy rather than resources. On the principle of 'better the devil you know', interest groups want a predictable, controlled environment.

But policy communities should not be seen in too cozy a light. The community may pull together when threatened by outsiders but left to their own devices the inhabitants will squabble contentedly among themselves. The more successful a community is in winning resources from the outside, the more there is to bicker over. More formally, routine policy-making consists in working out how organisations with different interests can be persuaded to accept a particular policy. For example, how can the government's desire to restrict immigration be reconciled with the employers' need for cheap labour? How can medical traditions of clinical autonomy be combined with administrators' concerns about the cost effectiveness of treatment? In traditional pluralist fashion, the objective in these negotiations is to deliver a policy acceptable to all, even if it is the first choice of none.

Policy communities are not entirely inward looking. In particular the participants in negotiations taking place in a policy community are not detached from the organisations they represent. The members of the community are representative of wider interests; that is why they are there. The civil servant must consider the likely reaction of the minister. The interest group representative must assess whether the membership will accept the proposal – or, more likely, how the members would react if they knew about it. The actors speak not for themselves but for their interests; a common focus does not mean common interests. This again detracts from a purely 'communal' interpretation of the policy process.

The term 'policy community' can also mislead in suggesting a gathering of equals. Although states differ in their autonomy, most have some choice over whether to allow specific groups to achieve insider status. The state can bring particular groups into the community and, with more difficulty, exclude them again. In minorities policy, for example, organisations such as the NAACP in the United States and the BLM in Japan found some government doors ajar in the 1950s and 1960s. Equally there is often a clear pecking order in these 'communities' with producer groups (e.g. trade associations) historically more influential than cause groups (e.g. consumers' associations).

Policy agendas

The striking conclusion here is how, within each sector, the agenda often shifts in a similar way at a similar time in different countries. For example, the agenda of health policy since 1945 moved from expanding access to controlling costs and then to improving efficiency. In industrial policy the agenda switched from policies to protect national industry to efforts at promoting national firms (or hosting transnational ones) which can compete in international markets. Many features of the law and order agenda have also found an echo in all four countries: more social tensions, an increased crime rate, more direct action and a growing emphasis on civil liberties. As a sector, minorities policy also moved up the agenda in all four countries in the 1960s and early 1970s.

One reason for common agenda shifts is similar patterns of industrial development which generate similar social strains. These then help to shape the agenda of social policy. For example, industrialisation has produced an ageing population in all four countries, which implies not only increased expenditure on health care but also a slower rate of increase in crime as the 18–25 year old cohort diminishes. These dynamics are then explored in international policy communities where sectoral specialists gather in such organisations as the OECD and the EC to compare notes. These bodies give some opportunities for specific emulations. Can the British system of cash-limiting hospital expenditure be applied elsewhere? Is the American experience of community crime prevention schemes relevant to Europe? This type of lesson-drawing is most likely in policy sectors with a strong technical and professional orientation. However, given the rapid flow of information around the liberal democratic world, more general policy developments can also diffuse across frontiers. The British experience with privatisation, for example, has been influential elsewhere.

In some sectors a standard model of shifts in the agenda can be developed. This can then be applied to individual countries so as to identify exceptions. For example, in health care Britain stands out as exceptional in that the agenda has never shifted decisively from access to cost-containment. The explanation of this is partly that the NHS never fully solved the problem of access and partly that it has been remarkably successful at containing costs. To take another example, law and order never emerged as a major issue on the Japanese political agenda. The simplest explanation for this is Japan's exceptionally low crime rate. The point, then, is that national differences can be used to explore exceptions to the 'normal' agenda in a particular sector.

Conclusion

In the countries and sectors we have examined, liberal democratic governments exert only limited control over developments. Whether impact is for good or ill, it is limited. When President Mitterrand sought important changes in the organisation of policing and medical care in France, he achieved neither, beaten by the power of entrenched professions. Changes within sectors are driven by more fundamental forces than government policy. In health, current improvements in the population's health owe more to changing lifestyles than to publicly funded treatment. In law and order, the crime rate responds more to trends such as urbanisation than to policing strategies. In minorities policy, improved life-chances for minorities owe more to changing attitudes than to legislation. And in industry, governments are just one of many influences on economic competitiveness (Indeed Grant concludes that 'industrial policy in most Western societies is a mess'.[10]) In short, liberal democratic governments operate at the margin, seeking to react to developments they do not control and which often they cannot even foresee.

At least this limits the damage. Just as medical treatment can sometimes be counter-productive, so too can intervention by government. For example, Britain's industrial policy of protecting declining industries may have slowed down the process of adaptation needed for long-term growth. Furthermore, even successful policies can generate new problems, unforeseen by their architects. The introduction of national health insurance to France and Japan gave virtually all citizens access to care but led to a seemingly uncontrollable cost explosion. And policies which are successful to start with can become a liability as conditions change. France's protectionist industrial policy helped to build national firms after the war but then became a counter-productive cloak behind which these firms sought to hide their lack of competitiveness.

None of this means that public policies are unimportant. They may not drive society forward but they are far from trivial. The contemporary liberal democratic state acts as a first aider, applying a band-aid to symptoms while cures are sought elsewhere or the problem heals itself.

For example, in law and order, the state may not be able to prevent inner city riots but it can at least quell them. In health care, the state cannot ordain healthy life-styles but it can at least ensure treatment is provided for the sick.

Nor should the purely symbolic aspects of policy be ignored. Putting police on the beat may do nothing to prevent crime (in fact it may worsen response time) but it does provide reassurance to many – and fear of crime is part of the problem. Longer prison sentences may assuage public concern even if they do not deter criminals. Thus the preference of governments for quick, conspicuous results should not be seen in a completely negative light. Even if it does nothing else, first aid does help the morale of the patient. But in general terms the liberal democratic state is reactive, only able to allocate resources to a problem after the problem has arisen, not before.

As Simmie notes, the policies of Western capitalist states 'are frequently characterised by structural contradictions, fragmentation and incoherence. These problems have proved to be persistent and difficult to overcome.'[11] Simmie attributes these failings to divisions among the institutions of the state and to the capture of particular departments by specific interests. While this is surely correct, the word 'failings' reflects a perspective on liberal democracy which not everyone would share. What appears to Simmie as incoherence in public policies would appear to most Americans, for example, as a desirable diffusion of power. The American system is based (if that is the right word) on organised anarchy. The underlying question is: what is the appropriate balance between effective and responsive government in a liberal democracy?

This book has not answered the question but it has suggested that the trade-off is a real one. Huntington was surely right when he said that 'governing and democracy are warring concepts'.[12] On the whole, effective government means flexible government. Industrial policy exemplifies this point. State-led industrialisation may have proved effective in Japan and France but the reins of the state have then to be loosened if an advanced economy is to prosper on the world stage. Japan and to a lesser extent France have shown flexibility in making this adjustment. As Hall and Ikenberry note, 'the ability to act flexibly – to intervene, withdraw, reform or abstain – is at the heart of state capacity'.[13]

But a flexible state needs room to manoeuvre. It must avoid the 'institutional sclerosis' which characterised British governments in the 1970s, hemmed in by powerful interest groups. A flexible state has to end programmes as well as initiate them. To do this, it must either have substantial autonomy from society or else form an alliance with powerful social groups. Both options involve some denial of democratic responsiveness, even if they do achieve results which are in the collective interest.

Take the case of Japan, which of our four countries clearly deviates most from a pluralistic, reactive liberal democracy. Japan's industrial success owes much to an intimate relationship between a small but flexible state and an effective business elite. So far this alliance has limited both the formation of popular demands and their expression through trade unions. The result is, as the Governor of Kumomoto put it, 'a rich country with poor people'. Japan's success in maintaining a low crime rate also owes much to a system of police supervision of daily life which would be unacceptable in Britain, France and the United States. If the balance in Japan is tilted towards effective rather than responsive government, the emphasis in the more *liberal* democracies of the West favours responsiveness. It remains to be seen which balance will be more appropriate in confronting the problems of the remainder of this century and the first decade of the next.

NOTES

1. W. Grant, 'Industrial Policy', in J. Simmie and R. King, eds., *The State in Action* (London: Pinter, 1990), pp. 25–42.
2. For example competition between the world's leading financial markets has led London and Tokyo towards the formal regulatory style favoured in New York. See M. Moran, 'Financial Markets', in Simmie and King, eds., *The State in Action*, pp. 43–58.
3. P. Cerny, *The Changing Architecture of Politics* (London: Sage, 1990), pp. 220–9.
4. Grant, 'Industrial Policy', pp. 40–1.
5. See for example D. Truman, *The Governmental Process* (New York: Knopf, 1951).
6. M. Olson, *The Rise and Decline of Nations* (New Haven: Yale University Press, 1982).
7. For example, public employment grew from 10 per cent of the British workforce in 1938 to 27 per cent in 1951, reflecting the continued effect of wartime mobilisation as well as post-war nationalisation of industry and the introduction of the National Health Service. For details of the growth of public employment in Britain and other countries see R. Rose, ed., *Public Employment in Western Nations* (Cambridge University Press, 1985).
8. For a detailed discussion of this and related terms, see S. Wilks and M. Wright, *Comparative Government–Industry Relations* (Oxford University Press, 1987), pp. 294–309.
9. H. Heclo and A. Wildavsky, *The Private Government of Public Money*, 2nd ed. (London: Macmillan, 1981).
10. Grant, 'Industrial Policy', p. 29.

11. J. Simmie, 'Varieties of States and Actions', in J. Simmie and R. King, eds., *The State in Action*, pp. 177–8.
12. S. Huntington, 'The United States', in M. Crozier, S. Huntington and J. Watanuki, eds., *The Crisis of Democracy* (New York University Press, 1975), pp. 50–118.
13. J. Hall and G. Ikenberry, *The State* (Milton Keynes: Open University Press, 1989), p. 97.

Appendix
Political outlines

This appendix gives a brief factual outline of the system of government in France, Japan, the United Kingdom and the USA. Each country is covered under these headings:

1 Constitution
2 Legislature
3 Executive
4 Judiciary
5 Electoral System
6 Election Results
7 Territorial Distribution of Power
8 Party System.

France

1 Constitution

The present constitution, setting up the Fifth Republic, was ratified in September 1958. It established a parliamentary regime with a strong presidency possessing independent political powers.

2 Legislature

Legislative power is invested in a bi-cameral parliament. This consists of the National Assembly, with 577 members, directly elected every five years and the Senate, with 317 members, indirectly elected every nine years (one third renewable every 3 years). The National Assembly is the more important of the two houses although its powers have been considerably curtailed under the Fifth Republic. Parliament's law-making powers are limited to civil rights, crime, taxation, the electoral system, nationalisation, local administration, education, social security, unions and property rights. All other fields fall under the direct jurisdiction of the government. Parliament has limited control over the budgetary process. Party discipline has increased since 1959 with the growth of a parliamentary majority supporting the President and a more coherent opposition.

3 Executive

France has a dual executive in which formal powers are divided between the President and the government headed by the Prime Minister. The President, who has been directly elected since 1962, is Head of State and also exercises considerable power as political leader of the nation and chief executive. The President appoints the Prime Minister who is usually the leader of the majority party in Parliament. The Cabinet is, in principle, nominated by the Prime Minister but in practice the President is very influential in appointing ministers. Ministers have to give up their parliamentary seat to a substitute if they are appointed to the government. The government is constitutionally responsible to Parliament in that its legislative programme has to be accepted by Parliament before it can be authorised. However, the government has considerable scope to introduce rules which only have to be signed by the President and Prime Minister.

Presidents	Dates	Prime Ministers	Dates
General de Gaulle	1958–69	Michel Debré	1962
		Georges Pompidou	1962–68
		Maurice Couve de Murville	1968–69
Georges Pompidou	1969–74	Jacques Chaban Delmas	1969–72
		Pierre Messmer	1972–74
Valery Giscard d'Estaing	1974–81	Jacques Chirac	1974–76
		Raymond Barre	1976–81
François Mitterrand	1981–	Pierre Mauroy	1981–84
	re-elected	Laurent Fabius	1984–86
	1988	Jacques Chirac	1986–88
		Michel Rocard	1988–91
		Edith Cresson	1991–

4 Judiciary

The ultimate court of appeal on the interpretation of the constitution is the Constitutional Council, which consists of nine members nominated by the government and all former Presidents who are ex-officio members. The Constitutional Council was particularly important in interpreting the respective powers of the President and Prime Minister during the period of power-sharing, 1986–88. The *Conseil d'Etat* (Council of State) is the highest administrative court and judges the legality of administration regulations.

5 Electoral system

The President is directly elected every seven years by a two-ballot system. If no candidate wins a majority of votes on the first ballot the two leading candidates go through to a second ballot.

Apart from the period 1986–88 all deputies have been elected on a single-member two-ballot electoral system. A candidate who wins an absolute majority of votes on the first ballot is elected outright. If there is no outright winner any candidate with more than $12\frac{1}{2}$ per cent of the vote can proceed to the second ballot, which the candidate with the largest number of votes wins. Generally, parties form coalitions and pacts between the ballots in order to secure their chances of being elected on the second round. Between 1986 and 1988 France had a system of proportional representation. The constitution provides for referendums which the President calls. There were five referendums under the Presidency of General de Gaulle. Pompidou held one referendum on British entry into the Common Market in 1972.

6 Election results 1958–1988

See table on p. 284.

7 Territorial distribution of power

France is a unitary state with a complex system of local government. There are some 36,000 local government *communes*, each with an elected municipal council and an indirectly elected mayor. The system was historically highly centralised with Paris ensuring a uniform system of government through nationally appointed Prefects who oversaw the work of local government. The decentralization measures introduced by Mitterrand in 1982 transferred some powers to local government by strengthening their financial and legislative powers and reducing the tutelage powers of the Prefect.

8 Party system

Since 1958 the French party system has become consolidated and polarised into two main camps around four major parties. For most of the Fifth Republic, coalitions have been formed at election time between the

Legislative elections 1958–1988
Number of seats won in the National Assembly

Parties	1958	1962	1967	1968	1973	1978	1981	1986	1988
Gaullist	189	219	200	292	183	153	88	145	128
Non-Gaullist right	Independents				FNRI				U R C
	132	33	42	61	55	U 137	63	} 129	} 130
Centre	57	MRP 55	CD 41	33	30	D			
					Réformateurs	F			
					34				
Radicals	13	39	—	—					
National Front/extreme right	1	—	9	10	13	11		35	1
'Unattached' right	—							14	13
Communists	10	41	72	34	73	86	44	35	35
Socialists							265	215	214
Left-wing radicals (MRG) }	62	104	118	57	102	114	14	} 215	214
Other left							6		27

Party labels

CD	Centre Démocrate	MRG	Mouvement des Radicaux de Gauche
FNRI	Fédération Nationale des Républicains Indépendants	UDF	Union pour la Démocratie Française
MRP	Mouvement Républicain Populaire	URC	Union du Rassemblement et du Centre

socialists and the communists, on the one hand, and between the Gaullists and the Independent Conservatives on the other. Between 1986–88 the National Front gained some prominence in the National Assembly.

Japan

1 Constitution

The present constitution was adopted in 1946, formally as an amendment to the Meiji constitution which was promulgated in 1889. The American authors of the document on which the postwar constitution was based sought to combine aspects of the British political tradition of constitutional monarchy and cabinet government with American notions of a written constitution and separation of powers.

2 Legislature

The bicameral Diet is, in the words of the constitution, 'the highest organ of state power and ... the sole law making authority of the State'. The stronger of the two houses is the House of Representatives which now contains 512 members alongside which works the House of Councillors – 252 members. The constitution gives the House of Representatives pre-eminence on matters of finance and foreign affairs and in the election of the Prime Minister. Both houses are served by a complex committee system modelled on that of the US Congress.

3 Executive

Under the post-war constitution the Emperor became merely the 'Symbol of State and of the unity of the people' and all executive power now rests with the Prime Minister. He appoints Cabinet members and is responsible for the selection of all senior members of the civil service. There is no constitutional limit on his tenure in office but rules of the Liberal Democratic Party concerning its president have restricted the time in office to two two-year terms.

Prime Ministers since 1964

Eisaku Sato	1964–72
Kakuei Tanaka	1972–74
Takeo Miki	1974–76
Takeo Fukuda	1976–78
Masayoshi Ohira	1978–79
Zenko Suzuki	1979–82

Yasuhiro Nakasone   1982–87
Noboru Takeshita   1987–89
Sousuke Uno   1989 (June–August)
Toshiki Kaifu   1989–

4 Judiciary

Following the principle of separation of powers the control of the Ministry of Justice over the court system was greatly weakened in the post-war constitution. Now the Supreme Court is ultimately responsible for the administration of the court system and the Chief Justice is the only appointment that is formally made by the Emperor (though acting on the advice of the Prime Minister). The Supreme Court is not only the court of last resort in civil and criminal proceedings but also may 'determine the constitutionality of any law, order, regulation or official act'. This power of judicial review has only been used sparingly. All appointments to the Supreme Court are subject to review by a popular referendum at the next general election.

5 Electoral system

The House of Representatives is elected by a system of single non-transferable vote in multi-member constituencies. All but one of the one hundred and thirty constituencies return three to five representatives (the exception returns only one). For one party to win an overall majority it must therefore field more than one candidate in most of the constituencies and these candidates will be competing almost as much against each other as the opposition. Representatives serve for a maximum of four years with the date of the dissolution being decided by the Prime Minister.

Each member of the House of Councillors serves for six years with half of the house retiring every three years. Elections are held in July. Two systems are currently in use. One hundred of the councillors (fifty at each election) are elected using a list system with the whole country acting as one constituency. Prior to the election each party lodges a list with the electoral authorities and seats are apportioned between the parties in accordance with the support the party attracts. The other councillors are elected by the prefectures each of which returns two to eight members. Some of these return only one member each time and thus have a first-past-the-post system but the rest operate the same system as the lower house.

6 Election results 1964–1990

House of Representatives
Percentage of votes (Number of seats)

	LDP	DSP	Kōmeitō	JSP	JCP	Other
Nov 1963 (467 seats)	54.7 (283)	7.4 (23)	–	29.0 (144)	4.0 (5)	5.0 (12)
Jan 1967 (486 seats)	48.8 (277)	7.4 (30)	5.4 (25)	27.9 (140)	4.8 (5)	5.8 (9)
Dec 1969 (486 seats)	47.6 (288)	7.7 (31)	10.9 (47)	21.4 (90)	6.8 (14)	5.5 (16)
Dec 1972 (491 seats)	46.9 (271)	7.0 (19)	8.5 (29)	21.9 (118)	10.5 (38)	5.2 (16)
Dec 1976 (511 seats)	41.8 (249)	4.2 (17)	10.9 (55)	21.9 (123)	10.4 (17)	5.8 (21)
Oct 1979 (511 seats)	44.6 (248)	6.6 (32)	9.0 (33)	19.3 (107)	9.8 (29)	7.4 (24)
Dec 1983 (511 seats)	45.8 (250)	7.3 (38)	10.1 (58)	19.5 (112)	9.3 (26)	8.1 (27)
July 1986 (512 seats)	49.4 (300)	8.8 (26)	9.4 (56)	17.2 (85)	6.4 (26)	8.6 (19)
Feb 1990 (512 seats)	46.2 (275)	4.8 (14)	8.0 (45)	24.4 (136)	8.0 (16)	8.6 (26)

7 Territorial distribution of power

Although the powers of local government were considerably strengthened by the post-war constitution, their influence remains weak compared to that wielded by the central authorities. In particular they are financially weak and rely heavily on central government funds to pay for new initiatives. Nevertheless when the local government units are under the control of the opposition parties there is a margin for innovation.

8 Party system

In the mid-1950s there were only two parties which had representatives in the Diet: the Liberal Democratic party (LDP) and the Japan Socialist Party (JSP). It seemed possible that a two-party system might emerge. The JSP split in 1960 and support for the JSP and LDP was to decline almost in tandem over the next twenty years, with the centre ground being occupied by the Democratic Socialists and the Buddhist Kōmeitō. Meanwhile the Communist Party revived to become a significant actor on the political stage by the end of the 1960s. The decline of the LDP was such that many were predicting the inevitability of coalition government in the

1980s. Indeed the LDP was kept in power 1983–6 only with the support of the New Liberal Club (NLC) which had split off from it in 1976. However, the NLC merged back into the LDP after its success in the 1986 election.

In the 1990s the multi-party system and the idiosyncratic electoral system will continue to ensure that the outcome of elections is unpredictable in the context of a political system in which the LDP remains the dominant if not necessarily the ruling party. During its forty odd years of monopolising political power in Japan the activities of the factions and leaders of the LDP have had far more impact on the decision-making process than those of the opposition parties.

The United Kingdom

1 Constitution

Britain is the only one of the four countries without a codified constitution – that is, a single document setting out constitutional principles. However, many constitutional matters are written down in statute law, common law and works of authority. The main principles of the constitution are the sovereignty of Parliament, the rule of law and a unitary system of government. Constitutional provisions are not entrenched and can be changed either by Act of Parliament or, in the case of conventions, by gradual modification of accepted practice.

2 Legislature

Parliamentary sovereignty means that Parliament can make what laws it likes. However, in specified areas European Community law takes precedence and regulations made under the European treaty have the force of law in Britain. The bicameral legislature consists of the House of Commons (650 members elected at least every five years) and the unelected House of Lords (over 1,000 members, making it the largest legislative assembly in the world though average daily attendance is under 300). Most Lords hold inherited peerages. Partly for this reason, the Lords accepts its subordinate position to the Commons, which remains an important political arena (e.g., Prime Minister's Question Time). The government is responsible to Parliament and cannot continue in office if it loses the confidence of the Commons. However, party government means the legislative process is largely executive-dominated though an extended system of Select Committees has improved the capacity of the Commons to scrutinise the executive.

3 Executive

The Prime Minister is the focus of the executive though the actual power of the PM depends more on political circumstances than on the constitution. The PM selects the two dozen or so Cabinet members. The Cabinet ratifies decisions and is collectively responsible to Parliament. Cabinet committees (whose number and composition are also largely determined by the PM) are a more important site of policy-making than the weekly meetings of the full Cabinet. The executive is organised into about twenty major departments and a large number of executive agencies. Departments are headed by ministers who are responsible to Parliament for their department's operation. In Scotland and Wales, the provision of government services is overseen by the Scottish and Welsh Offices, rather than being delivered through separate departments.

Prime Ministers since 1957

1957–63	Harold Macmillan	Conservative
1963–64	Alec Douglas-Home	Conservative
1964–70	Harold Wilson	Labour
1970–74	Edward Heath	Conservative
1974–76	Harold Wilson	Labour
1976–79	James Callaghan	Labour
1979–90	Margaret Thatcher	Conservative
1990–	John Major	Conservative

4 Judiciary

Given parliamentary sovereignty, the judiciary cannot overturn legislation, only interpret and apply it. There is no assessment of the constitutional validity of legislation as in the United States. However, the judiciary can declare executive actions illegal if they are *ultra vires* – that is, go beyond the powers laid down by Parliament. Judges are appointed by the executive and the head of the judicial system, the Lord Chancellor, is a member of the Cabinet. Despite these links between the executive and the judiciary, the judiciary is not perceived to be politicised, in a party political sense.

5 Electoral system

Within the five-year limit of a Parliament, the Prime Minister can choose the election date, a considerable advantage for the incumbent party. Elections to the Commons use the plurality or first-past-the-post system in

650 constituencies. This works against smaller parties with evenly spread support, such as the centre parties. The electoral system usually converts a minority of votes for the leading party into a majority of seats though the 'exaggerative capacity' of the electoral system is declining as the number of marginal seats falls. The gradual increase in the number of minor-party MPs (6 in 1959, 45 in 1987 including 17 from Northern Ireland who are no longer linked with the Conservatives) also means a party now needs a larger lead in votes in order to secure a majority of seats.

6 Election results 1959–1987

General Election results: share of the vote

Year of election	Conservative %	Labour %	Liberal/ Alliance %	Liberal vote per candidate (UK) %	Number of Liberal candidates
1959	48.8	44.6	6.0	16.9	216
1964	42.9	44.8	11.4	18.5	365
1966	41.4	48.9	8.6	16.1	311
1970	46.2	43.9	7.6	13.5	322
Feb. 1974	38.8	38.0	19.8	23.6	517
Oct. 1974	36.7	40.2	18.8	18.9	619
1979	44.9	37.8	14.1	14.9	577
1983	43.5	28.3	26.0	26.0	633
1987	43.3	31.5	23.1	23.1	633

Source: M. Harrop and A. Shaw, *Can Labour Win?* (London: Unwin Hyman, 1989), table 2.1.

7 Territorial distribution of power

Britain is a unitary state with a system of local government which has been modified in recent decades. A two-tier system of county and district councils operates in non-metropolitan areas while the two-tier system in the big cities (including London) was abolished in 1986. In metropolitan areas district councils now have most responsibilities. In a unitary state, local government cannot perform functions other than those specified by Parliament and local authority expenditure has been subject to increasing central control during the 1980s. The main task of local government is to deliver central programmes such as education. Local elections are largely a referendum on the performance of national government. Especially in the pro-Labour cities, local government became a major source of opposition to the Conservative administration in the 1980s.

8 Party system

To a large extent, Britain still exemplifies a strong two-party system. General Elections are about parties, not candidates; party discipline is still strong in the House of Commons; and the Conservative and Labour parties still see themselves as engaged in adversarial competition. There has been some weakening of party loyalties among the electorate and the share of the vote obtained by the two main parties fell from 93 per cent in 1959 to 75 per cent in 1987. But centre parties such as the Liberals and the SDP (which merged to form the Liberal Democrats after the 1987 election) have found it difficult to breakthrough in parliamentary representation, because of the bias in the electoral system. The Scottish Nationalist Party, with its geographically concentrated support, has fared better at the hands of the electoral system.

The United States

1 Constitution

The US constitution was drafted in Philadelphia in 1787 and adopted in 1789. It features two main principles: (a) separation of powers between the executive, legislative and judicial branches of the national government; (b) federalism – the division of power between the national (or federal) government and the states. Constitutional amendments must be approved by two-thirds of both chambers of Congress and ratified by three-fourths of the states.

2 Legislature

Legislative power in the national government is vested in a bicameral Congress, consisting of the House of Representatives (435 members) and the Senate (100 members). Each chamber is broadly equal in power and status, but the House of Representatives is traditionally pre-eminent on fiscal matters, the Senate on foreign affairs. The Senate must 'advise and consent' to the President's nominations of officials, ambassadors and judges. Foreign treaties require two-thirds approval by the Senate.

3 Executive

Executive power is vested in the President, who serves a term of four years (with a two-term limit). The President is Head of State, Commander in Chief of the Armed Forces and Chief Executive. Subject to Senate confirmation, the President has the power to make treaties and to appoint

Cabinet members, judges, ambassadors and other executive officials. He may recommend measures to Congress, and can veto legislation presented by it. A presidential veto can be overridden by a two-thirds vote in both branches of Congress but at the end of a congressional session, when much legislation is passed, there is no time to override, thus giving the President a 'pocket veto' (he just puts bills he doesn't like into his pocket). A President may only be removed from office if impeached by the House of Representatives for 'treason, bribery or other high crimes and misdemeanours' and convicted by two-thirds of the Senate.

4 Judiciary

Judicial power is vested in the Supreme Court, and lower courts established by statute. Appointed for life, the Chief Justice and eight other Supreme Court Justices are nominated by the President as vacancies arise and confirmed by the Senate. Constitutional interpretation by the Supreme Court has been a major means of adjudicating and adapting the constitution. Judicial review is most important in determining: (a) the civil rights and liberties of individuals and minorities; (b) the constitutional balance between the federal government and the states; (c) the constitutional limits on executive and legislative actions.

5 Electoral system

The US constitution disperses electoral power within the national government through separate methods of election, fixed terms of office and staggered elections. The structure of sub-national elections is determined by each state, though major federal intervention has been needed to enforce minority voting rights. Principal features of the national electoral system are:

(a) The Constitution requires that the President must be at least 35 years old, born an American citizen and resident in the US for at least 14 years. He is formally elected by an Electoral College, and indirectly by the people voting state-by-state. Each state has a total of votes in the Electoral College equal to its combined number of Senators and Representatives in Congress. This formula gives more weight to bigger states. Within the 538 votes of the Electoral College (including 3 votes awarded to the District of Columbia by the 23rd amendment), an overall majority (270) is needed to win. By unwritten rule, the presidential candidate who leads the popular vote in each state carries all its Electoral College votes. The Electoral College thus magnifies movements in the popular vote. If no candidate obtains a clear majority in the Electoral College, the constitution prescribes the election to be decided in the House of Representatives, the members from each state voting as one. So far, this has happened only once (in 1800).

(b) Each state, regardless of population, has two Senators, elected for a six-year term. One third of the Senate is elected every two years. Senators must be at least 30 years old, and are directly elected by first-past-the-post (until 1913, they were appointed by state legislatures).

(c) Members of the House of Representatives must be at least 25 years old, and are directly elected for two-year terms using first-past-the post, from districts of equal population. Congressional districts are reapportioned between and within states following each 10-yearly census. Representatives and Senators must be residents of the state they represent.

6 Election results 1964–1989

Presidential elections

	Winning candidate	Party	Percentage of popular vote
1964	Lyndon Johnson	Rep	61
1968	Richard Nixon	Rep	43
1972	Richard Nixon	Rep	61
1974	Gerald Ford	Rep	—
	(Appointed after Nixon's resignation)		
1976	Jimmy Carter	Dem	50
1980	Ronald Reagan	Rep	51
1984	Ronald Reagan	Rep	59
1988	George Bush	Rep	54

Congressional elections: seats won by major parties

	House of Representatives		Senate	
	Democrat	Republican	Democrat	Republican
1964	295	140	67	33
1966	248	187	64	36
1968	243	192	58	42
1970	255	180	54	44
1972	243	192	56	42
1974	291	144	61	37
1976	292	143	61	38
1978	276	157	58	41

Table (*cont.*)

	House of Representatives		Senate	
	Democrat	Republican	Democrat	Republican
1980	243	192	47	53
1982	267	186	45	55
1984	253	182	47	53
1986	258	177	53	47
1988	259	174	55	45

7 Territorial distribution of power: sub-national government

Federalism involves a substantial territorial dispersion of power between the federal (national) government and the states. Only limited powers were originally granted to the federal government (chiefly in relation to defence, foreign relations, regulation of the currency and inter-state commerce): the 10th amendment reserved all others to the states or the people. Though federal powers have been greatly expanded, each state retains its own constitution, elects its own governor, legislature and other officials, maintains its own criminal justice system, determines the structure of local government, imposes its own taxes and declares its own laws. Where federal and state laws conflict, the authority of the national constitution (as interpreted by the Supreme Court) prevails but this has not invariably favoured centralisation.

8 Party system

Each of the fifty states has its own party system, with the presidential election as a four-yearly focus for the national two-party system. At all levels of government, public primary elections are extensively used to select party candidates for office. Primaries, plus changes in campaign finance laws, have weakened party cohesion, making campaigning candidate- rather than party-centred. Particularly important in presidential elections, primaries have eclipsed the traditional function of the national party convention to choose the presidential nominee. The Democratic and Republican parties remain loose, heterogeneous coalitions of interests, with limited discipline and unity of aims beyond the pursuit of office. Electoral politics involves the interplay of many factors other than party loyalty and policy-making at all levels is pervaded by interest-group activity.

Index